NIKOS KAZANTZAKIS

RUSSIA

NIKOS KAZANTZAKIS

RUSSIA

A CHRONICLE OF THREE JOURNEYS IN
THE AFTERMATH OF THE REVOLUTION

TRANSLATED BY MICHAEL ANTONAKES
AND THANASIS MASKALERIS

Creative Arts Book Company
Berkeley
1989

CREATIVE ARTS BOOKS
ARE PUBLISHED BY
DONALD S. ELLIS

For more information contact:
    Creative Arts Book Company
    833 Bancroft Way
    Berkeley, CA 94710

Library of Congress Cataloging-in-Publication Data

Kazantzakis, Nikos, 1883-1957.
    [Rousia. English]
    Russia : a chronicle of three journeys in the aftermath of the
revolution by Nikos Kazantzakis; translated by Michael Antonakes and
Thanasis Maskaleris.
        p. cm.
    Translation of: Rousia.
    ISBN 0-88739-072-2 : $18.95
    1. Soviet Union—Description and travel—1917-1944.
2. Kazantzakis, Nikos, 1883-1957—Journeys—Soviet Union.
3. Authors, Greek (Modern)—20th century—Journeys—Soviet Union.
I. Title.
DK27.K2813   1989   88-38224
914.7′04842—dcl9   CIP

Manufactured in the United States of America

■ ACKNOWLEDGMENTS

The translators are grateful to Mrs. Helen Kazantzakis for her permission to translate *Russia* and for her subsequent encouragement and support; to Kimon Friar for reading the manuscript and offering many valuable suggestions; also to Peter Bien and Theofanis G. Stavrou for their contributions to this volume.

We also wish to express our gratitude to Columbia University for a Translation Center Award and to Salem State College for a Faculty Development grant, gifts that helped defray the cost of preparing the manuscript; to San Francisco State University for granting release time from teaching in connection with this translation project; to Mary Sucharewicz for her special assistance; to Katharine Fong for reading the manuscript with her keen editorial eye; to Nancy Riddiough for her superb copyediting; to Katia Siskron for her help toward a consistent spelling of Russian words and proper names*; to Professor Norair Taschian for providing answers to many of our questions on things Russian; and to Richard Elia and Kathleen Thompson for assistance with proofreading.

Michael Antonakes   *Thanasis Maskaleris*
Salem State College   *San Francisco State University*

---

* A note on transliteration and quoted passages from Russian authors:

Unfortunately there is no universally accepted system of transliteration for the Cyrillic alphabet. We used the Library of Congress system of transliteration, omitting the hard and soft signs. The exception in the use of this system applies only to names that have entered general English usage via another system, especially names of regions and nationalities, i.e., Moscow rather than Moskva; Bashkirs rather than Bashkiry, etc.

All passages from Russian writings that Kazantzakis quoted in his text have been translated from his Greek versions directly into English, without consulting Russian originals or existing English translations of them.

v

■ CONTENTS

■ FOREWORD

Like many other Western European intellectuals of the interwar years, Nikos Kazantzakis (1883–1957) experienced the irrepressible urge to make the "pilgrimage to Moscow," to observe "agonizing Russia" at close range and to assess the goals, problems and accomplishments of the world's "first socialist society." Like the rest of them, he enjoyed the attention shown him by his Soviet hosts and colleagues, and upon his return he shared his impressions through publications and speeches; but unlike most other visitors, Kazantzakis went to Russia repeatedly and traveled extensively throughout its vast land. Also, unlike most of them, upon his return to the West he did not join those who found Soviet communism a "God that failed" and did not contribute to the literature of political disillusionment, even though he had considerably modified his own views on Marxism and Soviet communism. He fervently claimed that he went to Russia (he preferred the use of the name "Russia" instead of "the Soviet Union") without any preconceived notions, as he wanted to witness for himself the great experiment of the century at work.

Kazantzakis first visited Russia during the Civil War of 1919 on a special mission for the Greek government to help with the repatriation of the Greeks from the Caucasus area. This trip clearly made an indelible impression on him, but it was his three visits between 1925 and 1929 that familiarized Kazantzakis with the political, social and cultural realities about which he wrote so eloquently in the volume at hand. For his *Russia* is one of the most engaging accounts to come from the pen of travelers to the USSR during the twenties and thirties. Kazantzakis was a tireless and insatiable traveler for whom journeying was a way of life and of learning. He worked indefatigably while on the road, inquiring, reading, writing in his notebooks or to friends, or revising drafts of his own work. Above all, however, he was a visionary artist, constantly in search of ideas and systems that could conceivably replace those of a bankrupt Western civilization or give meaning to one's existence. This was not unique to Kazantzakis. Intellectuals visiting the Soviet Union during this period usually projected on their new experience, and hence their reporting, their disappointment with Western institutions. But Kazantzakis went one step further. He felt that Russia would be fertile soil for his own gospel, that of the struggling and defiant spirit that aimed at building, incessantly building, a new world. This is an important detail to keep in mind as one reads this travel account, for despite his powers of observation and accurate recording of things observed, Kazantzakis as a visionary and an artist would not hesitate to describe a situation imaginatively and to give it epic proportions if this would help him to convey its essence or sense of urgency. For Kazantzakis aimed, above all, at capturing the mood of Russia in the years after the October Revolution.

Geographically he crisscrosses European and Asiatic Russia. Thematically he reports on a wide range of topics: revolutionary approaches to education, literature, the theater, dance and museums; he visits prisons and hospitals and inquires into the status of ethnic groups and women; he talks with prominent officials and intellectuals, Soviet as well as Western; he draws insights from the people in the streets. He is deeply moved by the huge Soviet effort to push a society to a higher level of historical consciousness, and he is virtually transported as he watches the celebration of the tenth anniversary of the Revolution in 1927. But 1927 also signaled an end to the "experimental" twenties, with the considerable flexibility enjoyed until then, and the beginning of regimentation in thought as well as in political and social action. And since Kazantzakis was above all an uncompromising thinker, relentlessly seeking freedom, the new atmosphere would create discomforting thoughts in him, even though he strove to appreciate the complexity of the transformation he was witnessing. He as much as suggested such misgivings in letters from Russia to his closest friend Pandelis Prevelákis: "What interests me is not man, the earth, and the sky; but the flame that consumes man, the earth, the sky. I must capture this flame." It was the same with Russia. He was interested in the flame that was consuming Russia and was concerned about forces that might extinguish it.

It could be argued that Kazantzakis, even though a non-Russian, nevertheless enjoyed a greater affinity with the Russian soul than did many other Western visitors. This was partly due to his special awareness of Russia's Orthodox religious heritage, having been born into an Orthodox family on the island of Crete. And it is worth reminding ourselves that, despite his conflicts with the Orthodox Church of Greece, and organized religion in general, Kazantzakis remained sensitively mindful of the individual's religious needs and above all was appreciative of the shaping influence that Eastern Orthodoxy had for the Greek and Slavic peoples. He therefore strove to assess the religious situation in the Soviet Union, as did many other visitors, by going to churches, religious museums and marketplaces, and even by visiting the editors of the antireligious journal, *The Atheist*.

Kazantzakis' assessment of the future of religion in the new socialist society was a grim one: Religion was on its way out, being replaced by a new communist liturgy. But as it turned out, those who eagerly predicted such an outcome were not entirely right. Faith and religious practice proved more tenacious than prophesied, and the new communist liturgy more vulnerable than anticipated. Yet there is no doubt that the situation at that time was an unenviable one for all religious groups that clung to their old ways. The following passage on the subject gives a sense of the keenness of Kazantzakis' observation, as well as an indication of the narrative skill characteristic of his travel account.

> Here in the Soviet Union, one very often finds the figures of the saints in the streets, in the hollow spaces in walls, or simply hanging on the doors of churches. They are neglected: Their clothes are shabby and dirty; their beards, unvarnished and unkempt. People have stopped nourishing them with prayers and offerings.
>
> I know a wooden angel who came unscrewed from the door of a church in a main street in Moscow. Someone had nailed him there to guard the entrance. Now he hangs there, with one wing down like a wounded bird. And a tin Saint Nicholas at a certain crossroads in Moscow has also become unhinged and now hangs precariously above the frozen sidewalk. When the wind blows, he squeaks and yells like a loose shop sign. No one cares enough to hold him by the legs and steady him or at least take him down altogether so that he will not continue to be tormented.
>
> The saints are hungry in Russia. The angels suffer pain as they hang between sky and earth. God wanders through the streets—homeless, unemployed, persecuted—like a bourgeois.

The passage, however, also suggests the subtle but painful dilemma in which Kazantzakis gradually found himself as he witnessed the relentless antireligious campaign of the Soviet authorities. As he pointed out, after his visit with the director of the weekly journal, *The Atheist*, he felt a strong intellectual and spiritual revulsion toward this exponent of atheism and his "scientific arguments." Experiences of this kind may explain the thoughtful letters Kazantzakis was writing to Prevelákis, on his reaction to the Soviet realities as they were gradually shaped by the advent of Stalinism. But he never published an account similar in style and content to those of Arthur Koestler or André Gide, which expressed disillusionment. A critical stance may be seen in his observations, but by and large he remained sympathetic to and understanding of the efforts being made to transform Soviet society, despite the fact that he was already moving into a post-communist stage in his thinking.

Kazantzakis' Soviet experiences and his reflections on them are in many respects unique, made even more so by the philosophical view that he brought to them. And even though one can get a glimpse of some of these experiences from passages in *Report to Greco*, Kazantzakis' spiritual autobiography, and *Toda Raba*, his novel inspired by the Russian Revolution, the present volume constitutes the most comprehensive recording of his varied encounters and thoughts on the subject. It is also one of the most insightful reports on Russia in the twenties, by one of the most inquiring spirits of the twentieth century.

Kazantzakis' account should fascinate devotees of travel literature. It should also give pleasure to those interested in exciting writing and story-telling. Finally, it should be of interest to students of Russian history and culture. The translators are to be congratulated for making it accessible to an English-speaking audience.

—Theofanis G. Stavrou

*Theofanis G. Stavrou is Professor of Russian and Modern Near Eastern History, and Director of Modern Greek Studies at the University of Minnesota.

■ A REMINISCENCE

Sixty years have passed since Nikos Kazantzakis wrote *What I Saw in Russia*, the title under which this book first appeared in Greece. During his visits of 1926, 1927 and 1928, he was witnessing the steps Russia was taking since the October Revolution, and I was with him during the last one of these three journeys.

We did not see any scenes of horror. We did not witness any killings on the streets, acts of violence or vandalism. Churches were closed but were not desecrated; icons were not burned, and no one destroyed the beautiful wall paintings of Rublev. In Moscow streets, we saw little icons of the Virgin built into walls that were still preserved under their glass covers. No one had cast a stone to break the glass in order to disfigure them.

Churches, museums and the palaces of the nobility were all beautifully maintained. During our stay at Borzhom I remember the little palace of the brother of the Tsar, Nicholas II. It was here that the Bolsheviks sent their prominent officials to rest and to relax. In the garden of the house not one of the large Chinese vases was broken. And within, the palace was filled with bibelots, ceramics and works of art, all in perfect order as if the original landlord still lived there.

In 1928–29, we cruised down the entire course of the Volga River from Novgorod to Tbilisi. We strolled in every town where our little boat stopped and anchored. We spent a good deal of time in Azerbaizhan, touring several days in Baku, Tbilisi and Batum. We also traveled in Armenia and in the Caucasus Mountains. Everywhere it was peaceful; the people, good-natured and courteous. However, I do remember an ugly incident that was related to us as we were traveling through Georgia. One night the owner of a vineyard uprooted all his vines because he was being forced to join a kolkhoz.

During this journey, which lasted almost four months, we enjoyed everything and were particularly moved by the many new and marvelous developments in the new Russia: day-care centers, kindergartens, schools, universities, hospitals, orphanages and homes for the elderly. There were also theaters, cinemas, opera houses and concerts with excellent orchestras and superb soloists. Moscow and Saint Petersburg were a joy to behold!

But there were also hidden wounds—injustices, hatreds, murders. Authorities in power often become corrupt and proceed to corrupt those around them. This is the fate of all peoples in every age. A folk-philosopher once told me: "Man cannot endure a contented existence!"

All peoples dream of love, justice and peace; few succeed in possessing them for very long. Much patience and much time are needed to change the nature of human beings. One day this too may come to pass.

But let us turn now to Nikos Kazantzakis, who gives us his insights about what he saw, felt and thought during his journeys into that vast and mysterious land—Russia.

—Helen Kazantzakis
January 1989

■ PROLOGUE

■ BETWEEN 1925 AND 1930, I went on three different journeys to the Soviet Union, and I stayed for a total time of almost two years,* traveling from Minsk to Vladivostok and from Murmansk to Bukhara and Echmiadzin.

I attempted in several books (*What I Saw in Russia,* two volumes; *History of Russian Literature,* two volumes; *Toda Raba,* a novel) and in a number of articles for periodicals and newspapers to pin down the landmarks in this difficult journey.

Today, as I collect in this book all the things that I saw and felt in this vast land, I do not want in any way to change anything. A new, after-the-fact arrangement would of course give my experiences a more logical coherence and a foresight easy to arrive at from the present perspective, but it would take away a certain spontaneous psychic sweep that they possess and all the fluff of virginal contact, virtues that I esteem in this kind of work more highly than a calm, logical analysis and the useless, well-intentioned effort to stifle the Russian flame. "When God raises a storm, pity the man who pours oil into the sea."

—Nikos Kazantzakis
1956

---

* First journey: October 13, 1925, to January 25, 1926; second journey: October 20, 1927, to December 22, 1927; third journey: April 19, 1928, to April 19, 1929.

1

■ INTRODUCTION

■ I SPEAK THE TRUTH, just as my eyes saw it. The moment through which we are passing is so crucial that each falsehood or omission would be a disgraceful action.

But if it were humanly possible that the whole truth—its luminous center and its pulsating nebula—could be fixed into words, this book would have to be harsh, visionary and terrifying. Whatever is happening consciously today in Russia is minor and uncertain compared with what is happening unconsciously, an activity beyond the awareness or even the wish of her leaders. As through a mist, we sense that cosmogonic events are engendered in this immense land of muzhik Russia. Unfortunately, we live only a short while and do not manage to witness the whole cycle. We can only guess—and even this in a brief flash—about the curve that lies hidden and then charges upward, along the ephemeral arc that is our age.

Whoever wishes to make a fruitful alliance with the Spirit that destroys and creates as it moves forward must love Russia entirely, deeply, without the wretched reservations of metaphysical thought or the minute investigations of mathematics and science.

The moment is critical. Exhausted but victorious, Russia is emerging from a terrifying ordeal, and bourgeois nations surround her with hate. The Idea has not as yet solidified into a firm body. It has not found its whole and clear voice. It still flows, searches and struggles to steady itself so that it can speak. The need to survive—that is the first concern. Russia is hungry and wants to eat. The world around her is aligning itself to attack her. She too must arm herself and be ready. Bread and tanks—these are her primary necessities.

Later, when the danger has passed and when she is fed and securely victorious, there will be time for philosophical discourses. Now, first of all, to survive.

And yet in this book that you hold, my reader, you will find a mind that puts prying and philosophical questions to the architects and the workers who are building the new Russia. They certainly have no time for philosophical discussion. They are building. At first I was still governed by the fine concerns of the bourgeois creature who has eaten and is satiated. Others work for him and he has the leisure to engage in discourse, for his mind to play. Time passed. I often went astray. I suffered, until the true face of Russia rose within me, filled with blood and light.

And now when I recall the entire vision in my mind, what moves me most deeply is this: In the bustling cities, in the snowbound villages and in the barren steppes of Russia, I saw for the first time visible signs of the Invisible.

When I say "Invisible," I do not mean a priest's God or a certain metaphysical consciousness or a poetic reflection of wish fulfillment. I mean the cosmogonic Force, which uses men as its carriers and beasts of burden—and before us the animals, plants, matter—in its forward surge, as if it had a purpose and had to follow a certain road. You sense, since they surround you here in Russia, the blind forces that create the eye and the light.

For this reason, my reader, I do not address myself only to your reason. I look for the movement within your being that wishes to drive the world forward in harmony with its own rhythm. And it is the stirring within myself I wish to transmit to you so that I can make contact with you. But since, in order to make this connection, I must embody my action in words—that is, to transform it into something inert—it is necessary before you begin reading to keep this in mind: Accept the words I use as something material—as if each one were a hard, dormant seed that holds explosive forces within it. In order to find out what I wish to say, you must let each word explode within you and in this way free the spirit it imprisons. Otherwise, communication cannot exist.

Crush the word; free the constricted strength within it, and then, my reader, you will discover this: Beyond logic, beyond discussion and clever debates, beyond economic necessity, social upheavals and political programs, above the Soviets and the commissars, it is the spirit of the historical epoch that we are living that surges and governs here in Russia, dark, blood-drenched and merciless in its search for light. From the most primitive muzhik to the holy countenance of Lenin, all are consciously or unconsciously its workers and collaborators.

A holy exultation has seized all who are constructing the new Idea, an awesome obsession. This is the most significant feeling that Russia gave to me. May I hopefully impart a little of this emotional experience to you. This open-minded book has no other purpose.

■ FROM ATHENS
TO ODESSA

■ AS I FINALLY LEFT THE GREEK COAST behind me, I began to breathe more easily. Behind me I left our shameless party disputes, our petty and somewhat comical political nonsense with its serious, tragic consequences, the choking atmosphere of contemporary Greece, and at last I began to enjoy the air of the free and uninhabited sea.

An intense curiosity and anxiety seized my heart. I was traveling north toward the mysterious land with its vast snow-filled plains where millions of half-Asian and half-European people, rich in paradoxical qualities—mystical and realistic, gentle and hardhearted, patient and revolutionary—are struggling. Entrenched in the earth and up to their knees in mud and blood, they are engaged in a pioneering struggle to open a new road for mankind.

What can be happening, I wondered, in these snow-capped regions? Have the "red snows," which the Bolshevik poets hail in triumph, turned purple from the new sun that has risen or only from the blood of the thousands of men and women who have been killed? Or does Russia continue to follow the same course as always, the one that her leading contemporary poet, Alexander Blok, who died from starvation, had always wanted for her: "Wilderness, meadow—and a bandanna on the forehead pulled down to the eyebrows"?

We shall see. No one has been willing or able, I think, to tell the truth up until now. The whole truth.

A mass of books has been written. Some praise, and others condemn. In some of them, "holy Russia" is a paradise; in others, she is a hell with all the Dantean circles of hunger, misery and madness.

5

One thing all friends and foes admit willingly or not: Man is undertaking a very difficult and bloody experiment in these lands. We hear cries of struggle and hope. Millions have died from sickness, from war, from hunger, but the people have not yielded. They fight with rage, determined to free the earth.

Hovering around the red threshing floor that is Russia, mankind, filled with fear and hope, listens and strains to see. Did the terrifying, bloody Idea bring a little more light, a little more justice and happiness to the village huts or to the workers' shacks? Did it uplift and soothe man's heart? Do the sons and daughters of Russia have more food to eat, and do they have more humane work to do? Do they breathe more freely?

Whenever politicians, industrialists, workers or journalists have gone to see for themselves so that they may enlighten others, they have returned with conflicting reports and have increased the confusion. And this has happened for two reasons:

Each one went to Russia carrying in readiness beforehand his own economic and social system and having one main purpose—to search and to find arguments that would support his system. And naturally each one, ignoring many things that he saw and adding others, managed with a fixed, narrow-minded, logical reasoning to illustrate that which before his journey he had considered a proven fact. A clear eye, not cold or indifferent but filled with love and detached wonder to find and speak the truth, has not been able as yet, it seems to me, to embrace the entire multifaceted countenance, all light and shadow, of Soviet Russia. Either the mind was fanatical and saw one-sidedly, from the right or the left, half the face of the truth; or the heart was mocking, unable to see anything without distorting it, naively inflamed or lost in lyricism and vagueness.

The second and most significant reason why Europeans

were not able, and may never be able, to understand Russia is this: An abyss exists between the European and the Slavic soul. Unlike the rational European, the Russian has a primordial gift with which he reconciles contradictions within himself that for the reasoning European are utterly irreconcilable. Above all, the European places the logical mind, the rational connection, the fruitfully practical use of the abstract idea; but the Russian places the soul above all else. The soul, full of light and darkness, in its rich, contradictory and complicated ferment, pushes man beyond the rational toward dangerous creation. The blind creative forces have not as yet arranged themselves in a logical hierarchy. The Russian is still mysteriously united with the primitive Mothers. Filled with earth and a divine darkness, he is, at the same time, pierced by a sharp light that burns him like a flame. For this reason, we must judge the virtues and the faults of the Russian with a different yardstick, and many of his actions should not astonish us. Even in his purest urge he can commit crimes, and in the midst of blood and vodka he can remain pure. The Russian is like the old man Karamazov: He has rich, primitive and overwhelming passions, but he also irresistibly fascinates us, for we sense that his soul is vast and that his heart is full of human warmth.

Among the passengers on the boat that was taking me north were two Russian men, a Russian woman and several Greek merchants who were returning to the richly profitable Russian ports. One Russian, pale and silent, was a teacher; the other was once a colonel in the Tsarist army. For years he had roamed the Balkans as a refugee. He tried all the vocations, went hungry, thirsted for vodka. His clothes were shabby, his cheeks were sunken, and his old fur coat hung from his shoulders like a tattered flag. But slowly all these hardships ended—ended or defeated his soul—his

anger against the Bolsheviks subsided, and now he was returning to his country, defeated but happy. During the day,
he played with a pig, a dog and a cat that he found on the
boat. He laughed to himself, spoke warmly to the animals,
smoked and constantly drank tea.

He approached me only once. He looked me over
thoroughly, pointed to his shabby clothes and his unraveled
sleeves and smiled. He glanced around with care. He saw
that we were alone. In a quietly emotional voice, he began
to recite some Russian verses. I understood nothing, and I
called one of the Greeks to interpret for me.

"They are verses of some Russian poet," he said.

"Good. What do they say?"

The wily Greek hesitated.

"Speak," I urged him. "What do you fear? We are alone."

The Greek, a lump in his throat, began to translate:

> *An iron curtain*
> *Is falling on Russian history with a crashing sound—*
> *The performance is over, the audience rises.*
> *Time to put on our fur coats and return to our houses—*
> *They turn.*
> *No more fur coats and no more houses!*

The Russian smiled again, shook his bald head and with-
drew to the stern of the boat. And the shrewd Greek winked
at me.

"Just look at his baggy trousers," he said. "He's going to
fill them out again in Russia!"

I engaged in a conversation with this cagey grandson of
Odysseus.

"What are your ideas about the Bolsheviks?"

"I'll tell you. In the beginning, when the storm broke,
we Greeks in Russia lost our senses. We trampled on one
another and fled. We came to Greece. Our country is good

and worthy, but there a man cannot earn his bread. You see, down there the men are clever like us. We can't outsmart them. What could we do then? We returned to Russia. The Bolsheviks are good too. Don't pay attention to what you hear. They're Russians too, naive and a little on the dumb side. . . . We'll find a way to manage things."

His small rapacious eyes were shining. Surely this wily Greek had already figured a way to extract fat from the new, lean Soviet cows. He spoke about the Russians with love. He sang hymns to their virtues, which were always a source of convenience to him in his business. They were unsuspecting, gullible and hardworking. Whatever one told them, they believed. They had rich fields—they planted them and you reaped. The eyes of this cunning Greek sparkled like those of the shepherd who calculates the amount of the meat, the fur and the milk of his herds at pasture.

In the same way, but with one word, the captain answered me when I asked him one evening how people were now getting along in Russia.

He smiled condescendingly, and he also winked his eye and said, "Pitifully!"

The Russian woman who was traveling with us was the colonel's wife. In their need, she had lowered herself by becoming a dancer in Salonica. Eventually she went hungry, became ill and lost her teeth. Although her blouses had holes in them at the elbows, her eyes gleamed with a mysterious bright blue. Her nose, tilted flirtatiously, gave an enchanting youthfulness to her withered and much-kissed face.

She wept and howled when her kidneys gave her pain, while at the same time singing in her shrill voice the light-hearted songs of the Cafe Aman. She twisted her waist, clapped her hands and stared with a languishing glance at the weather-beaten, weary men in the suffocatingly crowded salon.

We had left the Greek coast far behind us, and then in the turbid air of an autumn morning, a pale Constantinople rose out of the water. The minarets, grand and sharp, pierced the fog. It was drizzling. Saint Sophia, the palaces and the imperial harbor battlements, now in ruins, seemed to fade in the silent, oppressive rain.

We had all pressed ourselves toward the bow and, straining our necks, we watched. Each of us had a gleam in his eye for a different city. The Russians stared, deeply entrenched in a seethingly quiet ecstasy, just as a thousand years earlier their gigantic blue-eyed ancestors had viewed the palaces, the gold and the women of Byzantium. The two Greek merchants stared rapaciously at the harbor and asked about trade and contraband. As for me, my heart remained unmoved. In earlier times, passing by these legendary waters, I had heard my blood stir with tales, demotic songs and strong longings, and I felt heavy, warm tears from the icon of the Virgin falling upon my hands. Today this enchanting vision of homes and cypresses seemed mirrored in a far and improbable reflection, a fantasy created with mist.

For two days we watched the city from a distance and waited for the sea to calm so that we could sail on. I was glad that it was raining, that the Turkish gendarmes who came aboard as guards did not permit us to disembark so that we could stroll among the legendary cobblestone streets. Everything was in exact harmony with the stubbornly bitter disposition of my soul. I said, "With its palaces, its half-moons and its domes, this colorful city is a creation of my mind, which built it in the rain and decorated it with kings, mosques and cypresses to put temptation into my heart. But when I wish, I shall blow upon it, and it will vanish."

It was raining. The sea was a clear green, and the wind was still. At dawn of the third day, we set sail. We passed the Bosporus. The lush gardens grew sparse, houses became fewer in number, and on the left and right, the shores of Europe and Asia became rugged and uninhabited. We entered the Black Sea. The waves were pitching us up and down. The Russian woman grew pale and began to sing. She interrupted her song, vomited, and then, wiping her protruding withered lips with a huge red handkerchief, took up her song again.

That is how the days and nights went by.

Until finally one morning, we distinguished far in the distance, beyond the end of the horizon, a low, vague, dusty-green line—Russia.

■ ODESSA

■ "MOTHER RUSSIA! Mother Russia!" the two Russian passengers on the bow exclaimed as they watched the gray-green shoreline of their homeland growing before them and cutting through the wet air with greater and greater intensity.

Toward noon we could clearly see the neglected gardens, the green-domed churches, the tall houses. The Russian woman had locked herself in her room for hours now, and, when we finally entered the harbor, she appeared wearing makeup that was satanically clever. She had two blue circles around her eyes, a pale face and an overly red mouth. Wrapped in an orange silk blouse, she sat in the boat's salon, licking her lips without speaking.

The boat came to the side of the pier. Leaning on the bow, we all watched greedily. People on shore moved quickly along the pier, rubbing their hands to keep warm. Behind us we could see rows of many-storied houses, their windows shut. From the Customs Building across from us, a dozen officials and Red Guards appeared and came aboard. They searched everywhere, opened luggage, leafed through books, shook out clothing—all with politeness and without condescension.

"All right, you may pass!"

The officer smiled, stretched out his hand and indicated that Russia was before us. We were free to enter.

Let me not speak of the emotion I felt when I stepped on Russian soil. Many generations within me had yearned for this moment. Many of my ancestors on Crete, who had waited for centuries for the Moscovite to descend and

12

to save them, now exulted: "Keep your courage, my brothers. The Moscovite is descending!"

I walked through the wide streets with excitement. I looked, I listened, I touched—I was happy. Heaps of melons on the sidewalks, piles of red apples; few men—pale and in a hurry; painted women, barefoot children, now and then an automobile; the stores filled with goods—a few displays with luxury items, others filled with books; and everywhere pictures of Lenin with that sarcastic smile, sharp as a knife.

Your first impression, a profound one, is the silence and loneliness in the wide, open streets. The stores are all open, and yet they appear closed. They are filled with things, and yet they seem empty. Clearly stamped on every face is the exhaustion, the pallor of hunger, the deprivation and the fear—which do not exist now, but which sorely tried the people during the early revolutionary years without mercy.

You feel that all of Odessa has bled profusely. She has been seriously ill, but now you sense that life is running through her veins again; the day has again found its regular pulse, the men are beginning to be happy, the women are smiling, the cheeks of the children are red again—the streets, the trees and the people are slowly recovering from their sickness.

A certain holy, calm silence penetrates you, the way it happens when you enter the room of a dangerously sick man who has now taken the upward road. His fever has fallen, and he has now begun to eat and talk. I recall a few years ago another city that I saw, at a crucial moment for her as well—Vienna. What a difference! Vienna was dying, and all the establishments for easy pleasure were open day and night—the dance bars, the rousing Gypsy music and other obscene spectacles. Many women stirred in an atmosphere redolent with flowers, sweat and cocaine.

Odessa did not fall into such corruption. She was

wounded and in danger, but now she starts out again and lives. The bread is fragrant again in the ovens. People again have clothes, shoes, coal, meat—all the indispensable needs of life. At night there is very little activity; the exhausted city sleeps. In the trolleys, on the street walls, in the schools, in the courthouses, in the clubs, there are colored posters: laborers at work; women breast-feeding their babies; children going to school; farmers pushing the plow; Lenin leaning over the masses, at one time smiling and quiet, at another, angry and frantic, with a spasmodically disfigured face. You think his lips are those of a prophet. What comes forth from them are not words but burning coals.

You are also impressed by the number of Jews here. Odessa is one of the few Russian cities in which the Tsars permitted the Jews to remain, and now, as you walk through the streets, you are surprised by the shrewd dark faces, the beaked noses, the black, darting eyes and the goatlike lips.

My Greek companion who was showing me the city cursed when he saw the "unbaptized" and spat on the ground. A deep hatred and a merciless professional rivalry separated him from this "dangerous" and powerful race.

"Ptui! May they vanish from the face of the earth!" he grumbled. "It's not enough that they crucified Christ. They also took all our jobs!"

Wearing his torn shoes and his patched, baggy refugee trousers, he walked beside me, staring at everything with a sharp and rapacious eye. He was happy that he had returned to his poor "Mother Russia." After noticing certain businesses and asking their prices, he began to plan where he would open a store, dreaming about how he would buy new trousers and order new shoes. And then cautiously, without the "Reds" getting wind of it, he would again pile up rubles and become a native. This was his dream. Today when he got off the boat, he fell down and kissed the

Russian earth, and when he first put the murky black rye bread into his wide mouth, he could not hold back his tears. Greece shone in his mind like some far-distant idea; Russia for him was Mother, the "Poor Mother" as he called her warmly, and he loved her, searching and struggling to find her breasts, as if she were, in truth, a kind and contented cow filled with milk.

"Let's go to the Red Alley," I said to him.

I wanted to see the small house where the Society of Friends* first assembled. On the ground floor the cobbler was working.

I grabbed this shifty, cunning Greek by the arm.

"In this poor little house that you see," I said to him, "the first meetings of the Society of Friends were held. Three simple men, merchants like yourself, gathered one night on the upper floor and took an oath to destroy the Ottoman Empire. They did not have money or an army or what wise men would call a brain. Turkey was all-powerful. She had all of Asia Minor, Egypt, Arabia, Syria, all of the Balkans. Her armies had almost reached the gates of Vienna. And these three simple Greeks planned, behind the windows that you are looking at right now, to seize the Sultan, bring down Turkey, free Greece and take us all into Constantinople!"

The Greek listened but did not speak. We climbed into a carriage, and he accompanied me as far as the station for Moscow. Night had fallen, and the houses were sinking into the darkness. Men and women returned to their homes hurriedly. On the corners, beggars played harmonicas and softly sang Ukrainian folk songs. A freezing rain slowly fell on the large, noble looking city.

---

* Secret organization of Greeks founded in Odessa to work for the liberation of Greece from Ottoman rule.

When we reached the station for Moscow, and I turned to say good-bye to my friend, he took my hand, very much moved.

"From the moment you showed me the little house of the Society of Friends, I became a different person. I now fear nothing. Though I was once rich here in Russia and lost everything, I return now with holes in my pants and without shoes—but I vow to you that I will become very rich. I have found a way. I will do big things—you will see—because I know that whatever a man's soul desires, he can accomplish."

And this is how this unbeatable, crafty Greek transubstantiated within himself the Society of Friends into a business enterprise.

■ KIEV

■ NIGHT. IT WAS RAINING. The train jolted forward. Opposite me sat a middle-aged man dressed in working clothes—a shirt with a leather belt, high, heavy shoes, a shaved head. We started to talk. He was a professor at the University of Kiev. We spoke about Russia and Greece. He hoped some day to fulfill his dream to see the light of Greece; I was realizing my dream of losing myself in the dark North, deep within the snow. We smiled when we considered the insatiable nature of man, who always yearns for that which he does not have, and we happily discussed how it was that on this demonic, unquenchable thirst, and on the incurable malady, man builds all his hopes and all his accomplishments.

Thus from time immemorial and with this risky and uncertain yearning, life managed to leap from the plants to animals, from animals to man; and now with an all-encompassing groan it pushes us—sacrificers and at the same time victims—to destroy our present societal and spiritual equilibrium and to seek a new, uncertain and dangerous but higher, we hope, kind of balance.

When we reached this point in our philosophical confession, my companion grew silent. I eagerly wanted to relate these general principles to the contemporary Russian problem, but the professor would not speak. He took two apples from his pocket, ate them peels and all, and then, wrapping himself in his coat of cowhide, stretched along his bench and said good-night.

In the morning we woke up in the boundless black soil of the Ukraine. Every so often we saw farmers steeped in the rich soil, plowing with their heavy, thick-boned horses.

17

There were no rocks or hills or forests. At some moments the eye could discern slender white poplars or hungry crows in the sky. Through the fog we could distinguish the villages scattered in the endless plain. There was always a church in the center with its painted green, pear-shaped dome; and huddled around it, the low village houses; and on the outskirts, a shepherd standing tall amid his sheep.

At each station, smiling village girls with slightly tilted noses and dewy blue eyes, wearing multicolored blouses and thick woolen shoes, sprang up to meet us. They held trays loaded with glasses of hot tea, buckets of milk or baskets filled with apples, pears, bread and butter. A few boys leaped on the train and sold inexpensive little books: the *Alphabet of Communism,* works of Lenin, Trotskii, Bukharin, proletarian songs, popular advertising pamphlets on the cultivation of the soil or the sicknesses of man.

For a few moments the station was filled with laughter and noises. The passengers got off the train and filled their teapots with boiling hot water. But the whistle of the engine quickly sounded. The train set forth, and we moved again into the silent, damp, black-soiled Ukraine.

I watched in silence, mulling over in my mind the enormous body of the Russian land. High in the North, the dark, dense forest: firs, beech, elms, linden, oak. Then in the South, the vast steppes of the Kazakhs unfold: regular, monotonous, with those sacred hills, *kourgan,** that cover the bones of the old heroes. Farther to the south, the steppes turn to sand at the mouth of the Dnepr, to silt north of the Crimea and to salt around the Caspian. Wave after wave of the awesome, wild steppes with their half-savage people— the Circassians, the Nogai, the Kalmyks and the Tatars. Farther down at the shores of the Caucasus and the Crimea, the sun shines, and the vineyards, the olive trees and citrus

---

* A hill raised at a burial site.

trees blossom. Nothing is missing in Russia. All the animals and plants, from the most northern to the most tropical, live easily in the boundless Russian land.

Natural boundaries do not exist. The land stretches out the way the sea does, and the desert molds the image and the spirit of man to its likeness. To these plains and to these steppes the Russian owes his expansive nature. In the eyes of her people, Russia is a whole world. "Of what foreign land do you speak?" a certain character in Gogol's *The Inspector General* cries out. "From our town you can travel three years in a horse and carriage and never reach a foreign land!"

The Russians love to travel in their vast land. In the very early times, they loaded their gods and their children in their canoes; they entered the big rivers, and like children they enjoyed changing sites, food, climate and manner of life.

A mixture of many races created the giant Russian mosaic: Slavs, Varangians, Germans, Lithuanians, Armenians, Greeks, Jews, Poles, Tatars, Mongolians, Kazakhs . . . New blood was infused into this great land continually. Conquerors came and brought order to the chaos. There were two especially great organizers:

The Varangians: They came down in their oblong canoes from the frozen North Sea, moving along the great Russian rivers, building forts on the banks, all the way to the Black Sea. They seized whatever they could in their journey, and they reached Byzantium, where they eagerly sold their goods: sheep furs, amber, honey, wax, livestock, slaves— male and female.

The Slavs who lived along the banks of the Dnepr were an agricultural people, who had patriarchal families that were good, hardworking and savage. They worshiped freedom and were ready to risk their lives in heroic fashion. They were good to strangers and loved to dance and sing with a passion.

Their customs were simple and primitive. A woman was a slave to her husband, and the children were the property of the father. The worship of the ancestors was their religion; every head of a family was a priest, and the elders presided over their sacred ceremonies.

Their most important holidays were two: the festival of spring in which they asked the gods to bless their sown fields, and the feast of autumn in which they thanked the gods for the harvest. Temples did not exist. The places of worship were the forests, hills, springs and rivers. When they were defeated in war, they did not surrender. They committed suicide by slitting their stomachs, believing that if they died from wounds inflicted by the enemy, they would work forever as slaves in the future life.

Anarchy. Chaos. They battled among themselves, killing one another for centuries, until as Nestor, the oldest Slavic chronicler, states, they sent a message to the Varangians to come down and make order out of their anarchy: "Our land is rich and large, but we have no order. Come then and put us in order." That was their message to the Varangians.

The Varangians came down. They built towers and castles. They made the Slavs into serfs; they became feudal lords. They did not interfere in any way with the family and social life of the local people or with their customs or religion. They wanted only obedience and taxes. They took it upon themselves to defend the Slavs from nomadic pirates and from their own internal anarchy.

The Byzantines: The Varangians organized the Russians' external affairs; the Byzantines organized them internally, cultivating their intellectual and psychological strengths and giving them a civilization: the alphabet, writing, art, religion—they owe all these to the Byzantines.

First Olga, the widow of the Russian chief Igor, went to

Byzantium and was baptized. "Olga glittered in Christen-
dom," writes a Russian chronicler, "like a morning star. She
shed a very sweet light upon it. She shone upon the nonbelievers like the moon at night. Now she ascended into the
Russian sky, praying to God for the sons of Russia."

Her wild son Vladimir, once he had ruthlessly conquered
the tribes around him and had enthroned himself at Kiev, sent
envoys to the various neighboring rulers to see and report on
what gods they worshiped so that he could choose. They
went to the Alamans, but they did not like their gods. They
went to Moslem sultanates, but when Vladimir heard that the
prophet of Mecca forbade his followers to drink, he angrily
exclaimed, "Mohammed's religion is unacceptable because
the Russian people feel a great joy when they drink!" When at
last the envoys reached Byzantium, their minds were stirred
with admiration. "We don't know," they wrote to their king,
"if we are in heaven or on earth. Such beauty! Surpassing the
imagination of man."

Emperor Basil, the Bulgar Slayer, showed them the
palaces, the churches, the contests at the Hippodrome, the
holy feasts, the liturgies. He loaded them with beautiful
gifts and at the end offered his sister Anna to Vladimir as
wife. Amazed by such wealth and power, the barbarian
Russian prince had himself baptized at Kherson in the
Crimea and had flocks of his followers baptized in the
rivers of the lands about him. Anna, the refined daughter
of the renowned Theofanos, took scholars, priests, artists
and architects with her and traveled north. She passed the
endless fields; she slept in the small primitive houses. She
awoke in the morning among snows and kept moving
northward, carrying in her delicate hands the civilization
of Greece, hoping to transplant it into the black soil
underneath.

The seed took root. Not many years passed before

churches and monasteries arose from this rich land. Their walls were covered with paintings and mosaics. The old rough habits grew tame, and from Kiev to old Novgorod the face of Russia was illuminated.

In the morning we reached the old capital of Russia, Kiev. From a distance we could discern the golden domes shining like pointed Tatar helmets in the light fog.

A holy place. Like the other old cities, she drips with blood. For how long did her first good fortune last? Two centuries. And then suddenly the Tatars fell upon her. They burned the churches, slaughtered the men, seized the women. Literature and the arts then sought refuge in the monasteries. The highest ideal was to abandon the world and become a monk. Many castrated themselves to save their souls. The monasteries became rich; the monks became leaders. They made agreements with the Tatars and as partners exploited the peasants.

The sun was shining. We got off the train. We strolled hurriedly through the famous city. Rich parks, cheerful Ukrainian faces, exciting colors. The Ukraine is the smiling face of Russia. On the 25th of March, the young girls in many towns climb up on the roofs and *call out to Spring.* They entreat her to come early, to bring the sun again, the birds and the flowers. These lyrical greetings to Spring often take a dramatic form. The women divide themselves into two choruses. One group calls for Spring; the other answers as Spring.

The Ukrainian dances are full of life, passion and grace. The men and women dance together. Their dance is often a dramatic pantomime, an erotic chase in which the woman refuses the man, flees and then returns. At the end she is happily defeated, and the dance breaks out into a triumphant whirl.

I went into the churches: darkness, the smell of incense, old Byzantine icons of our Virgin gone to foreign lands—all the golden imprint of Byzantium still embedded like a rock in the very being of contemporary life. No one now disturbs these fossils, nor do they bother anyone. At one time they constituted a living organism filled with hunger and strength. Now they are simple and cosmetically harmless decorations. The Bolsheviks pass before them and barely turn their heads to look at them. Once in a while, a few anachronistically impassioned worshipers go by and pay tribute to them in secret, as if they were committing a sin— or as if they were afraid.

At noon we boarded the train and the journey began again. After a thousand years we move north again, not to give light but perhaps to receive it. Here new leaders have destroyed the old political and spiritual structure of Russia. They are creating a new way of life with which they struggle to renew the world. With agony and excitement, with confused logic that was also full of contradictions, I was going now to these new leaders, to live the new reality, and to see if they had brought any kind of change to the material life and the heart of man.

As previously in old cosmogonic epochs, we now have learned that new gods have been born in the North, and we have come from afar to bow before their cradles. With me on the same train, peasant delegates were arriving, sent from their local Soviets; Czechoslovakian workers; Turks and Bulgarians; and even two silent and mysterious Japanese. Each one brought his anxieties, his hopes and his questions—these are the gifts that modern man brings to the newborn god.

I approached the two Japanese, both of whom were architects.

"We have read about the new schools of Russian

architecture, and we are going to Moscow to study them. Several technical problems are tyrannizing us, and we hope to find a solution."

I listened to them and happily remembered the old words of the Magi: "We saw a new star and we followed it."

I passed the second night with these thoughts, and we awoke to find ourselves in the deep snows. The fir trees were motionless, frozen in crystal. The stone houses had disappeared, and we now saw wooden huts with their inclined straw roofs. We had finally traversed the Ukraine and were now entering Great Russia.

The peasant faces appeared heavier, more like the soil. The villages looked crushed and bleak. Life changed its rhythm to one that now seemed more broad, deep, primitive and sluggish.

Wrapped in their cloaks of cowhide, the muzhiks with their low foreheads wait—silent, greasy and hairy. They look like demons who live in the snowy forests, and who at the same time seem lower and yet holier than man. These peasants hold the fate of Russia, and perhaps not only of Russia, in their gnarled, hairy hands. They are a dark, many-headed, rigid mass. In the very first line of battle, a few souls stir and struggle; they toil and groan. Behind them a raw bulky mass, blind, yet certain, pushes and is pushed.

In my mind I recalled the sparkling figure of Lenin, all light and flame, and I saw before me the dark mass that he had leavened—the muzhik. I now thrilled to reach my destination as soon as possible in order to see those two primordial antagonists and collaborators—the Spirit and the Flesh—wrestling in the enclosed red arena of the Kremlin.

The thick snow fell, covering the plowed land. The seeded grain nourished itself in silence and certainty. Every so often a pitch-black crow flew fiercely toward the roofs of the people to find something to eat.

I looked at Russia, and the words of Ilia Erenburg, filled with sorrow and pride, came into my mind:

Unclean and swollen from hunger—blood and pus flow from your open wounds. Russia, you have lain yourself down with groans and sighs. They have taken the delirium of your birth for death. The wise, the satiated, the clean, have jeered you. Their inner vitals are barren; their petrified chests are empty. Who will accept the holy inheritance? What Promethean hand will seize the half-smothered torch, rekindle it and take it further? A difficult birth, a great holy moment. Neither the sea foam nor the blue sky will give birth. Out of this black wasteland, washed with our own blood, a new, powerful age is being born. Believe in us. Receive it from our hands. It is ours and yours! With one breath, it will wipe out all the boundaries. In the dark midnight of the city, forgotten, under the shroud of snow, life lies hidden. And it was fated that a people will water the barren breast of the earth with its holy blood. Your enemy will come to you, O Birth-giver—to kiss your bloodied footsteps in the snow.

I stared and stared, anticipating. I felt that my gaze had acquired the wide blue depth that one sees in the eyes of those who live on the endless plains. I was staring, and suddenly around noon, golden domes appeared in the distance under a gray-black sky.

We were approaching and finally reaching the new Jerusalem of god the worker, the very heart of the new Promised Land—Moscow.

◼ MOSCOW

◼ I WANDER AND NEVER FEEL SATIATED as I watch this multicolored, multigerminated chaos—Moscow. Before I begin the toil to find what is hiding underneath this fascinating surface, I let my eyes enjoy this unexpected sight with the simplicity and happiness of a child.

Let us walk a little and take a turn around Moscow. The Bolshevik doorman at our hotel bends over and helps us with our rubbers, just as if masters and servants were still in existence. It is cold and sleet is falling. The sparrows and the foxes have taken refuge in their cozy nests, but thousands of vagabond children in Moscow do not have a hut in which to find warmth. These young proletarians watch me without any hostility as I pass wrapped in my fur coat. I console myself with the thought that they will grow quickly, more quickly than all other children in this world, and they will strive to take my fur coat away from me.

A well-dressed gentleman—a tall, rigid old lord—stands on a corner near the hotel, selling an amber pipe. Suddenly, another old man on the opposite sidewalk sees him. He splashes through the mud, rushing to greet him with great emotion. He clasps his hands. The fallen lord smiles quietly and kindly, and he speaks, repeating that noble word that is filled with the old Russian spirit, *"Nichevo! Nichevo!"* (It does not matter!)

> *There exists in history a wound larger than glory—*
> *a handkerchief kissed by a million lips—*
> *In the human forest of Moscow—*
> *where ideas are heaped upon one another—*

trees are burned by lightning and words
are like brittle leaves . . .

I was surprised that I remembered the words of that mystical Russian poet, Kluiev. I whispered them as I left the presence of the two fallen noblemen behind me.

The Kremlin rose in front of me: the heart of Moscow, and today, I believe, the heart of the world. In Red Square, the astonishing Cathedral of Saint Basil, and outside, the platform where Ivan the Terrible stood, his executioner decapitating rebels and liberty-loving boyars. He wanted to humiliate all the noblemen in order to create a firmly unified state; but at the same, he loved the humble people, and he listened emotionally when the ragged wandering bards sang the popular ballads in his court. An angel stood on his right—the boyar Nikita Romanov, brother-in-law of the Tsar and an ancestor of the Romanovs. A devil on his left—the bloodthirsty Maliuta Skuratov.

One of the ballads narrates how Ivan conquered Kazan:

He had dug under the wall of Kazan. He heaped up barrels of gunpowder. He put fire to the fuse. But the powder would not explode. On the walls, the Tatars laughed and showed their behinds to him. "Ha! Is this, my dear Tsar, how you are going to take Kazan?" The Tsar was furious. He ordered the gunners to be hanged. An old man asked permission to speak to him: "My lord, have patience. The wick burns quickly in the open air. Underground, it burns slowly." And, just as he spoke, Kazan staggered and fell, totally demolished. And the Tsar rejoiced. To each gunner he gave fifty rubles, and to the old man he gave five hundred!

Other ballads relate the dark private life of Ivan—his seven wives, some of whom he had killed, others whom he had locked up in monasteries; his son, his successor, whom he slew:

> Ivan the Terrible walked back and forth in his palace. He stared from the red window, combing his black hair with a fine comb. He said: "I brought the throne from Tsargrad [Constantinople] to Moscow. I was the first to dress in imperial purple. I conquered Kazan and Astrakhan. I dealt a blow to treason at Kiev; I destroyed it at Novgorod. I will strike at it again within the motherland in Moscow with its white walls."

Then a boyar gets up:

> "Tsar Ivan Vasilievich, you crushed treason at Kiev and Novgorod, but you cannot crush it in Moscow. It is inside your palace—it sits at your side—it eats from the same dish with you—it wears the same clothes as you do—the traitor is Tsarevich Fedor!" Ivan is furious. "Don't I have any trustworthy butchers?" Maliuta jumps up. "Do you want me to raise my arm to strike? He seizes Tsarevich by the fingers of his white hands, which are covered with rings, and drags him to the river Moskva. . . .

Rich and contradictory the soul of Ivan—brutal and pious, daring in imagination and drawn to the fine arts. In his letters to Prince André Kurbskii, and to the abbot of the Monastery of Saint Cyril at the White Sea, he reveals his cunning nature, his sarcasm, his vulgarity, his unbridled insults, his fear of God and his erudition. He is the first Russian writer to uncover and expose his ego in all its nakedness.

In one of his letters, he describes how he suffered as a child under the boyars:

> How I suffered from nakedness and hunger! We children were playing. Prince Shuiskii, sitting on his throne, leaned on his elbow and stretched his feet on our father's bed. They took the vast treasure that belonged to our father and our grandfather. They melted it, made sets of gold and silver plates from it and had their names engraved on them. . . .

I gaze at the golden domes of the churches of the Kremlin, the red walls with the heavy fortress doors decorated with the red star at the lintel where once upon a time the icon of the Virgin smiled—and I hasten to leave the bloody medieval past. I enter, relieved, into the contemporary scene, so full of life.

All of the East is buried in the snow. Businessmen of the Middle East with heavy turbans; Chinese, wrinkled like monkeys, sell charming wooden and silver toys. All the sidewalks are occupied by men and women who sell fruit, books, bibs for children, plucked chickens, small statues of Lenin. Young women with cigarettes in their mouths sell newspapers. Women workers pass by with red kerchiefs on their heads—stout, crude women with Mongolian features and eyes. Half-naked children with domed astrakhan hats. Churches with green or golden domes, Tatar walls, medieval castles, and next to them, modern skyscrapers. And this inscription on the walls, on the churches and on the streetcars: "Proletarians of the world, unite!" And suddenly toward the late afternoon, above all this unsettled din, the deep-sounding Russian bells announce the Vespers that persist in living on.

Chaos—your first impression!

Moscow is the perfect incarnation of the Slavic soul.

Without any urban design, it grew like a forest around its central red nucleus—the Kremlin. The first things built on this sacred Russian hill were the palaces of the king; next to them, the golden-domed churches of God. Quickly spreadding out its tentacles from the Kremlin, the city took hold beside the river and connected itself to the Tatar wall. And later, with time, it overflowed and spread out again. Oblique and irregular roads opened up. Churches and houses were daubed with warm colors. All of the races of Russia and the Orient came and wedged their souls without any logical pattern in the immense and always open-ended Russian mosaic.

Eastern architecture allows its palaces and cities to grow freely like a forest, without geometric harmony but with the irrational and complex surge of life itself. Similarly, a fixed Russian reality does not exist; it is always becoming. It is a river that flows, and as it moves, it opens and creates its own riverbed. There are many contradictions, things and creations that are logically inexplicable—remnants of primordial things that die slowly, others that had an abortive birth and yet others that are just beginning to live, with all of the awkwardness, uncertainty and grace of the newly born.

Here in the heart of an immense land inhabited by more than the hundred different ethnic groups that are nurtured by it, contradictory forces live together with a complete ease that is incomprehensible to the Europeans. In the churches, in the window displays, in the museums, in the life of the home and of the street, you are glad to search and find diverse tributaries issuing from afar.

Here is the Ukraine with her carpets and her many-colored pottery. Here is the Crimea with her charming silk embroidery, the strong Tatar breath on metal and leather. The Caucasus brings its precious enameled silver weapons, belts, buckles and earrings; Azerbaizhan and Daghestan, their silks, beautifully embroidered with flowers and wild animals; Central Asia, her rich rugs, where each race patiently weaves its unique geometric rose. And finally the hairy hermits of the North, wrapped in their sheepskins, who come and contribute their primitive engravings on wood and bone.

These are what Asia brings. And from Europe come ideas, theories, systems and a powerful need to bring some kind of logic to all of this Asiatic madness. In the streets, the schools, the offices, you meet somber men who are all method, action and rationality, totally different from the Russian personalities—inert, hysterical and mystical—that great Russian literature has made familiar to us.

Today, a new type of Russian is being forged by the new Idea.

And thus a second fundamental impression governs you as you walk through Moscow. Here in this exotic city, people are struggling to reach a synthesis. Painfully and with an ardent obstinacy, they are striving to subdue all of the Eastern chaos within and without them with an austere, logically assembled Idea.

You see you have entered a city of fanatic believers. In no other city in the world can you find these stern and resolute aspects on people's faces: the burning eyes, the tight, stubborn lips, this intensity and this religious fever for work. It is as if you have transported yourself into a sullen medieval city that is all castles and battlements. The enemy draws near and the knights arm themselves behind barricaded doors. Similarly, in Russia you breathe an air of warlike readiness. Whether you enter schools, universities, ministries or factories, or you partake in celebrations or lectures, you always sense an atmosphere filled with preparation for battle.

Here they work and they struggle. They are preparing themselves with a persistent faith. A great fear and a great hope hover above their heads. You rarely hear a careless laugh here. You do not meet the unemployed promenading in the streets. And toward nightfall you do not see women gossiping in public, nor do you find cabarets in the evening, dancing halls or urban dens of paid pleasure. Truthfully, something terrifying lies waiting in the air. One of the fearsome flaming Cherubs of the Second Coming, all eyes and sword, stands on the ramparts of the Kremlin—like a medieval chimera on the Gothic steeples—and guards Moscow.

I follow the crowd. The clerks finish their workday. The streets and trams are filled with hurrying, silent new Russians with their leather belts outside their shirts and their shabby sheepskins. I intercept their glances; I catch the glitter of their faces in the faint light of the autumn afternoon; I observe their decisive violent gestures. Slowly, slowly, I discover a deep inner uniformity in all of these moving crowds. And this is third fundamental impression that seizes you in Moscow: The individual retreats and submits to an order that is above the individual.

And then your hope or your fear increases. You sense something invincible and pitiless, something like a natural force that propels all these dark and, as of now, incoherent masses toward an all-powerful unity.

Night came. It was cold. Suddenly on the main road in Moscow, a savage battle song resounded in the air. At the end of Sverdlov Square, a battalion of the Red Army appeared. They wore their pointed Mongolian caps. Their steely gray overcoats reached to their feet. Their faces were burning like fire. At their head marched their leader, and he first began the wild song. Just as he passed before me, I saw his mouth twitching like an epileptic's. The veins in his neck were swollen, and perspiration dripped from his forehead, despite the frosty air. For some time he sang by himself, brandishing his sword in the air, and as he walked, you thought he was dancing, so frantic was the rhythm of his body. He sang alone, and suddenly the soldiers took up the wild tune, and all of the quiet street resounded.

As I watched the Red Army pass and felt its breath upon me, Roerich's angry prophetic song burst forth within me:

May fear overcome you when the Immobile One
Stirs. When the disorderly winds
Create a storm. When the mouth of man
Is filled with senseless words.
May fear overtake you when in the ground
Men bury their riches like treasure.
May fear overcome you when masses
Gather. When all learning is
Forgotten. When you do not have a piece
Of paper to write down thoughts. Oh, my neighbors,
How badly you have enthroned yourselves!
Your madness has called the most
Abominable of all women, "Beloved!"
Little wily ones, as you dance,
Prepare to suffocate
In your dance.

The Russian army passed by. The air quieted down. But I was able to see, this night in Moscow, that which I yearned to see: not heaven or hell, but the earth—the earth, whose masses have struggled for millions of years with their sweat and blood amid dangers, treacherous terrains and false steps—to move forward and upward. In our time this struggle of the earth is more evident, more prophetic and more crucial here in Russia. In other periods it was in other lands. Today the great Combatant—some call it God or spirit and others, matter—has centered all of its energy, that is, its agony and its hope, in this pioneering, tortured *Matushka*—Russia.

■ THE NATIONALITIES/
THE JEWS

■ IT IS A GREAT JOY to walk through Moscow and watch the bizarre, mysterious races strolling through the din of its streets: Tatars with alluring serpentine eyes; Jews and Armenians with their wily, restless expressions and their full and insatiable lips; Varangians from Arkhangelsk wrapped in cowhides; tall, slender, bone-sculpted Kazakhs; short businessmen from Turkestan with their long-haired sheepskins; gay, handsome Georgians, given to wine and women; and behind them, Turkomans, Circassians, Uzbeks, Bashkirs, Yakuts, Kalmyks, expatriate and distant brothers of ours who smell like horses.

All of Asia circulates in its capital, Moscow. In this crucible, life mixes the blood of many races. In the richness of crossings, it sometimes fails, sometimes succeeds, as it struggles to create a new and unexpected human type. We will not live to see the fruits of this new pan-spermic fertilization, but a mind that can look ahead across a long period of time takes pleasure walking in Moscow, because it can distinguish the new human elements that rush restlessly and spontaneously like spermatozoa toward the ovum to create a new civilization.

More than a hundred nationalities have their roots in Russia, and each one has its own language, its customs, its habits and its own separate psychic makeup. How did Bolshevism attempt to give some kind of order to this complex and dangerous Babylon?

When I reached Odessa, one thing truly surprised me: the strong nationalistic thrust of the Ukraine—its books, newspapers, shop signs, conversations, all on Ukrainian identity, ambition and ethnic pride. The entire race that for centuries suffocated under Tsarist tyranny was now breathing freely.

At the historic Greek School of Odessa, I had a similarly pleasant surprise. The director of the school, an austere and fanatic Greek communist, said to me, "The law requires that all of the lessons be given in the Greek language. No one can be appointed as a teacher here if he cannot teach in Greek. Each nationality goes forward on its own road."

When he saw that I was surprised, he smiled and said, "The communist democracy does not push for uniformity among the various national groups, but strengthens the ethnic character of each one. The communist Idea is a rich harmony of different voices. Each voice is free, but at the same time, it is harmoniously submissive to a totality."

Recess. The children—boys and girls—play, laugh and fight in the large schoolyard. They play, laugh and fight, and their teachers are with them.

"This is the big difference!" my ascetic-looking companion with the shaved head continued. "The Tsarist political program tried to Russianize all of the nationalities that lived in the empire. It did not permit schools to teach the native tongue, but only Russian. It did not allow the publication of books and newspapers, the production of theatrical works or the presentation of lectures in the local language. Ethnic character had to atrophy, and the Russian soul had to be superimposed by force on all of the national cultures.

"But the Bolsheviks broke these chains. A few days after the Revolution, the Declaration of Rights of the Peoples of Russia was published, signed by the Russian, Lenin, and the Georgian, Stalin:

"'All of the peoples of Russia are independent and equal.

"'Each ethnic group has the right to shape itself culturally as it wishes.

"'All special ethnic privileges are abolished.

"'All of the ethnic minorities have the right to develop freely.'

"A brave, daring and historic proclamation, which was not only the product of a supreme ideological consciousness, but also clever and fecund political practice. The boundaries that up until now separated the dominant ethnic group from the others were removed. Races as rulers and races as slaves ceased to exist. Workers and peasants from all of the races became friends. Each ethnic consciousness was liberated.

"Ethnic schools were founded in each region. The linguistic idiom of each race became its official language. For the first time, books were written and newspapers were published in various, and up to now uncultivated, ethnic local tongues. Eighteen ethnic groups—Iakuts, Chuvashes, Circassians—did not have an alphabet. They were given an alphabet in which books in the mother tongue were published for the first time.

"Many half-savage tribes were now enlightened with schools and learning. Before the Revolution, all of Tatary had only 75 schools, in which only the Russian language was taught. Now ten years later, there are more than 2,000 schools, in which the national Tataric language is taught. In Turkestan under the Tsars, only 300 pupils attended the local schools. After ten years of freedom, there are 673 schools with 45,000 students, and in addition, there are 1,596 kindergartens, orphanages and vocational schools for thousands of students.

"Millions of books, newspapers, illustrated pamphlets and magazines are printed each year. The work that is going on in Russia to awaken man is astonishing. Enemies disregard it or ridicule it. Blind followers exaggerate it. But both of them are wrong. The work that is occurring here for ethnic groups is very significant but very difficult and has not as yet produced all of its fruits. That is to come."

My companion grew silent. For a long while I kept think-ing how successfully the Bolsheviks, with their enlightened policies, managed to get the support of all the ethnic groups who up until this time had lived in Russia in mutual hostility and scorn. When enemies from within and without strove to endanger the new Idea, these ethnic cultures always took the side of those who gave them, after so many centuries, their ethnic freedom and their human dignity. That is how the Revolution was saved.

Later one of the Soviet leaders explained to me in greater detail: "Of all the possible solutions that could be given to the complicated problem of the nationalities, we have chosen the one that not only suits our Marxist ideology, but is also the most opportune politically and economically. Certainly there are dangers, but we know them, and we are doing all we can to overcome them. How? By teaching communism to our uneducated and half-educated people.

"Communism does not eradicate or level off the special characters of each individual or ethnic group. On the con-trary, it enhances and protects whatever useful and unique contribution each individual or ethnic group can make to the communal whole, because we know that all individuals and peoples mutually complete one another through cooperation; and that uniformity impoverishes the collective body.

"The more communism understands this principle, the more certain our harmonious symbiosis becomes. We teach our different ethnic groups not to concern themselves about whether one is a Jew or a Turk, Ukrainian or Tatar, but to care about one thing only: whether one is a com-munist or a bourgeois. The individuals in the first group, no matter what their nationality, color or race happen to be, are comrades; those in the second, even if they are our parents, are enemies.

"And we are striving to solve the problem of our national

cultures with the only method that can bring permanent results when it comes to cutting the Gordian knot: the light of education. Enlightenment—that is our sword!"

And the Jews?

This destined race, which has spread out its nets over the whole world and is often in first place—because it has great strength—for both good and evil, is still accused today as it was twenty centuries ago of wanting to overthrow the existing world order.

Even educated men frequently support this view: "The Russian Revolution is the work of the Jews. It is a gigantic satanic conspiracy of the Jews against the Christian civilization." What role then did this "dangerous" race play, and what role does it still play in the historic feat of the destruction of the old society and rebuilding a new one in Russia?

In order to be able to give a correct answer to this question, we must clearly understand the following: What is the psychic and moral nature of the Jews, and what were the stages of their historical formation worldwide and in Russia in particular?

The Jews, because of historical forces that have acted upon them for centuries, have acquired a psychic makeup that is unique among the peoples of the earth. Study their history over the last two thousand years, and you will understand that they, following powerful biological laws, found it necessary to overdevelop certain strong good and bad attributes in order to survive so many persecutions.

Through the centuries the Jews were the most despised of the races. They were not permitted to live in certain cities. Where they were tolerated, they were crowded into the most filthy quarter, the Jewish ghetto, and were isolated there like lepers. They were scorned, beaten mercilessly and denied the most basic of human rights. Suddenly, for whatever cause—a child disappeared, or the leaders of an area in debt to Jews found it in their interest to do them in, or because it just happened to be Good Friday—raving Christians attacked, broke the gates to the Jewish quarter and slew thousands of Jews.

Thus they lived for centuries in constant mortal agony. It was natural, therefore, to develop defensive strengths and to nourish certain exceptional qualities.

First of all, a hatred against the state. Any state. The massacres and the injustices made them revolutionaries out of necessity. In their cellars, they dreamed about how they would tear down the established order—and for them every order was unjust—and bring justice to the world. With their blood, their tears and their hate they engendered a messiah who would someday arrive in all his might to liberate them. For them the state was an organized injustice; for, in truth, no people on earth have suffered to the same inhuman degree the tyranny, the greed and the injustice of the strong. Because they could not find recourse in their physical strength, they cultivated their intellectual powers to an extreme degree in order to save themselves. Except for the mind, they had no other weapon. Intelligence, intrigue, patience, endurance, were for Jews qualities of prime necessity because not only did success in society depend upon them but their very lives did as well. Only the most brilliant, the most patient and the most cunning could escape from so many enemies and survive. Fierce and cruel for centuries was the law of selection that operated on the Jews.

There was another factor that contributed to the formation of the Jewish character—their dispersion. The Jews were not, like other groups, tied to a particular homeland. They were scattered throughout the world, and everywhere they experienced the same humiliations and persecutions. Theirs was a very bitter experience, and all forms of authority seemed to them equally unjust and had to be overthrown. And thus the Jews carried everywhere the burden of the Diaspora and the "thirst for justice," creating a revolutionary nucleus in every society.

It was only natural that each revolutionary kernel would have secret and continual contact and cooperation with every Jewish revolutionary element in its region, with all Jews, and generally with revolutionaries in all regions. Out of its very nature, this revolutionary structure became international.

Whenever a revolution broke out in any part of the world, it was natural for Jews to play a central role in it. The slaughter of Jews often followed, which again bathed them in blood and made the steely Jewish race even more pliant and powerful.

And so, under persecution and terror, the Jewish people acquired the ardent consciousness of martyrs by fanatically gathering together around their God, the terrible Jehovah, who torments his people because he loves them, engraves everything worth knowing on copper, remembers the good and the evil—and who will descend one day, Lord of the Mighty Powers, as avenger of his people and conqueror of the earth.

This faith that the day is coming, that the hour of justice and revenge is approaching, has saved the Jews for centuries.

Such in general was the condition of the Jews in the world. In Tsarist Russia their fate was even worse. They were only allowed to live in certain areas, especially along the western and southwestern borders. Every so often fanatical mobs arose, and with priests and Kazakh horsemen in the forefront began the pogroms, the horrible massacres of the Jews. And when they did not kill them, they treated them as accursed, unclean and dangerous beings. They did not permit them to educate themselves, placing great obstacles before them when they tried to enter schools and universities.

And yet we see an astonishing thing when we look at official statistics of the Tsarist era. Although there were no more than seven million Jews in all the empire, the total number of Jews who knew how to read and write was about equal to those who could do so in the remaining population of 160 million.

It was because the Jews knew that intellectual superiority was for them a matter of life or death; that education, the most powerful weapon, was one instrument that could defeat the awesomely dark forces of their enemies. They devised, therefore, a variety of schemes so that they could educate themselves. In the universities, the Jews were not allowed to exceed five to ten percent of the student body. What then did they devise? They found young Russians, registered them as students, paid their fees, and with this apparent increase in the number enrolled, the Jews achieved the right to have more students. Imagine now with what zeal, sense of responsibility and noble pride these Jewish students would taste and absorb the forbidden fruits of learning.

And so the Jews, working within the awesome darkness of the Russian masses and seeking to awaken and to open new and more just roads for man, unwittingly serve the profoundly messianic yearning in the Russian soul: the passion to save the world.

But how? In what way? All agree that Russia has assumed this messianic mission, but beginning with the period of Peter the Great, opinions are split in two. Some, the Slavophiles, argue that Russia is a unique world between Europe and Asia and must follow its own road, a different one from that of Western Europe. Her religion, her tradition and her soul are entirely and qualitatively different. "If the brotherhood of peoples," say the Slavophiles, "and if beliefs in truth and goodness are not delusive phantoms but life-giving and eternal truths, then moral superiority does not belong to the Germans, the conquerors, but to the

Russians, the simple peasants." Europe, they say, is a cemetery; all the large souls have died, and only the soulless, practical and selfish "grocers" survive. Russia is the woman of the Apocalypse. When the sun falls upon her, she becomes fertile and bears a son. The son that Russia will give birth to is the Logos, the Word that will save the world.

In contrast, the Francophiles support the view that Russia must, out of necessity, follow the evolutionary stages that Europe went through. Only Russia must pass through these more quickly so that she can adapt to contemporary necessity. The redeeming work of Peter the Great was not finished. For this reason she suffers. "We have not had our own internal evolution," said Chaadaev, a leader of the Westernizers. "We grow but we are not maturing." The password for Russia is not "Back to holy Russia!" but "Forward toward Europe!" The old social and economic rules of Russia are completely backward. The theocracy is a stage that mankind has surpassed. The need now is to industrialize the land, to create a bourgeois class and to prepare the ground for a civilized, modernized and bourgeois democracy.

They differ on the way that Russia should follow to carry out her messianic mission. However, Slavophiles and Westernizers throughout the nineteenth century agree on this: Russia, whether she follows her native sources or European trends, is destined "from heaven" or from historical necessity to save the world.

You feel that this race still overflows with unused vital forces. She looks at the old world and does not like it. With her faith and with a kind of creative naivete, she wishes to tear it down and build something new on the wide footpaths of the Slavic spirit. The agonizing question of the most progressive and representative souls in the Russian land is: "How will the Russian be saved?" This query quickly broadens and flows past its Russian boundaries to the universal question: "How will man be saved?"

The messianism that has kneaded the Jewish people for centuries has fused with the messianic spirit of the Russian soul and has taken at present its most modern, articulate expression and is shaking up the whole world.

This is the reason why the Jews played such a crucial role in the Russian Revolution. Their educated elite were practically as many as the others in all of Russia. They were not just the most genuine revolutionary elements; they were the only ones who could provide the most fanatical leaders to a revolution that had an international character and that wished to destroy the ruling powers by proclaiming justice, equality and freedom. They fought in fact to forge into reality the perennial hopes of the Jewish people.

It was a Jew who was the prophet of the new religion— Marx. It was a Jew who was the ardent apostle of nations— Lassalle. All of the contemporary leaders in Russia, whatever their beliefs, are simply commentators and practitioners of *Das Kapital,* the Marxist New Testament. Lenin, that solid, pure Russian type, always felt an obligation to remain faithful to the spirit of Marx. "There is no such thing as Leninism," a professor at the Communist Academy of Moscow told me the day before yesterday. "Lenin simply carried out the Marxist commandments."

What the Jews have given to the Russian struggle is the passion, the searing flame, for the Idea, and their invincible, combative endurance. With each step here, I leap from one world to another when I speak with a Russian or a Jew. Yesterday I went to the Communist University. The Russian general secretary welcomed me. He was blond with very mild features, his blue eyes flooded with a serene light. He spoke quietly, with a calm conviction, about the organization of the university, about the students and about Soviet higher education. I was ready to leave when someone opened the door with a violent thrust. Another professor entered. He had black curly hair, and eyes that were all afire—a Jew. After he entered, the atmosphere changed instantly. The Russian got up for a moment to bring me a book, and the Jew quickly enthroned himself in his chair and began a violent conversation, full of passion and polemics, that lasted for hours. With admiration I watched this representative of an explosive people who hid and trembled for centuries, but who now joined the struggle, armed to the teeth and thirsting for vengeance and justice. We are living in a crucial and transitory period. You feel that the Jews today have a specific historical mission: to tear down the old world. Our planet is now in the constellation of the Jews.

Ideas, convictions and traditions crumble. The class that created a civilization, adjusting the world to its interests, is organizing and arming itself to defend it. A class that until now has known only oppression and injustice is rising and wants to be free. What other race is better prepared than the Jewish one for such a work of vengeance and justice? For this reason, many great scientists, philosophers, economists, journalists, men of action, are Jews. How long will this intellectual dominance of theirs prevail? Just as long as the transitory period through which we are passing.

One day they asked the Jewish economist, Rathenau, "What will be the consequences of Russian communism?"

"A terrible massacre of the Jews," he answered.

■ WORKERS AND PEASANTS

■ "FATHER, WHO MADE the railroad?"

"The Minister, my dear."

One day last century, this conversation was heard on a train by the poet Nekrasov, who called his Muse one of "vengeance and pain." These few words stirred his heart so strongly that he wrote a fiery text that evoked a tragic vision: From the soil where the railroad tracks were strewn sprang thousands of workers—hungry, exhausted, shivering—who had died laying the tracks. There is a holy indignation in the poet when he describes how the workers labored from dawn until night, how the foremen whipped them and how contractors cheated and underpaid them. A Second Coming was the resurrection of these workers whose bones creaked when they heard the bugle call of the poet.

"There will come a day," proclaimed Nekrasov, "when all the workers will rise from the Russian earth!"

That day has come. Indignation has mounted and mounted, and the heart of man can no longer contain it. A few years after this song was written, Tsar Alexander II was assassinated and the tyrannical Alexander III assumed the throne. He limited the freedom of the press, choked the freedom of the people, hunted down the Jews without mercy, Russianized the ethnic groups by force and terrorized Russia.

One would have thought that freedom had drowned in its own blood, but as always, freedom springs from the most oppressive slavery. It is exactly during this reign of terror that Russian industrialization begins. Thousands of peasants go to the cities for work. The working classes multiply. And along with these economic shifts, the Russian society also changes. The intellectuals and liberals no longer hope that with the abolition of serfdom the people will be free. A new, completely modernized form of tyranny makes its appearance in Russia: capitalism.

The workers concentrate themselves in certain regions of the country. They slowly realize their strength; they organize themselves and raise their voices. They seek to improve their lives. This new generation, unlike the past one, does not concern itself with poetry and romantic stories. It listens with faith to new theories, which reveal that out of historical necessity, and not because of an ideological change or a philanthropic gesture of the bourgeois class, it will take power into its hands. Karl Marx penetrates the Russian land.

New violent ideological conflicts break out. Must Russia, like Europe, experience, though at a more rapid pace, the stages of economic evolution—feudalism, bourgeois capitalism, proletarianism—or can she, by leaping over all the intervening stages, enter into socialism at once?

The communist society—with its common ownership of the means of production and its abolition of classes and the state—is an ideal that is impossible to make real from one day to the next. It requires great preparation: the intensive education of the people, the extermination of all internal and external opposition, the subordination of individual freedom to the interests of the whole community. Until this preparation is carried out with time, what power shall rule during the transitional period from capitalism to communism?

With his usual perspicacity, Marx asked this question and gave it the only possible answer. In between a capitalist and communist society, there intervenes a period when revolutionary change transforms capitalism to communism. There will be then, politically, a transitional period when the state can take only one form: the revolutionary dictatorship of the proletariat.

Today Russia is passing through this transitional interval. Communism does not exist as yet in this pioneering nation. We must not forget this very simple truth if we wish to understand the problems that arose and why they were sometimes solved in non-communist ways in contemporary Russia. The mission of the proletariat's dictatorship requires it to crush all opposition, free the workers themselves from old habits and force them to create new ones. In this way only will the people later construct the ideal communist society.

In this period of transition, violence is at times necessary. "You don't create a revolution with white gloves," Lenin proclaims. "The Communist Party is not a school for naive schoolgirls. The dictatorship of the proletariat means war, a merciless, endless war against the capitalists until death."

The means of production during this transitional period do not belong to the whole but exclusively to the state organization of the proletariat. It monopolizes only temporarily the means of production. The class struggle does not disappear. Organized as a state, the proletariat amasses all power with an iron discipline; it puts pressure on the bourgeois class. It does not permit it a single liberty and wants to destroy it, transforming it with peaceful means or with force into the proletariat.

With such a sword in hand, the Russian Revolution undertook to solve every economic, social and political problem since its first days. And slowly, after dangerous and cosmogonic eruptions, it molded, around the ever-flaming communist nucleus, the solid habitable crust of today's Soviet Russia.

There are two basic internal problems that will determine the fate of today's Russia: the peasants and land reform, and the industrialization of the country.

For us to thoroughly understand the Russian problems, we must always keep this in mind: On November 7, 1918, there was not only one revolution. There were two, and indeed, two revolutions that were altogether different: the revolution of the peasants against the feudal landowners, one clearly of the bourgeoisie; and the revolution of the workers against the bourgeoisie, a socialist one.

The two revolutionary forces united in the moment of common danger. As soon as the common enemy was destroyed and the danger no longer existed, the comrades in arms during the hour of necessity separated. Lenin had proclaimed to the peasants: "The land belongs to those who work it. Go and take it!" The peasants attacked. They killed or drove out the privileged. They distributed the farms. Before the Revolution, one-third of the land—and the most barren—belonged to the peasants; that is, to one hundred million farmworkers or more. Two-thirds of the most fertile land was controlled by a very small group of idle notables. The Revolution brought justice.

But the peasants, as soon as they divided the land and became small landowners, got tied to their farms and did not feel any obligation to the few workers who continued to demand new sacrifices. "Why do we need more risks?" said these peasants. "Haven't all the aims of the Revolution been realized? Wasn't the land given to all the workers?" They now refused to continue supporting the new demands of the Revolution.

The struggle began between peasant and worker: the worker, impetuous and impatient, ready to make sacrifices but representing hardly ten percent of the Russian population; the peasant, sluggish, egotistical and self-interested, resisting like a stubborn animal, refusing to work for others and struggling slyly and rapaciously to exploit others and to bring wealth to himself.

The village people with their petit bourgeois mentality refused to help the socialist cities. Each peasant was concerned with his farm only and did not wish to work for the collective good. He did not wish to send his surplus wheat to the workers. He hid it and the government had to take it from him by force. The peasants then began to sow only that which they needed to support themselves.

This passive resistance of the peasant was extremely dangerous. How could he be forced to produce more? And if the most fertile provinces did not reap larger quantities of wheat, far exceeding what they needed, how would the remaining provinces be able to survive? And how would there be exports, which would make the purchase of essential industrial products possible?

But the peasants resisted with a fierce stubbornness. The situation reached a chaotic impasse: Hunger and misfortune were rampant; factories shut down; rebellions broke out; wheat was burned and workers were killed; leaders pleaded, threatened and struggled to enlighten the peasants, but they crossed their arms, refusing to work for others. The Soviet Idea was in peril. There was a need for a quick reconciliation between the peasants and communism. But who would have the courage to propose veering the communist Idea to the right?

Lenin, at this crucial moment, saved the Soviet Idea. What distinguished this man was his astonishingly simple yet sharp contact with reality; in the midst of the most complex chaos, he could pinpoint the most direct and certain road of action. He was not blinded by theories or servilely stuck to dogmas. In the deepest sense, he could understand and apply Marx's precepts: "Our theory is not dogma; it is a guide for action."

Lenin was indeed a true leader. With a unique clarity and courage he identified the weaknesses in the application of pure communism. "At the economic level," he admitted, "we had the biggest failure and made the worst errors. But how is it possible to begin an enterprise for the first time in history without mistakes and failures? Without careful forethought, we wanted to enact decrees about state-regulated production and the communist manner of distribution of products in a land of petty owners who wanted to adhere to exploitation and profit. Life revealed our mistakes to us. To prepare the transition to communism, we must first prepare a series of transitory stages—state capitalism and communism. Ideological enthusiasm is not enough; personal self-interest is needed to build a solid bridge on which the petit bourgeois will pass. It is impossible to reach communism in another way and to lead millions of people in this new life."

Many fanatics were indignant when they heard Lenin's pronouncements. But Lenin persisted. "Russia," he said, "is not yet ready for the complete application of the pure Idea. It is necessary, therefore, in view of the economic, social and psychological stage through which Russia is passing, for us to carve out a new economic policy. We must arrive at a compromise, not because we wish to damage our Idea, but because we wish eventually to fulfill it completely."

One day he stated this thought in his own simple but striking writing style: "What does the person do who wants to lift a sack of flour but cannot because of its weight? He empties half of the flour, lifts it, and later, the other half. We must do the same."

"The important thing," he proclaimed in a resounding voice, "is not that we have driven out the landlords and the capitalists. That we have accomplished with relative ease. The significant thing is to wipe out the small producers. It is impossible for us to kick them out and to eliminate them. We must compromise with them and must transform them—perhaps after many years of educational and organizational work—into active members of our communist society. For these small producers and merchants envelop the proletariat in a petit bourgeois atmosphere. They penetrate it, corrupt it and decompose it. Every day and every hour these petit bourgeois reconstruct capitalism in a quiet, imperceptible manner. We must come to an agreement with them if we wish, by working vigilantly, to subdue them."

"What will the bourgeoisie of the world say? What a shame for us to turn backward," the ideological fanatics shouted.

"Let them say what they want, let them ridicule and abuse us," Lenin answered. "We don't regret our mistakes for an instant; we will fight until death to correct them.

"Whoever attempts," he said, "to overthrow the international bourgeois class—a task much more difficult and complex than the most furious of national wars—and at the same time refuses to make compromises, taking advantage of the conflicting interests of his enemies, making friendships and allies that are insincere and uncertain but useful for the moment, is absurd. It's as if he wants to climb a steep and inaccessible mountain but does not deign to follow an oblique path on which to proceed and even to turn back at times. Instead he insists on climbing straight up directly to the peak."

Lenin's view prevails. The peasants are allowed to manage their harvests as they wish. Those who are hardworking, bright and thrifty grow wealthy and become kulaks. They now begin to exploit their fellow villagers. They use some as workers, to others they lend money or buy their harvests in advance. Slowly, slowly, they enslave them economically.

The ambitions of the kulaks grow audacious. As they prosper and gain strength, they attempt to intervene with increasing energy in the political life, hating, as is natural, the communist ideology. Thus a new danger appears. Lenin speaks about the kulaks with an intense hatred: "The kulaks are the most brutal and inhuman of exploiters. In other lands they have brought back the feudal lords, the kings, the clergy and the capitalists. These vampires have amassed great fortunes by raising the price of wheat; they get fat feeding off the poor peasants and workers. They drink the blood of the people."

In the midst of the two extreme factions of the villagers—the kulaks and the proletarian farm workers—stirs the large mass of middle villagers. Their only desire—and their daily effort—is to become wealthy and to climb into the ranks of the kulaks. They are conservative, struggling with treacherous ways to get their hands on the means of production. They become usurers, exploiting the labor of the poor. The greedy and unscrupulous soul of capitalism raises its head again.

"This is the moment," the fanatical leaders clamor, "the time to attack and destroy all the capitalist elements and wipe out the kulaks."

But how will this attack take place? Trotskii, consistent with his conviction that only the worker can have a pure communist ideology, cries out: "We must turn against the peasant. The worker and not the peasant must become the regulator of Soviet Russia."

But Stalin, who is in power and at each moment confronts the immense difficulties the Idea meets in its peaceful applications, answers: "There is not one peasant, there are three: the poor one, the one in the middle and the rich one. The poor one is our friend; the middle one can become our friend; the rich one is our enemy. The thrust of my policy is to strengthen and to organize the poor and the middle peasants, getting them to participate more and more actively in political life. We must also fight the kulaks as soon as we can replace them without endangering our struggle. How? With state and communal cooperatives and with our technology. At the same time, we fight them methodically with nonviolent and nondangerous methods: We deny them the right to vote, refuse them loans, impose heavy taxes upon them and give farm equipment on a priority basis to the cooperatives."

"Communism means: Soviet rule plus electricity." Here again Lenin correctly found the only solution. "Only when the peasant is surrounded by electrical wiring will he become a communist. The biggest hope and weapon for communism is industry." The great leader theorized that "electrification" was the only method, not only for reconstructing the land economically, but also for making the peasant into a communist. The peasant will stop being a small owner of the old type and will now become an agricultural worker. Only a large state industry will eliminate small private manufacturing; agricultural cooperatives will drive out private commerce; industrializing the agriculture will force the kulaks out of existence.

As a result, Soviet Russia turned to the only solution open to her: the industrialization of the land. After a few years, Russian industry surpassed its pre-war level. But this is not enough if Russia is to survive. She must continually compare her industrial production—quantitatively, qualitatively and economically—not with her pre-war status but with the contemporary industrial production of Europe and America.

The capitalist world, equipped with more advanced machines, with finer technical specialists and with awesome organizational strength, produces more, better and cheaper industrial goods than the youthful Russian technology. How will contemporary Russia be able to reach the production level of capitalism? And she must not only reach it but surpass it if she wishes to root out capitalism and replace it with communism.

The crown of victory goes to the society that secures the highest standard of living. Will the capitalist nations give Russia the necessary time to develop her economic and industrial potential and to exploit her vast natural resources?

The capitalist nations know full well that time is on the

side of the new Russia and yet they will never manage to unite themselves and wage a successful war against her. For indeed they do not have either spiritual or economic cohesion. Russia, during this beneficial truce, mobilizes all her strengths toward reconstructing herself in order to surpass her adversaries. Will she have time?

The moment through which Russia is passing is grave. Peace is essential in order for her to continue her technological development and at the same time—for she is certain that she will be attacked—her military preparation. Will her opponents give her time?

Russia has aspirations, and her hopes are based on her army (the capitalist nations know that it is strong and fanatical); on the absence of harmony among her opponents (the capitalist nations do not just hate the Soviet Union; they hate each other, and, at a crucial time, there will be capitalist nations that will ally themselves with Russia); and on the fear capitalists have that if such a war breaks out, it can quickly turn into one of social struggle.

Tragic indeed is the situation for the two opposing worlds. One is not yet ripe and is asking for a time period of several years to prepare and consolidate itself. The other has overripened and knows with dramatic clarity how disastrous peace can be for it and how equally dangerous a state of war will be.

We have reached a fecund turn in history when an old world staggers, crumbling, and another, a new one, struggles to ascend. In these crucial moments, whatever happens, either from friends or enemies, fatefully collaborates, consciously or unconsciously, with the world that is rising. Nothing can happen in the epoch in which we are living, whether we want it or not, that will not help the Soviet Union.

■ THE RED ARMY

■ THE RED ARMY is not dressed in red. The Red soldiers wear gray capes that reach to their feet and pointed, gray, woolen helmetlike caps. The only red is a red star on their caps.

The Red Army was born out of necessity. For three years the Red Revolution battled unceasingly with internal and external enemies. The bourgeois world fell upon the new Idea to drown it in blood. Enemies rushed in from every vast border: from the north, the naval and land forces of England; from the west and southwest, Poles, Germans, Finns, Estonians, Lithuanians, Czechoslovakians, Serbians, Greeks, Italians and Rumanians; from the southeast, the English again, and the French, the Americans and the Japanese. The capitalists of the world had sensed the danger. If they permitted the Soviet Union the right to exist, they would be lost. It was necessary to make every sacrifice at once, to wipe out the new Idea.

All the dangers were not just external. The capitalist nations helped to organize all the reactionary groups within Russia—with men, munitions, staff and abundant financing. They hurled the exhausted land into a bloody civil war. The fierce revolts of Kornilov, Denikin, Wrangel, Iudenich and Kolchak burst forth.

This period, which lasted for three whole years, was indeed a critical one of mortal danger. Without money, exhausted from war, hungry, wretchedly dressed and disorganized, the faithful to the new global creed stood up and banded close together around the Red flag. They understood the need to create a new army and to start a new war. Those who managed, with satanic skill, to dismantle the Tsarist army, who proclaimed the brotherhood of man, the war against war, were now forced to organize their own army, one with an iron discipline and with a fanatically warlike spirit. Otherwise, they were lost.

No revolution ever succeeded or ever will, Lenin emphasized, unless it makes the dissolution of the competing army its first priority. For the army is always the defender of the ruling class—the capitalism of our epoch. And at the same time no revolution can establish itself and thrive if it does not create a new army of its own, the defender of the new order. Armed workers now stood as the nucleus of the Red Army, an armed living cell of the new social hierarchy.

The struggle to establish a new proletarian army was a very dramatic one. Since March 1917, the Bolsheviks had begun to arm workers and poor peasants. They entrusted weapons only to these two groups. After a few months, Kerenskii forbade recruitment, but he soon needed to resort to the proletarian army to wage war against Kornilov, who was defeated. The scanty Red Army took courage and began openly and more systematically to organize itself. Committees in factories compelled their workers to do military training, and there was a rapid and enthusiastic conscription.

At the same time, the remaining members of the old army and navy were subjected to an intense propaganda. Hundreds of thousands of officers, soldiers and sailors joined the ranks under the Red flag. The October Revolution broke out; it was victorious, and Lenin signed the decree to organize the proletarian army: "The Red Army of workers and peasants should be composed of those who are organized and who have the consciousness of their class. This new army will form the nucleus of a larger force composed of all of the armed people who will confront the coming social revolution in Europe."

The organizing genius of Trotskii worked miracles. This astonishing Jew emerged as the father of the Red Army.

From month to month, the armed strength of the proletariat grew larger and larger. In April, 1918, the Red Army had 106,000 men; in August, 392,000; in December, 790,000; in April, 1920, 3,660,000; and by January, 1921, 5,300,000.

Faith and merciless necessity created the Red Army and led it to victory. It fought barefoot, hungry, without adequate munitions and with novice commanders. And three years later, the miracle, that is to say the very reason for its life, became a reality; all of the internal and external enemies of the new Idea were scattered.

After their victory, the Red soldiers returned to the factories and to the land to continue the struggle in other sectors.

In what way does the Red Army differ from all the other armies in the world? There are, I believe, four fundamental differences:

1. The Red Army is unique in stressing that equally as important as military training is the education of the soldier as a human being and especially as a communist.

Both political and military instruction begin at the start of service. However, two years before the future solider is inducted, he undergoes military gymnastics and schooling in general education. In two years the uneducated learn how to read, and in this way no one enters the Red Army illiterate.

Once the soldier is assigned to a specific unit, he receives two hours of instruction daily in general culture and one hour of instruction in communist theory. In each barrack there is the famous cultural organization of the new Russia—the Club, a large room decorated with red flags and a photograph of Lenin and with a copy of the *Stengazeta (Wall Newspaper)*, in which soldiers record what specifically pertains to their lives. In the Club, there is a library and a reading room where discussions, theatrical presentations, concerts and holiday celebrations take place. Here they also receive representatives from other army units.

2. The discipline of the Red Army is ironclad during the hours of duty; however, when not on duty, the soldiers are cordial and familiar with their officers. The isolated and arrogant officer class no longer exists in Russia. Everyone, officer and soldier, comes from the ranks of the working people.

And thus we come to the third distinguishing feature of the Red Army:

3. Only the working citizen has the "right" to enlist in the Red Army. All those who live off the labor of others—businessmen, priests, kulaks—are not entitled to bear arms. The Red Army is recruited only from the proletariat, and it represents only those who work. And thus it is necessarily a staunch defender of the Soviet Idea.

4. The Red Army does not see itself as an organization of the Russian proletariat only, but rather as a representative of the world proletariat. For the first time in human history, a regular army of a certain nation is being taught that it is not an army for one national culture but one that has international responsibility. Red officers and soldiers understand that they belong to a global ideology that extends beyond every national and ethnic boundary toward an international class consciousness. For centuries in the whole world, the oppressed class has experienced injustice and suffering; the proletariat of Russia has a duty, since it was the first to become free, to help, with its Red Army, the other proletarians of the world to gain their liberty.

Just as the idea of fatherland engenders enthusiasm in the armies of all the rest of the world, the idea of an international proletariat fires the Red Army. The new cry that mobilizes the inner resources of man is filled with an invincible strength because the energy of the new communal hope is still unspent.

Communist ideology, of course, is against war. But the Red Army has come into being out of necessity, and it alone has the power to save the newborn Idea from its vigilant and rabid enemies.

At the international congress recently in Moscow, many voices were heard decrying war. But the air was filled with the widespread belief that the capitalist nations are preparing a crusade against the Soviets.

More than a thousand representatives—workers and intellectuals from all over the world—came to express their views. War is coming. What must we do? The immense hall of the Central Union of Syndicates was filled with a strange assortment of inflamed faces from the white, black and yellow races. In the past, the rich businessmen and noblemen had their private club in this edifice. They got drunk here, told their scurrilous jokes and played at their green tables. Today, representatives of the world gathered here to give an answer to this agonizing question: What can be done to avoid a new world war?

The congress convened for three days. Many voices were heard—from the European sounds to the guttural cries of Africa, to the birdlike screeches of Siam and China. Almost all of them supported the view that there was a need to launch a huge propaganda for peace, to proclaim war against war, to organize the working masses by preparing them to throw down their arms when the moment of the mobilization arrives and to refuse to kill the working brothers who are in the opposing battlefield.

This perception I found exceptionally dangerous. And even though I was swept away in this turbulent atmosphere, I was able to subdue my aversion for public speaking, and I expressed my opinion:

"The propaganda in favor of peace that you propose seems to me to be excessively optimistic and dangerous. The hope that we will be able to organize the working masses of the world so that they will refuse at the crucial moment to go to war can bring us to our ruination. I am certain that the workers will all turn to slaughter and proletarians will again kill proletarians.

"It is necessary, I believe, to confront the danger head-on. You say: 'Tell the masses that if they organize themselves they will avert the new world war.' I propose: Let us inform the masses that a new capitalist war will surely break out. The capitalists who govern the bourgeois nations know that war is to their advantage, and it will start. Do not believe in propaganda for peace. Do not have any hope that we will escape a new war. It's coming quickly and surely. Proletarians of the world, prepare for the new world war!

"Deep is the gap between these two proposed opinions. If we follow the first one, we push nations toward an optimism that may again prove fatal. Immersed in their well-intentioned hopes, they may, without realizing it, find themselves again in a war that they naively thought they could avoid. If we follow the second view, the peoples of the world will not fool themselves with false hopes, and their purpose will not be negative and utopian—how to escape war—but positive and realistic: When war comes, and it will surely do so, how can we transform a capitalist war into one of social struggle?"

The conference ended. The thousand representatives from forty-three nations rose as one person and began to sing the "Internationale." They all sensed that this Russia was the great Mother in danger. An African from Sierra Leone next to me was laughing and crying, and as he sang his savage cannibal jaw rose and fell. The Chinese hardened their blinking slanted eyes. The Germans and the English—straight-necked, broad-chested, blond and ruddy, were glowing, perfect types of the white race. And in the midst of all, with their prominent cheekbones, their small noses and their fiery, slightly slanted, half-Eastern, half-European eyes, with their very keen judgments and frantic enthusiasms— merciless realists who put into action the most mystically passionate goal—circulated the Russians.

For a moment, the Ecumenical Councils of the early Christians passed through my mind. A similar mixture of all races, a similar emotion of brotherhood and fervor. Greeks, Jews, whites, blacks, did not exist; all of them, in the first whirlwind of the Idea, had actualized the highest aspiration of a divided world. They had become one.

■ RED JUSTICE

■ WHAT IS RED LAW LIKE? How is justice rendered in Soviet Russia? Did the Revolution that overturned the old economic, social and political relationships manage to bring a new, superior and broader content to the meaning of justice? I wonder.

I visited a courthouse where I followed a trial for a considerable time. The courtroom was very simply furnished: wooden benches, a small table covered with a red cloth, and on top of it, two large portraits, one of Marx and one of Lenin. On the walls, large red letters: "The people's public court enforces justice for the people. It battles the bourgeoisie and defends the poor." "Long live the union of peasants and workers!" "Proletarians of the world—unite!" Just like the army, justice is a battle weapon in the hands of the proletariat.

A large wall painting of poor workmanship decorated the wall: workers with hammers, peasants with sickles, a powerful woman in the center holding a Red flag and all, beside themselves, rushing into the snow.

The defendants, two young workers, arrived; they were seated. Very few observers—two young girls, a family with their infant children, five or six old men. A moment later the three judges appeared. The presiding judge, with a heavy, peasant physiognomy and a good-natured simplicity, tried to appear stern and frowned as he sat down. To his right sat a plump and jovial woman with her hair in a bun. To the left of the presiding judge, a young worker whose manner was somewhat abrupt and comical took his seat. He wore a red Garibaldi-like shirt, and a tuft of hair fell across his forehead à la Napoleon.

The trial began. The accused, alone and without lawyers, spoke quietly. The presiding judge asked them questions, attempting to discover the truth. You sensed that his intent was to settle a question of law and not to smooth over an unpleasant incident in a way that would satisfy everyone.

The whole scene recalled a primitive rendering of justice. The judge sits under a tree and attempts in a capable and paternal way to dig down to find the truth, and later, in keeping with the simple and firm logic of the good *pater familias*, he makes the decision.

This simple manner of bestowing justice is characteristic of today's Soviet Russia. Immediately after the Revolution, the complicated procedures that had slowly strangled the substance of the law were abolished from the courtroom. The tight net of the Tsarist courts disappeared. The old system of law was abolished and a new, revolutionary one was created.

A large area of jurisdiction is left to the judge. The purpose of the court is not to find and enforce the naked letter of law and to fit an incident into a specific article of law but to judge each arising matter by considering its social aspect. When the interest of the community requires it, the judge not only has the right but also the responsibility to deviate from the written law and to fulfill the unwritten law as his conscience dictates. The judge in the Soviet land is not a passive and heartless enforcer of the law. He is, when the communal good demands it, the legislator of law.

The Russian judge also has this prerogative: In civil cases, he is not required to judge, governed by the "submitted and proven evidence," but to seek and find the deeper truth in every way.

Legal procedural rules have become considerably simpler, but even if these were done away with, essential justice would still be possible. And often, because of this simplification, a litigant does not have the need for a lawyer. The judge then explains to the litigant how to defend his rights.

The way courts are constituted, the manner in which judges are appointed or dismissed, the creative directive given to the judge to seek the fulfillment of the communal good as the highest law, are in harmony with the anti-individualistic principles of Soviet ideology. All individual rights are subordinated to the general good. Bolshevism is a merciless enemy for every individualism; it recognizes the individual only as a means to a higher end. Individual liberty, the famed sanctity of private ownership and the legal autonomy of each person must submit to the needs of the whole.

Murder, theft and injustice are not punished chiefly because they represent punishable actions against the individual. They are condemned above all because they subvert and injure the collective body. If the prosperity of the whole demands it, then the violation of individual freedom, the seizure of property, exile and execution are considered applicable and legal procedures.

Thus, as in other manifestations of the new life in Russia, so in the area of justice, many notions that are deeply rooted in us have been shaken, and others have taken their place, always based on the general immutable principle: The supreme rule governing human relationships is the interest of the whole.

The individual as individual has no rights. He is not free, inviolable, endowed from birth with so-called "natural rights." Because the individual is a member of the whole and nothing else, he is obliged to carry out a certain mission within that communal whole, and only as he fulfills it does he have rights. Natural rights do not exist; communal rights do. No one is free to do as he wishes with the productive means in his possession; if he has land, he is not free to leave it uncultivated. According to Red law, only as he tills the soil does he have rights; if he does not, he loses the rights he has over that land. Red law does not protect the free disposition of the owner's property for the benefit of the owner; it only protects the fulfillment of the communal responsibility that any ownership entails. Individual rights have validity and are protected only as long as they do not come into conflict with the interests of society; if there is a clash, individual rights are abolished.

Just as in all the manifestations of Russian life, in the area of Red justice, too, the general rule that governs the experimenting and changing Soviet society has such intensity that it is transmitted like a musical rhythm to all the other living branches of the total organism.

There is a faith here. You may question whether it is correct or whether it is to your interest or not. You cannot deny, however, that it exists. Faith always has this elemental and profound consequence: It unites, creates solidarity and orders the most heterogeneous organizations and the most rebellious and complex institutions toward the same direction. The discipline, simplicity and obstinacy that characterize the legislators and the executors of the law here have sources much deeper than individuality.

A severe, inflexible, unrelenting rhythm governs Soviet Russia, a force that elevates morality and justice beyond individual happiness.

■ THE RED PRISON

■ THE PANAYIS SKOURIOTIS* of Soviet Russia is like our own, a vigorous, dedicated man with a fiery fanaticism for the main goal he has set for his life: the reform of the prisons. Blond, with blue eyes overflowing with joy, he is like those men who, governed by a large passion, satisfy it and rejoice. Happy and energetic, he swept me into his car and brought me to the large prison outside of Moscow.

In the dense morning fog, the houses and churches shone with a pale immaterial glitter like exotic edifices built from smoke and dampness. The electric lights cast a dim glow on the streets and on the frozen store windows. Crows flew silently overhead and sat in trees crystallized by frost. There were fewer homes now as we rode through the fields outside of Moscow. We arrived at the prison.

During the entire ride my new companion explained how Soviet Russia is confronting the very difficult problem of the prisons and the imprisoned:

"There are two basic principles: the rehabilitation of the convicted, and employment:

"Each jail has a school for the illiterate so that every prisoner who is released will know how to read and write. Each prison has its theater, cinema, library and recreation room where there are discussions, lectures and theatrical performances, and where prisoners can read and educate themselves. Each prison has its own *Wall Newspaper,* which the convicts themselves publish with complete freedom on all matters pertaining to their material or spiritual lives. The

---

* Panayis Skouriotis (1881–1960), director general of the prisons division of the Ministry of Justice in Greece.

66

convicts are divided into different groups, each of which undertakes a particular task. There are groups for education, politics, economics and health programs. Others concern themselves with literature, music, holiday festivities. All of the members are convicts, and only their president is a state employee. At the same time, we pay particular attention to the body and its health: cleanliness, sun therapy, good breathing, gymnastics, hikes.

"In accordance with our second principle, all convicts who are able must work. The work requirement is not used as a form of punishment, but as a means for human and vocational development. For this reason, the work a particular prisoner does suits his inclination and ability. Physical or psychological punishment is forbidden, not only because it opposes our Soviet principles, but also because it hardens the prisoner, exacerbating his hatred for society. Experience has shown us that nothing is more beneficial to the imprisoned man than respect for his individuality.

"As soon as the convicted man enters a prison, the director and the department heads in education or in the work areas meet with him. They talk with him, study his character, his education, his vocational abilities. The next day we give him a pamphlet, which sets down his rights and his obligations.

"The prisoners are placed in three classes: the lowest, the middle and the highest. Each convict must fulfill a certain number of years in the class to which he is assigned before his directors permit him to enter the next higher level. His time frame in the same class or his transfer to another depends upon the progress of the prisoner in this work and in his conduct, and in general upon his reaction to the corrective system.

"His advancement to a higher class carries certain privileges with it: The rules of discipline are relaxed; the prisoner can be released before the years of his punishment are served. Those who are in the lowest class may have guests and receive mail every fifteen days; those in the highest, every day. Those who advance to the highest class earn greater freedom in the manner they use the money they earn and in buying food, clothing and books. Those in the middle class are entitled to seven days leave during the year; those in the highest class receive fourteen. Also, the farmers with good conduct can be granted an absence of three or four months so that they may go to their fields to assist in the harvest. Those months are counted as part of the prison term.

"We have different types of prisons according to the various needs for the protection of the community:

"Correctional: These are subdivided into detention houses; correctional facilities; agricultural, vocational and industrial colonies; special solitary centers; transitional corrective houses.

"Medical/pedagogical: workhouses for minors and for offenders who are youthful farm workers.

"Therapeutic: facilities for the psychologically and physically ill; institutes for psychiatric therapy, hospitals, et cetera.

"The Soviet corrective system has launched still another significant innovation: Until now the idea prevailed that the courts were the only regulators of the penalty. For us, however, the judicial and corrective authorities are equivalent programs of a unified penal policy of the state. The work of the corrective authority does not have a mechanical character. It has become something creative.

"Immediately after the trial, the central responsibility is transferred to the corrective system; the correctional staff begin their study—psychological, physical and spiritual—of those convicted. They classify them, determine special regulations. They utilize different approaches for each category, techniques both corrective and educational.

"And most importantly, they not only can change the manner of executing the judicial decision but can also shorten the prison term defined by the courts, thus radically transforming the system of social protection. Soviet Russia has shaken the conviction that judicial verdicts are inviolate. The administrative groups can, depending upon the conduct of the convicted, radically modify the punishment.

"With these measures we are trying not to punish the criminal but to enable him to work cooperatively within the human community. We teach him how to read and write; we heal his spirit and his body; we teach him a skill to enable him to live and feel useful in the society at large.

"We do what we can to conquer the darkness in the mind and in the soul of man."

In the midst of the thick fog, I saw the northern eyes of my companion glowing like two flames. We entered the large prison yard.

The building is old, vast and isolated in the plain. Some prisoners chop wood; others carry coal. The director greets the "prison comrades" cordially. We enter a long, well-lighted corridor; you get the impression that you are not in a prison but in a quiet, well-run factory.

We open one door after another, and we always find ourselves in front of a new workshop. Here the printshop undertakes, with the seal of the prison, to publish books. Further on is the book bindery, then the carpenters' shop, the shoe shop, the machine shop and the bakery. The prisoners themselves bake, fire the ovens, cook and wash. They greet us everywhere with a pleasant cordiality. There are no guards with uniforms or weapons. There are a few guards dressed in civilian clothes. The prisoners also wear whatever clothing they like. Nothing suggests that you are in a prison.

Learning that I am foreigner, many of them, because of curiosity and a strong human interest, draw near me and ask me about my country. What is going on down there? Are there people who still exploit others? Are there comrades who are suffering? What action are you taking to enlighten and free the people? They question me, grasping my hands.

They look at me eagerly and wait. But I answer vaguely.

In the machine shop, a convict stood in the corner with his hands crossed. "This one doesn't want to work," the director explained good-naturedly. "In a few days, he will get bored and feel ashamed. He will envy the others and go to work. When a convict arrives, we ask him if he wants to work and where. A few respond that they have no desire to do so, and we leave them alone. Each one is free. But we strive to help the unoccupied, along with those who work, and always after a few days, they come to us themselves and ask us to give them something to do."

We went to the clubhouse. At one time it was a church; a few religious wall paintings above the altar have managed to survive. Now it is decorated with Red flags and Red slogans. And in the back, where the Holy Table once stood, there is now a marble bust of Lenin; on its right, a wooden copy of his monument in Red Square; on its left, an impression of the peasant hut where Lenin had found refuge when he was being pursued by the agents of the Tsar.

When we entered, the prison band played the "Internationale." The stage curtain opened and about forty half-naked athletes appeared and began to perform various difficult gymnastics.

"One of our biggest concerns," said the director, "is to teach our prison comrades how to breathe correctly, to exercise their bodies and keep them strong and clean, and to live in the open air as much as possible. This is, as you can see, why they are so ruddy and energetic."

It was noon. We all sat at long wooden benches and ate together—soup, meat with potatoes, tea. The convicts came from their workshops; they washed themselves and sat in good spirits and ate with us.

I spoke to the director: "We too in Greece are striving, sometimes with work, to improve the body and soul of the imprisoned. We too are aware of the theoretical views you are putting into practice, and we are trying to realize them. I have a friend who has dedicated his life to this important mission. His name is Panayis Skouriotis."

The director shook his head: "This attempt exists throughout the world. All the theories are well known and circulate in the air of our epoch. In every land, we can find a pure and fiery idealist who will sacrifice his life to put them into action. But I believe it is in vain. The bourgeois nations cannot achieve a significant change in this area. The prisons are a part of the whole fabric of society, and no basic reform can take place if it is isolated.

"In the bourgeois societies, punishable acts very often have their root cause not in the individual disposition of the offender but in the sum total of the existing social conditions. In most cases the society pushes the criminal toward his offense. And when it shuts him in prison, he has a deep conviction that society and not he is the criminal. He is the victim. And this belief fills him with bitterness and hatred. With this psychological attitude, it is only natural that he resists every attempt that society makes to rehabilitate him.

"The bourgeois effort for reformation cannot be either integrated or continuous. It is in the character of a bourgeois society that it never wants—because it is not in its interest—to awaken completely the soul of man. It is not in its interests to have people see how they are being done an injustice and by whom, nor should they realize the power within their own hands. For this reason, whenever a pure effort breaks forth in any national or social segment, that attempt is, out of necessity, isolated and precarious. It is the result of the notions of some nonconforming idealist. It is always met with organized and furious opposition—open and covert—and it quickly fizzles out."

The other day an acquaintance of mine, a cunning and reactionary Polish Jew, responded with a sarcastic smile when I recounted my visit to the Soviet prisons and all the admirable things I saw each day: "When Potemkin took his imperial mistress, Catherine the Great, on tour, he sent ahead ready-made villages of cardboard and set them up where people would pass. Village men and women, dressed in bright costumes, sang happily under the trees. They played balalaikas; they danced and drank to the Empress. They were not villagers. They were actors whom Potemkin had hired. And fat, lovesick Catherine wept with emotion and mirth.

"So do the Bolsheviks promenade in Moscow—the city of cardboard, actors, balalaikas; Moscow, the big showcase of Russia—and they present you (the Russians are by tradition excellent stage masters) with several well-made, cleverly arranged spectacles: schools, sanatoriums, prisons, courts. The factory sirens whistle as you pass by, giving the impression that they are operating unceasingly. The same agricultural machines always go through the streets that somehow you by chance are passing through also. And you dopey Europeans gape and fall into the newest system of the Potemkin trap—the 'Karl Marx trap.'"

My friend laughed sarcastically and stared at me with his small cunning eyes. A light shiver shook my body. Amid the ardent and fanatically faithful who work with love and obstinacy, there also exist the infidels—highly cultured and malevolent. They know everything; nothing can fool them. Very cleverly, they undermine and denounce the "holy ruse," without which no one can ever lay the foundation of a new faith.

These fine-mannered unbelievers have all the answers. However, they forget one thing: Only by yearning, deceiving and being deceived—in other words, by believing—can man change the face of the earth.

■ THE RED SCHOOL

■ I LIKE TO WANDER ABOUT the Red schools and talk with the teachers, all of them young and cast in the same mold: hair cropped short, blouses with leather belts, high boots. They do not know many theories, and my intellectual and somewhat indiscreet questions annoy them. They have not studied at the higher levels because they did not have the time. They were fighting. For their present mission, they do not need extensive education; such an education could even be a dangerous luxury. All they need is the enthusiasm and the religious fervor to live the historical moment we are passing through and to do their immediate duty.

A teacher, weary from my questions, said, "We want to create fighters, not wise individuals. This generation that you see sitting at the desks or shouting in the yards has a specific and immediate mission: to fight. Therefore, we are arming it. To fulfill its purpose, it must remain physically strong, and it must learn how to use deadly weapons, to run machines and to advance toward its goal without evasions and hesitations. We have no need for excessively intellectual analyses, theoretical games and erudition that cannot be transformed into defensive and offensive weapons. Don't ask me any more questions."

In all the schools that I visited, I could breathe the air of this combative preparedness. The new generation being raised in today's Soviet schools will play, I am quite certain, a frighteningly militant role in the immediate future.

In this particular area, Lenin opened the road that Russian education follows with such fanaticism and faith: "The smallest action in the schools, the tiniest step in rearing and education, must be absolutely in harmony with the struggle of the classes." And Kamenev, another leader, proclaims: "The Red Army of teachers must have only one purpose: to transform the school into a weapon for the proletariat."

The school has always been a weapon in the hands of the ruling class, and each new upcoming generation is always taught that which is in the interest of this class. Religion, ethics, history, science, art—all are taught in a way that serves the interests of either the church, the kings, the nobility or the bourgeoisie. The theory behind the school's purpose was always this: to create "good citizens," that is, good defenders and servants of the ruling class. For this reason, every new attempt by pioneering reformers to give a new purpose and content to education was always hated; it was brief and attacked without mercy. The "new school" always presupposes a new social and political situation, a radical change in the whole society. And in today's capitalist societies, whatever schools desire to serve a higher socialist ideal and a broader and more enlightened perception of morality, religion and justice are condemned to savage persecution and eventual failure, since their roots hang in the air.

Therefore, only in the Soviet Union, where the class of the proletariat has seized power, can new schools succeed. And in this lies the great value of studying the Soviet school.

There are two major goals in this new education:

Negative: to fight the bourgeois class, to eradicate in the children every perception and habit that is bourgeois. "And in the schools," thunders Lenin, "we have an obligation to overthrow the bourgeoisie. We proclaim openly: A school that is divorced from the political life is falsehood and hypocrisy."

Positive: to accustom children to the idea of joint cooperation, to lay the foundation in their minds and their actions of the principles of the new communist society.

According to the official Soviet program, the public school must: awaken in the child an active interest in whatever surrounds him and create a need for him to explore all natural and social phenomena; teach the child to ask science to give answers to all of his questions; accustom the child to live and work in a harmonious rhythm with the whole society; transmit to the child a certain amount of scientific knowledge, which will allow him to educate himself on his own and to adapt himself fruitfully to contemporary everyday life and to each necessity.

What chiefly characterizes the new school program is not its pedagogical method but its educational goal. It gives an entirely new and objective purpose to the intention, the thought and the energies of the student. And this purpose is inseparably linked with the social and political reality of Russia. The children of the worker and the peasant do not go to school to learn more than their social equals so that they can become doctors, lawyers and scientists and thus, as in a capitalist society, climb out of the class in which they were born. Here in Russia they go to school to obtain a better consciousness of their class, so that they can enter its struggle as aware defenders. In their faith, they gain a fanatical belief that they have a duty to free the working classes of the whole world from ignorance and slavery. And this is the second major characteristic of Soviet education. It gives to itself an international mission, a worldwide responsibility. Today's young pupils who sit at their desks and who play in the schoolyards of Russia acquire the conviction that they are the pioneers in a new view of the world, that men and women are not classified as Russians, Americans, Chinese, Christians, Muslims, whites, yellows or blacks. People are either perpetrators or victims of injustice. And these young pupils have a duty, when they grow up, to bring justice to the world.

For this reason, in the oath children take as they enter

school, they make a serious and proud promise: "I will work with the worker and the peasant. I want to fight the common enemy with him. I want to help so that the Idea will prevail. I want to be a faithful and useful co-worker with my older comrades. That is why I am in school."

To forge a future warrior who will overthrow the international capitalist class and, at the same time, to create an enlightened collaborator for the new society—that is the double purpose of the Soviet school. That purpose is pursued with the most certain pedagogical method. It begins with the most simple questions and answers, but it is always deepening in its scope by keeping the student in constant contact with contemporary realities. It arms him, according to his mental and psychological strengths, with all the aspects of knowledge, techniques and habits that will serve him in his revolutionary mission. The Russian teacher works with the unshakable conviction that through the Soviet Revolution, mankind has definitely entered a phase of social revolution as well. He struggles to arm this new generation with the most contemporary weapons necessary for a revolutionary fighter in this crucial moment of history.

Therefore, whatever is taught to the student—history, sociology, science, art, technical skill—has a specific and immediate purpose. The present critical turn of the world is the focus of educational concern. Soviet education has little interest in scientific theory but cares about that aspect of science, history and knowledge that has practical usefulness in the social struggle.

At the same time, children in school practice the cooperative self-control and self-government that constitute the foundation of the future communist reality. The Soviet school nourishes and strengthens the child's social instincts, habits of cooperation, group efforts and enjoyments—emotions that go beyond narrow egotistical individuality. And the games of the children are selected with great care in

order to strengthen the will, to awaken the need for mutual
service and cooperation, to accustom the child to undertake
responsibility.

The pupils together with the teachers run the school.
They punish, reward and judge themselves as well. Through
their own independent council, they oversee the orderly
function and hygiene of their school. They are in the forefront during celebrations of the Revolution, join in military
parades and take part in the mass meetings of the workers.
At the same time, they help the peasants with their tasks by
plowing, sowing, harvesting and threshing. Children of
farmers and factory workers become friends. They get to
know each other well by being together. They correspond
with one another and their contact becomes more cordial.
And thus the city and the village become aware of each
other, and slowly love grows between them.

The life of the young Bolsheviks now extends beyond the
up to now ordinary duties of the student.

According to the official program, the child who has
completed grade school must have acquired the following
habits and knowledge:

Training in orientation: land orientation—he must know
how to find accurately any point of the city or the country
on a map. Time orientation—he must know the time required to cover a distance on a geographical scale. Size and
quantity orientation—he must know how to measure and to
calculate, how to use the weighing scale, the yardstick and
all the instruments of measurement. Quality orientation—
he must be able to judge the quality of things of primary
necessity. Intellectual orientation—he must know the mech-
anism of government in his land, and finally, he must be
able to use the electric car, the train, the post office, the
telegraph, the telephone.

Training in analytical work: He must be able to draw a
plan for a yard, a house, a street, an area; to design simple

objects; to write a composition on any subject; to draw up a bill, a statistical account, a bill of lading, a newspaper column.

Training in domestic tasks: personal hygiene, housework, washing, ventilation, disinfection. He must be able to mend clothing, to wash inner and outer garments, to cook simple meals and to give first aid.

Training in the use of tools: He must be able to repair furniture, to dismantle, clean and reassemble simple machinery. He must know how to use electricity.

Training in agricultural tasks: He must know how to care for domestic animals and plant life, how to cultivate the land (sow, water and harvest) and how to fish and hunt.

Training in scientific awareness: He must be able systematically to observe certain phenomena; to make entomological and mineralogical collections; to use dictionaries, indexes, catalogs, newspapers, guides, libraries, et cetera.

Training in political and social issues: To participate actively in the meetings of his school, to concern himself with his group, to take minutes, et cetera, to carry out by himself and with others the mission entrusted to him by the group. To organize clubs, festivals, lectures, picnics, propaganda for a certain issue; to work cooperatively as editor of the *Wall Newspaper;* to classify magazines, newspapers and press cuttings on a certain subject.

Such is the program—astonishing from the perspective of our bourgeois routine—that the official Soviet educational system expects from the graduate of the primary school. This system that sharpens the five senses of the child to the utmost and prepares him for the future struggle is called Leninist.

"What is this Leninist system?" I asked a teacher one day.

"To see clearly," he answered, "the material, moral and spiritual world around you and to employ it for your immediate objectives: the destruction of the worldwide bourgeoisie and the creation of a communist society."

The schoolchildren around us were skating on the snow-covered yard. The teacher looked at me and his eyes were shining.

"Would you like to speak to a pupil of Lenin?"

Without waiting for my reply, he shouted, "Ivan Mik-hailovich!"

A slender stripling, flushed from the game, detached himself from his group and ran toward us. He wore a red tie and had the badge of Lenin on his chest. He balanced himself on his pointed ice skates with a graceful agility and saluted.

We began to talk. He was a Pioneer, a communist Boy Scout. When I asked him to explain the life of the Pioneers, his eyes glittered.

"Last summer we went to a small village. All day long we helped our comrade villagers with their work. We did the mowing, reaping and threshing. We carried the wheat. We grazed the sheep. At night we met with the village youths and talked to them about Lenin. Later we lit fires around our camp, set up guards and went to sleep.

"One night some other Pioneers, who had encamped on the opposite hill, wanted to seize our flag. They set out secretly at midnight, crawled along the crops and reached our guards, who on this night were two girls. They charged and gagged one of them with a jacket, but the other managed to blow her whistle. The whole camp rose to its feet at once. We ran to catch the invaders in the place where they had hidden. We lit torches, we searched, and there they were, the wise guys, sprawled out in the fields. We rushed at them; there were more of us and we captured them. They confessed that they had come to see if we were protecting our flag well. They asked us if they could stay awhile to warm themselves at our fire and if we would then allow them to return to their encampment. We gave them tea and boiled potatoes, and when they were leaving, we said: "Stay alert! We're going to come and take your flag!"

The young Pioneer laughed, made a big turn on his skates and then glided back and stood in front of us.

"And did you take it?" I asked.

"What?"

"Their flag."

"How could we take it! Don't you think they had posted guards, too?"

He laughed again. I held his shoulder. "I want to know, comrade," I asked him, "how a Pioneer is different from other children."

He became serious immediately. "A Pioneer," he answered, "never tells lies and is never afraid. He endures hunger and cold and he obeys his leader. He doesn't smoke, doesn't chew sunflower seeds and brushes his teeth. He goes to the villages. He helps the peasants and talks to them about Lenin. We are all, those of us who wear the red tie, children of Lenin."

"And who was Lenin?"

He gave me a severe look and then continued, "We Pioneers write to other children in Germany, in America, in China, wherever they wear the red tie, even though it may be inside their shirts and does not show."

"But why?"

"Because their countries are not yet free. When we grow up, we will send messages to each other so that we can join forces in a revolution to save mankind."

"To save them from whom?"

"From whom? From the capitalists, from the kings, from the priests!"

He blushed. His boyish eyes were staring at the snow-covered trees in the distance. He again turned toward me.

"Are there in your land," he asked, "men who exploit other men?"

Night had come. A dense flock of crows flew over us and then perched on the crystal-covered branches.

The boy waited for a moment. When he saw that I did not answer, he made a turn on his skates and went to join his companions.

I turned to the teacher. "Why aren't all the children of Russia Pioneers?"

The stern face of the teacher broke into a smile.

"It isn't easy," he answered. "It must not be so easy that any boy who wants to can become a Pioneer. The Pioneers are a battalion with difficult demands, and a young boy must train and must be able to pass through many trials to be worthy enough to wear the red necktie.

"We have three battalions: the October Children (six to nine), the Pioneers (nine to sixteen) and the communist youth groups, the Komsomols (sixteen to twenty-three).

"Each branch of the October Children has a Pioneer as a leader and is obedient to him; each company of Pioneers has a Komsomol as leader. Apart from the school, this leader has absolute authority over the children. He leads the excursions, gives them communist training, undertakes with them a political enlightenment in the countryside and habituates them to collaborative work and living.

"If a young man passes this long triple service—Octobrian, Pioneer, Komsomol—he is ready to enroll in the highest and most responsible ranks in Soviet Russia: the Communist Party.

"The role of our generation is to overthrow the bourgeois class, but the October Children, the Pioneers, the Komsomols, must achieve a much more difficult task—the creation of a new society. We tore down the corrupt house. The new generation has the mission of building a new one that is honorable and comfortable. We demolished the unjust economic system in our land. The new generation, holding on to the technological strengths of the capitalist world, has the duty to create the new classless economic life. We abolished the old morality whose foundation was the God of capitalists. The new youth must give us a new one whose basis will be man, whose heaven will be the earth and whose future life will be the terrestrial life.

"The responsibility of the young, not only in relation to Russia but to the whole world, is huge, and thus it is correct that the selection of these children be done with such strictness."

I said good-bye to the teacher and took to the snowy streets of Moscow. By now the crows had all gone to their perches. Thousands of many-colored electric lights brightened this swarming, mysterious heart of Soviet Russia. During all the days I had allotted to the schools, I sensed more and more that here in Soviet Russia a terrible weapon is being forged—a fanatical army of students, workers, villagers and women is in training with a definite and uncompromising goal: to tear down the old world and to build a new one.

Capitalists, priests, kings, swordsmen and scribes of all the world—beware!

The other night I went to a children's theater. I was thinking: "Tonight at least, at the theater, I will see children laughing and playing freely, without being concerned about slavery and economic injustice and without asking and answering questions like grown men."

The theater was crowded with boys and girls, and there were red neckties and rosettes of Lenin everywhere. An energetic, high-spirited Komsomol had climbed on the stage and, standing in front of the still-closed curtain, spoke with good humor and explained the program to the children: "Quiet! Quiet! Now, you will see!" He gave an interpretation of what they would see, gave them instructions about what they should do, when they should intervene on the stage and take part in the drama. The impatient children yelled, shrieked and stomped their feet.

Red paper masks were passed out to all the children, and in a twinkling of an eye, they tied them to their excited faces. The atmosphere changed instantly. Behind their masks, the children grew fierce; behind this Red communist uniformity, individual differences disappeared. All of them were now being swept away by the same identical burning enthusiasm. Their eyes were anxiously fixed on the curtain.

The stage curtain opens. All of a sudden a fast-moving, violent and naive drama bursts forth on the stage. In America the first inhabitants, the Indians with their multicolored feathers and their chocolaty skin, proclaim a revolution. They can no longer tolerate the bestial American capitalist who exploits and kills them. Several children with red neckties then appear and speak, encouraging the revolutionaries. They raise the Red flag. An airman enters. He turns on a small device and the voice of the earth is heard: The women are crying, the workers are shouting. The myriad-voiced sound of the despairing, victimized masses increases in volume until, suddenly, a triumphant cry explodes a name like a thunderbolt: Lenin!

At this moment the fascists rush in, dressed in black with skulls and bones painted on their chests. They set up their cannons and prepare for the assault. The revolutionaries are in danger. And then, in one wavelike motion, the entire audience of children, body and soul, rises to its feet. Angry children with their red masks climb on the stage, merge with the Pioneers and the Indians, and together they strive to tear the fascists to pieces. The unfortunate actors playing the fascists roll down into the orchestra, jump over the seats and rush toward the doors to escape.

The children, standing straight but panting and uproarious from the agitation of battle, now inflate their small chests and sing the communist hymn as though possessed.

The theater emptied as the children went out into the corridors. They talked in shouts and did not want to leave in order not to separate from one another. The director of the theater, a slender, energetic woman with short fiery blond hair, lit her cigarette and, breathing the smoke out of her wide nostrils, asked me, "So how did our children's theater seem to you?"

Shaken and unnerved, I answered, "These are not children. They are tiny merciless men and women. You've sucked out the dew of their childish souls. You don't allow them to play a moment unless the game has an immediately propagandistic purpose. They don't play; they are in training."

The director laughed sarcastically. "I know. You want fairy tales—fantastic birds, fairies, dragons, kings and blonde princesses. You want to fill the heads of children with a nonexistent fantasy world and to make them wander in the depths of the sea or up in the clouds but never on the ground; in that way you blur their eyes so that they never see the truth."

I got angry. "What appears as fantastic to us," I answered, "is for the child the deepest and most palpable reality. He rides astride a bamboo reed. We adults see it as a reed. For the child, it is a horse, the most authentic horse that exists. Myths and tales are the deepest and the most inexhaustible source of creative power for the child. He has his own world, one that is altogether different from ours. We must awaken that world if we want children who are whole—that is, children who will later become men and women."

The director threw away her cigarette. She shrugged her shoulders. "You come from a very old world," she said.

"There is no communication between us. Our theater does not intend to stimulate the imagination or to make children yearn for the invisible and the useless. Our children's theater, like our schools, has a definite, vigilant and firm intent: to create a new, militant and determined soul in the children, one that will enable them to see the real world clearly, to distinguish accurately what they should hate and for which ideas to struggle and to die.

"We are creating a new world. You call it severe, fanatical, confining. And yet we call yours unjust, hypocritical and dishonest. Yours has all the refinements of decadence, the eloquent wisdom of old age; ours, the savage intransigence, the naive vitality of youth. Choose. But you can't. One is destined to follow the youthfulness or the old age of his race."

It was a joy for me to hear this wild, ardent Slav, and to make her speak out even more, I answered her harshly. Slowly, even though we did not want it to happen, the tone of our voices grew angry. We were two armies, two adversarial worlds, one confronting the other. I laughed.

"I am not such an ancient Greek as you think," I said. "I'm from Crete and we Cretans are very African; we have unspent, barbarous strength. Glory be to God."

"Let it be so!" said the Slav, her lips still tight. "You may be able then to understand what we want and how we want it. For someone to know us and to become a comrade, it is necessary that the blood in his veins pulse with the same rhythm as ours. That's what is essential. Discussion is simply a sickness of the old."

She looked at me with that vast and mysterious glance of the Slav. And I blushed, as if she had cast a flaming communist mask upon my face.

■ WOMEN IN RUSSIA

■ MOSCOW IS A CITY where you sense that the proletariat is sovereign. In the streets you see leather work jackets, worn collars, rough hands. Here you do not meet strollers who loiter, dandies who flirt, women who look like peacocks. They all walk with a quick step for a definite purpose. They come and go, each with a clear mandate like bees.

The word you hear the most often is *rabotat* (to work), in all tenses and persons of the verb. You feel as if you have entered into a hardworking, restless behive. Everyone is burning with the fever of work. Out of necessity, anyone who does not work here is something outside of nature. He cannot lean on any institution or custom for security. Of course there are some functionaries of the New Economic Policy, *nepman*, as it is called, who have managed to profit here by exploiting the others. And of course there are wealthy here, although very few. But how different from the rich throughout the world! Here the rich can eat, drink and dress better than others, but they have no strength or influence in society, politics or government; they are suspect and their place is uncertain. All honors and powers are found in the hands of those who work. The "materialistic" worldview of the Bolsheviks brought this unexpected ideal to fruition: the contempt for wealth.

You walk through the streets and listen to the conversations. Russia is the only place in the world where the talk of men does not revolve monotonously and painfully around the subject of money. Here people have found relief from this universal nightmare. Why should they talk about riches? In Soviet Russia, no one can acquire farms, mines, factories

86

or houses. No one can import and export or play the stock exchange for profit. They all struggle, each at his job, to work better in order to contribute to the general economic betterment; only when the whole society prospers can the individual feel an alleviation of his pain and a sense of prosperity. The cost of living will go down, wages will go up, the working conditions will improve, the hours of leisure will multiply. They have all become a single family. When one member of a family gets ahead, all the other members prosper with him.

Another shame that degrades capitalistic societies is absent here: nauseating eroticism. The chasing of pleasure, the sickly sentimentality, the persistent and shameless talk about women—all the symptoms of a decadent civilization—are unknown in this pioneering Russia of workers and peasants. Love, as when it blossoms in each healthy individual or society, has been placed in the high and special place it deserves.

Thus the two powerful passions that cheapen and wear out the contemporary souls of man, the pursuit of money and erotic desire, have lost their strength in Soviet Russia. Other worthy thoughts that are qualitatively superior here occupy the minds of the individual and the masses.

It was snowing. I walked quickly and anxiously, thinking about the new concerns of man. They are never absent. They just change and shift their direction, and from this movement one can judge the worth of an individual or a civilization.

As you turn a corner in order to reach the great Sverdlov Square, you see a grade school on the street level. I rise up on my tiptoes and look into the window. The walls are covered with red flags, and on the flags are pinned many photographs, cards, sketches, newspaper clippings that present Lenin first when he was a plump, charming little boy with curly hair, and later as a young man, all freshness and seriousness, and then, higher up on the walls, the violent, sarcastic, impetuous aspects of Lenin with his worker's cap, his mouth open as he speaks to the masses, his fist raised in the air.

I can only make out the head of the teacher. She must be about sixteen, dressed like a worker with a red kerchief over her hair—a face without femininity or charm but concentrating persistently on the Idea. Millions of women here have faces that are fierce; their femininity has been transformed, shifted from its sexual center to new and sterner areas.

While going to the Museum of the Theater, I kept thinking about this new attempt of man to go forward one step. It snowed incessantly. The mouths and nostrils of the people were steaming. Electric lights were turned on even though it was midday. On the sidewalks, old men and women sold apples, chickens, pictures of Lenin and peasant toys made from yellow wood with green decorations.

A prominent Russian lord had dedicated all of his life to the task of gathering together whatever pertained to the theater: stage scenery, costumes, posters that faithfully depict how theatrical works were played during different periods, manuscripts of great actors, silk slippers of famous dancers, fans, gloves, cigarette cases . . . He had filled his rich, imposing building with this theatrical booty. The Revolution came and said to the landlord: "All these treasures that you have gathered you can no longer keep egotistically only for yourself. They belong to everybody. All have the right to see and enjoy them. For that reason, I seize them. I also take possession of your building, and I make it a museum. Since you know the theater well and love it, I make you the director of the museum."

The old nobleman accepted, and now he himself was leading me through the luxurious chambers. As he showed me the various objects, he explained the nature of the posters, the manuscripts, the slippers, with perception, love and nostalgia. For hours I relived with him the wondrous development of the Russian theater. The old nobleman brought old actors, beautiful actresses and famous dancers back to life for me.

I said good-bye and prepared to leave. In a dark corridor, I stumbled into a young woman. I began to ask her pardon in the little Russian I had in my command, and she answered me in faultless German, laughing at my commotion. In the half-light, I made out the upturned Russian nose, the small blue eyes, the short blonde hair.

We went outside. She was pleased that I was from such a distant land. In the midst of this frozen, snow-filled afternoon, Crete, it seemed to her, was a sun-washed rock in an open blue sea at the end of the world. She knew hardly anything about Greece, either the old or the new one. Of course she had heard something about Pericles, Plato, Venizelos. But they all appeared to her as products of a pleasure-loving bourgeois fantasy.

She took out a cigarette. She approached a driver who was sitting in his snowsled wrapped in his sheepskins and took a light from his cigarette. As she greedily inhaled the smoke, I saw her heavy Slavic features and her thick-lipped mouth in the light.

"Where are we going?"

"I am hungry," she answered. "Let's go eat."

She took me by the arm, and we went down into a very clean basement restaurant. The celebrated national borscht soup was brought steaming to us. I saw my companion eating happily and hungrily, totally involved in this high bodily ritual. What a powerful, unfeigning animal! I admired this well-built woman, so much like the millions of other young women of Russia, as she sat next to me, knee to knee, with that passionate Russian openness that smashes all boundaries—just as wretched Europeans chance to do for a few moments, either when they are lovesick or when they are drunk.

When we finished eating, the woman lit another cigarette, and now that she had satisfied her appetite, she spoke enthusiastically. She was a clerk in a state office; she lived alone. Her mother had died in the Great Hunger; her father, who had married again and had fathered other children, worked far away in a mine in the Urals. We talked about marriage, and she expressed her opinion very bluntly.

"If I love someone, I will take him as husband and stay with him as long as I love him. During all of that period, I will of course remain faithful to him, since I love him. When love ends, I will leave him. I too have my morality, just as you, the bourgeois, have yours. But it is different. You allow a woman to deceive her husband, provided she does not create a scandal. You permit a woman to have many men secretly, just as man can have women. For us communists, this is not possible. Our morality is honorable and difficult; yours is convenient and immoral."

I stared at her open-mouthed. She laughed.

"Of course," she said. "Do you think we Russians are still in the Domostroi period?"

"What is this Domostroi?"

"It is an old family code of the fifteenth century. It defines the obligations of the Christian head of the family, from the highest realm (belief in the Holy Trinity) to everyday matters: how he will tailor his clothes and save the remaining pieces and how to make good beer. The woman is a slave. When she disobeys, her husband must beat her mercilessly with a whip. You strike her with the whip, this frightful Domostroi commands, and as you beat her, you give her a warning: The whip hurts, and at the same time it is healthy. And be careful. No one must see or hear. Such was the woman's lot in Russia. A slave. That is how my father beat my mother. But now . . ."

A little girl, pale and snow-covered, entered, selling the evening newspapers. A vagabond sneaked under a table, looking for cigarette butts. Suddenly he got up, grabbed the leftover bread and ran off.

"All these starving creatures," I said to my companion, "are the result of casual marriages. Don't you pity them?"

"In three years," she answered, "there won't be a single ragamuffin in the streets. The state will gather them up, educate them and give them skills. All these children you see will become the best communists. Of course some will die from the cold and from hunger. But Russia is a large place."

Suddenly I truly realized that Russia is huge, fecund, invincible and, like the earth, is constantly renewing herself. Just a few years ago, five million people died from hunger, and even more were killed in the war. But new millions of children sprang up from the soil and replaced the dead. If you figure it out, the gains are bigger than the losses.

We got up to leave. In the restaurants here you cannot sit long engaging in conversation; there are hungry people standing over you, waiting.

"We will pass this evening together," I said to her. "I like to hear you talk. It's as if I'm traveling and exploring Russia with you."

The young woman laughed. "You sound like a poet," she said and eyed me suspiciously, then she immediately shrugged her shoulders.

"*Nichevo!*" she said. "What is your name?"

"Nikolai Mikhailovich. And you?"

"Tatiana Ivanovna. Where shall we go?"

We went to the Jewish Theater. They were playing *A Night in the Old Marketplace* by the Jewish poet, Perez. The stage curtain rose: a medieval marketplace, Gothic homes, hanging iron lanterns, pointed windows. Rabbis, priests, thieves, merchants and whores gather together, tangling in verbal jousts. They agree, they scatter and then mix together again. They all invoke God, some Jehovah and others Christ, and in the name of their God, they maneuver their suspicious enterprises and satisfy their miserable, petty passions. And at the end, a huge broom appears unexpectedly on the stage and sweeps them all away.

The actors played with superb skill. What strength, what an understanding of and identification with other souls. What demonic gaiety! My companion had perceived one thing only, but in greater depth than I. The old God, who once protected these rabbis, priests, thieves, merchants and whores, had been swept away. He no longer existed.

"And do you know who held the broom?" she asked when we were outside in the snow-covered street.

"Who? I did not see anyone."

"Lenin. You did not see him, but I did."

I was pleased. The legend keeps solidifying around the name of a man who was alive until just yesterday. It takes on the force of Saint George who killed the beast to save the princess—the soul of man.

We climbed into a snowsled. These carriages are narrow, hardly big enough for two. So that you won't fall, it is necessary to hold your companion, even if she's a woman companion, tightly about the waist.

It was snowing. Around the streetlights, you could make out the snowflakes falling thickly and silently, covering the trees and the earth. My voice trembled when I was bold enough to suggest to my companion that we go to her house. She broke into laughter.

"And you tell me that you are not bourgeois. Like you're asking something horrible. Let's go."

I was thrilled to see the home of this modern Russian woman. When she turned on the lights, a portrait of Lenin—fine, mercurial, sharp like a knife—shone on the wall. There was also a small divan covered by a red piece of calico, a table loaded with books and pamphlets, and on a furniture shelf, a heavy plaster bust of Marx with his short, thick and priestlike beard.

She lit a small copper samovar. She opened a cupboard and took out bread, butter and smoked fish. We ate, drank and talked with simplicity and warmth, just as if we were old friends. We spoke about Lenin. And suddenly the eyes of Tatiana Ivanovna filled with tears of exasperation and impatience. When will the Red flag cover the world?

She asked me about Greece and about my friends. How we work, what we do to awaken and save our people. And suddenly, over the tea, the butter, the thick slices of wheat bread, I felt, as I never had before, the awesome presence of the Idea.

We had forgotten that we were man and woman in this humble little room. We talked until dawn about man and his unjust suffering and about the obligation we had to elevate life just a little, as much as we can, before we die.

"Tatiana Ivanovna," I said to her, as I drew the calico curtain at the window just a bit, "it's daybreak . . ."

■ MARRIAGE AND LOVE

■ A YOUNG WOMAN, who had finished her studies with a degree in electrical engineering, has invited me this afternoon to her home. An austere workshop for learning: science books, equations and algebraic formulas on a small blackboard above her bed. Vera Grigorevna is twenty-two years old. She is thin and tight-lipped. She is wearing thick glasses and a Tolstoi blouse. We talk.

"Are you a member of the Communist Party?" I ask.

She sighed.

"No," she answered, "I was not able to join. I applied for membership twice, but the party did not accept me because I am from a family of intellectuals. No one in my family, unfortunately, has ever worked with his hands."

"What do you believe? What purpose do you give to your life?"

"I believe in matter; only that exists. I think my role is to become active and productive for the whole society in the field I have chosen for myself."

"When you say 'matter,' do you think that the word explains something? Don't the words 'matter' and 'spirit' seem to you masks that cover our ignorance? What exists behind these convenient words? What is the essence?"

Vera Grigorevna laughed. She looked at me somewhat ironically. "The essence has never concerned me. What shall I do with it? That too is an invention of the bourgeois. I am a scientist, not a philosopher. Phenomena are enough for me. Those we must control and use to give prosperity to the masses; that is the purpose of our science."

A shiver passed through my spine. It was as if I were speaking to a cold and fully-armed organism from some other planet, a more advanced one where the great freezing process had already begun.

After a little silence, I asked, "What are your pleasures, Vera Grigorevna? You are twenty-two years old."

"To work productively."

"Yes, but when you are not working."

"I always work."

"And love?"

"It doesn't play an important role in my life. I am not a sentimentalist. I don't have time. Here in Russia, the rhythm is swift, time is valuable, the needs are great. Emotional love needs time and a certain leisure. It's good for the bourgeois. My biggest joy is not to get a husband, but to work, knowing that I'm not a parasite and that I can contribute something to the whole society. I will love certainly; I am not a complete ascetic. But it will be simple, without love talk and wasted time."

"Is love then a kind of Swedish gymnastics?"

Vera Grigorevna knit her brows, and for a moment her serene blue eyes glistened with severity.

"I know what you're thinking," she said. "That we are restrained and dry, that we don't have poetic and secret longings, that we are not lovesick doves on the roof tiles. Better narrow-minded and strong beings than open-minded, poetically excited emigres and mystics. We have suffered much, Nikolai Mikhailovich. A few years ago, Russia was dying. Now she is recovering from a massive hemorrhage. She needs to eat, drink and strengthen her bones. After a century or two, come by, and we can philosophize. And maybe then I'll have time. Maybe we can even begin the love confessions. But now look . . ."

She showed me the open notebooks, the blackboard above her bed filled with algebraic equations, the poverty of her room, the unheated stove.

I got up, feeling that I was unjust in wasting her time.

She gave me her hand, and it seemed that this cold, tense hand came from another shore opposite from mine. I shivered. I sensed an abyss between us. What abyss? The leap that Russia had made.

Truthfully, the rhythm of life in the Soviet Union is very severe. A great threat and a great hope hang above everyone's head. Men and women are dedicated, focused on their work. They have to solve problems of immediate need. They do not have the time or the spirit for erotic pursuits. Love for these strong organisms is a physiological function like hunger and not the persistent idea and dizzying concern of people who have overeaten.

When evening darkens, you do not see the lamentable spectacle that dishonors capitalist cities: the painted, hungry "sisters" who chase men on the streets. During the Tsarist period there were famous brothels here, and their inauguration involved great pomp and ceremony, the presence of the police and the blessing of the local priest. In the Soviet Union, such dens of shame are no longer permitted. Of course there are women who sell themselves. When they are caught, the man who pays is punished.

This selling of the body is rare. At first you are surprised, but as you breathe in this new atmosphere, you eventually understand the reasons why.

Here, in the Soviet land, the passion for luxuries that pushes women all over the world toward dishonor has disappeared, at first out of necessity, but later out of habit and out of new inner concerns. Woman here, dressed very simply, without gold and feathers, has found new, superior styles of coquetry and has placed on a higher level her innate capacity to attract men.

Another reason that prostitution has ceased to flourish in Russia is that the sexually arousing shows and reading materials that infect and rot capitalist societies no longer exist. In the cinemas and theaters you will never see works that titillate the imagination and the flesh. They are now institutions of the state whose function is to educate the masses. The political, economic and cultural elevation of the people is a task of primary importance in Russia, because if the people are educationally nourished, the communist Idea will take root and thrive. The capitalists rush to the centers of their cities to be entertained and excited; here the masses gather to learn and become educated.

In the same fashion, each printed form has a stern educational content. For a book to be published in Russia, the manuscript must be submitted to a special editorial committee, which gives its permission. The publication of a book, periodical or newspaper that does not serve the educational improvement of the people is very strictly forbidden. Pornographic materials are completely unknown in the new Russia. Those who hold a pen in hand here must learn that they have a great responsibility.

Furthermore, all women work here. When they do the same job, they get the same wages as the men. New curiosities have awakened within them and new preoccupations have emerged. They elect officials and they are elected; they play a role in the Soviets. They follow issues of collective interest with a responsible attention and awareness. They are no longer unoccupied, suffering from boredom and losing their souls and bodies in the powder room and in flirtations. A fresh new wind has blown inside the souls and bodies of women, and this wind is stirring a new and unexpected kind of nobility in their lives. The freedom during the early revolutionary years intoxicated them and drove them to shameless excesses. It is now getting a sense of proportion, a restraint, and is taking on its most austere profile: the face of responsibility.

■   ■   ■

Those women who are experiencing this new life at a deeper level are struggling with a missionary fervor to awaken this new awareness of responsibility in the millions of women in the cities and villages. The teachers above all, as well as the workers, the students, the members of the Komsomols, are leading this women's liberation movement with fanaticism and a method. A mass of newspapers and periodicals are published which are geared only to women; some only for workers, some for peasant women, and others in various local languages for the half-savage women of the numerous and varied races in Russia.

In this vast, primitive land, it is a difficult and arduous task to awaken women from an age-old lethargy. But those women who have become enlightened and are opening the way by going forward have patience, determination and unshakable faith. Niurina, one of the brightest of the women who have undertaken this immense task, spoke to me the day before yesterday in her office.

"Don't forget, Nikolai Mikhailovich, that we here are passing through a transitory period. The old woman is not dead yet and the new one has not as yet found her definitive viable mold. In a changing time, there are, just as in the evolution of species, many abortions and caricatures, many excesses and imperfections. The final form has not been set. But with time, all these manifold searches will settle into a stable and fruitful type. Don't be in a hurry. How many years have we been free, and how long have we been working? Give us time. And we will create a new woman—companion, wife and mother."

"And marriage, Vera Nikolaevna?" I asked.

She laughed. "What bile and ink have been spilled over the Bolshevik marriage. People outside Russia think that marriage does not exist in our new society, that a woman can have as many men as she wants, a man as many women as he can handle, and that the society is falling apart? Uneasy capitalists spread these reports and they poison their unfortunate and unenlightened masses. They ignore the fact that there is no country where there are so many obstacles in the way of such a polygamous herding together as in Soviet Russia."

At that moment a young woman, slightly built but energetic, entered the office. Aquiline nose, short raven-black hair and fiery almond eyes. She sat at the opposite table and opened a briefcase filled with papers. I sensed that she too was from that mysterious race that shakes the world, the one that brought one messiah and is now giving birth to another. For a moment she lifted her eyes toward me as if she were weighing what I was worth, why I was living and what I was contributing to the struggle. And then she quickly bent over her papers, still panting from her running pace.

Niurina spoke to her quickly, gave her instructions, handed her a thick envelope and then turned to me: "This is Itka Khorovich, my assistant," she said. "She's taken over the informational services in the countryside concerning Soviet marriage. It's a difficult job, but we are going ahead."

"What are the chief characteristics of Soviet law concerning marriage?"

From the moment she had come into the office, I was stifling, as if a merciless spirit had suddenly entered, had weighed my soul and, finding it worthless, had cast it aside.

"The religious wedding," answered Niurina, "has of course been abolished. A mutual declaration by a man and a woman in a public office stating that they want to marry is sufficient. Polygamy is prohibited. A woman's property remains hers after the marriage. Each partner has an obligation to provide for the other when destitute and unable to work. Married or unmarried mothers have the same rights. Legitimate and illegitimate children have the same rights. The parents are obligated to provide for the physical health and spiritual education of their children until they are eighteen years of age. The children are obligated to support their parents when they are in need and unable to work. When one of the partners wants a divorce, it will be granted. But the economic consequences are such that one observes this unexpected thing: Divorces are not so common as you think in Soviet Russia. The Soviet family has been strengthened by this enlightened synthesis of freedom and responsibility.

"It is the first time in human legislation that the rights of a woman have been protected by such broad guarantees and that marriage has been given such supra-individual significance. Nor do we make women common property. We don't take children away from their parents or destroy the sickly. Nowhere in your capitalist world is a woman protected with such understanding and love as wife and mother; and nowhere is her ability to contribute to the whole of society so strengthened.

"We never forget the enlightened words of Trotskii. 'We must strengthen marriage if we are to raise the worth of the individual. The degree of civilization of a nation is proportionate to the support it provides to the mother and therefore to her children.'"

■ THE ENLIGHTENMENT
OF THE PEOPLE

■ PERHAPS WE CAN DISTINGUISH the various important combatants who struggle for the ceaseless renewal of life.

First, at the lowest level of initiation are those who contribute the most to bring evil to its highest point, and thus, without realizing it, the strongest apparent enemies of a future world are at the same time its most effective collaborators. As the capitalists, the priests, the old generals, the judges and the kings cultivate injustice and falsehood, they swell the wave of anger and give impetus to the storm.

At the second level of initiation are those who ask for the "conflagration" in order to tear down the old, to plow the land so that it can be ready for the new seed. They blindly hate the old class—its economic, social, ethical and spiritual structure—and work with absolute faith for a new order.

At the third rung have climbed those who have cast the seed in the plowed, bleeding land.

Having completed her necessary and long service to slavery, Russia has gone beyond the first level. By carrying out her bloody mission of the communist battle to its conclusion, she has gone through the second stage. And now, as she enters the third phase, she begins the most difficult task: to create a new society.

For this reason, the study of this many-souled, many-seeded land has never been so revealing and so useful in a practical way as now. Earlier, during her first frenetic, revolutionary years, Russia was more tragic, more fascinating for poets, philosophers and spectators. Now it is an attraction for economists, politicians and scientists. All the capitalist nations

101

could help themselves and extend their existence for awhile by studying how a new power system can be channeled, and how it can invigorate fatigued social organisms.

An acquaintance of mine, an official of rank in the Commissariat of Hygiene, took me to a place where I could observe a truly original and enlightening piece of propaganda.

It was a large hall adjacent to a factory filled with male and female workers. The men with their caps pulled down on their heads and the women with their babushkas sat close together, eating sunflower seeds and apples. All had their eyes fixed on the upstage curtain and waited.

Suddenly the curtain rose in front of us and we were in a Soviet courtroom: a long table covered with a red cloth, high red chairs and on the walls, portraits of Marx, Lenin and Rosa Luxemburg.

My escort explained, "These are the courtrooms of public health. You will witness a true drama. Three judges, the prosecutor and defense counsels will soon arrive—all of them doctors, male and female, who, after they have finished their workday, undertake to present certain appropriate theatrical works in front of workers and peasants to teach them how they might protect themselves from various illnesses. All these workers in the audience have come here not simply to look and pass their time, but to judge, enter into the drama and make a decision. All the people you see here are the jury."

At that moment three judges, the public prosecutor and the lawyers came on the stage. The president rang a bell; the trial began. A door opened again and the defendant entered—a worker who had married and infected his wife. She died in childbirth. Pale and disgraced, he confessed his error and asked for clemency. His mother-in-law entered, a tall, strong woman, who proclaimed a bitter denunciation and demanded that the killer of her daughter be condemned. Witnesses rose, the prosecutor spoke, the lawyers gave legal opinions.

Those in the audience followed the proceedings with intense attention. They agreed, disagreed; opinions took different turns. You sensed that this drama was not a playful fantasy. It was alive and frightening, taken from the ordeals of their pain.

The proceedings ended. The president presented these questions to the jury; that is, to the whole audience:

"Is the defendant guilty because, before he married, he contracted the disease?" The men shouted, "No!"; the women, decisively and with feeling, "Yes!"

"Is the defendant guilty because he married before he received medical care and thus transmitted the disease?" All of them, men and women, responded unhesitatingly, "Yes!"

"Are there mitigating circumstances?" For ten minutes there was a heated discussion to find an answer to the third question. The women, merciless, and many of them perhaps with personal lessons in these matters, would not accept any reduction in sentence; the men, lenient, argued that the defendant, having expressed regret, should be acquitted.

"I would support acquittal," shouted an old lady, raising her hand, "if his repentance could return the dead woman to life!"

The old lady's cry was victorious.

When the court made its decision and the assembly adjourned, everyone's face was excited. During this evening, all these souls had lived an awesome drama of contemporary life.

As we were leaving, the doctor, who depicted the president of the court, spoke to me when we reached the street. "We have had excellent success with this type of presentation. A theatrical rendition influences and enlightens the people better than a lecture, a film or a book. We have put together a repertory of drama that we have adapted and simplified: *The Prostitute* by Margueritte, *The Syphilitics* by Maupassant, *Ghosts* by Ibsen. We also have other simple, original and moving works that aim to make people aware of the ruinous results of alcohol, consumption, syphilis, malaria, uncleanliness. We do what we can to transmit a little light to our comrades who still find themselves in darkness. We would like this light to be more abundant and to move more quickly. But enlightenment always takes struggle and moves very slowly. We know this, and that's why we work patiently and persistently. Eventually we are certain that light will conquer."

We moved along the snow-filled roads of Moscow. We passed Red Square. The golden domes of the Kremlin gleamed under the frozen starlight.

My companion sighed. "Russia is boundless," he said, "and the people are still steeped in ignorance and superstition. That's what the Tsars wanted. Let me mention two incidents so that you will understand: In 1923, we learned for the first time that there was an unknown race living in complete isolation in a deserted, lost corner of Siberia. They used water only for drinking and never for washing the body or their clothing. The public health mission who discovered them immediately began to inform them of the need to wash and to bathe their bodies. But no one listened. Finally one person, the bravest, was willing to wade into the river to bathe. But his fear was so great that when the water reached his neck, he died. All of that community angrily fell upon the public mission, and the doctors barely managed to escape."

I laughed. But the doctor shook his head. "I can't laugh," he said. "Listen to another example, equally tragic, or if you like, comic. In many villages the peasants, when they plan to move from their homes or to take a journey, take a certain number of lice with them as an amulet because they believe that these terrible parasites are incarnations of their ancestors!

"That is our people. This is where the whip, illiteracy and economic slavery have brought them. You can understand now what an awesome responsibility confronts us and what difficulties we encounter trying to enlighten such masses. But faith conquers all, and we shall win."

I was very much moved as I heard my evening's companion speak for some time with clarity and passion about the godlike crusade that the few in Russia had undertaken to save the many. An extensive network of Soviet public health has spread itself throughout this gigantic land. In each factory and in each ministry, in all the schools, the barracks, the living quarters of the villages—this public health corps informs and supervises hygienic regulations to see that they are put into practice. As many as possible mobilize themselves for this informational task: clerks, scientists, workers, students, schoolchildren, soldiers . . . Popular pamphlets are published—some for workers, others for peasants, for young men, for young women, for mothers. Lectures and discussions are set up in the factories, the schools, the barracks, the villages. Everywhere. Exhibitions are transported from village to village, from city to city, in which you see colored impressions in plaster that reveal the terrible results that tuberculosis, syphilis, swamp fever and alcoholism have on the body. There are multicolored wall posters where the best Soviet artists portray simply and dramatically how a bad habit, a chance episode, a bad companion, can result in these terrible illnesses and how we should fight against them. The cinema plays the most significant role in this public health propaganda. It makes clear the most abstract notions, and the most illiterate and unenlightened peasant opens his eyes and quickly accepts its influence without any mental effort.

"You see," concluded this Soviet apostle of health, "that

we employ the latest methods of communication, the same as a private company would use if it is to succeed. In order to lengthen the lives of their clients who have paid for coverage, American insurance firms send numerous informational booklets to them. Every so often, they mail them instructions on how to live, how to eat, how to breathe, how to sleep. They spend millions on this propaganda in order to amass, through the longer lives of their clients, an even greater profit. Soviet Russia is doing the same thing to protect its citizens."

I listened and was moved as I understood with how much risk, courage and obstinacy the light struggles to pierce the darkness. I turned to my companion who now silently continued in his head the battle to make another Russia, another world, a better and more enlightened one. A despairing cry rose up within me. I tried but was unable to keep it within me.

"Toward what goal is this struggle of man moving?" I asked my companion.

But he, surprised, turned and looked at me without answering.

The next day I wandered into a museum of art and followed the crowds of village men and women who stood in groups, gazing the way their bulls and cows would look with their large eyes at the divine paintings of Rembrandt. They were brought in flocks from all parts of Russia. They were dragged into the museums, the libraries, the theaters. Before them went the ardent young guides who struggled to stir up the lump of mud within these hard peasant heads.

A young man of twenty, with his blue shirt, his glittering eyes and his curved Jewish nose, stood today in front of this mass of people, attempting to explain Rembrandt: What is art; why do artists paint; who was Rembrandt; how he loved people; how he suffered in his life; how his creditors threw him out of his house even though he was an old man; how they sold all that he owned and left him in the streets because he could not pay them . . .

The peasants listened to him, some with heads bowed and others with stretched and stiff necks. Every so often the face of a young peasant woman would light up a bit, her mind stirring for a moment; another peasant would at last comprehend something that he had been hearing for so many hours. Something stirred like a little insect, like the seed of a flower in the rich mud of their brains. And the young guide was sweating. He leaned over them. He yelled, "They have often told me that all of our hopes depend on the education of the people. The enlightenment of the people, a thing of great danger to capitalist countries, is for us the only salvation."

For this reason, one of the first concerns of Bolshevism is the teaching of reading and writing to the millions of illiterates. Thousands of associations have been set up with the title: "Wipe out illiteracy!" Members journey from village to village. They stay for three or four months, teaching as many as they can how to read and write. They entrust to those they have taught the duty to teach others. They leave and move on to another village.

Students, teachers, clerks, workers—all have taken on the task of educating each group in a certain area. A holy crusade has been launched against illiteracy. And its purpose is not just to teach the uneducated how to read and write, but also to awaken within them a consciousness of their class, to push them into taking a place in the Soviet rebirth of the nation. Nothing is taught, not even a phrase, that does not intend to enlighten them and to educate them in the communist way.

At the same time, they awaken in these unorganized minds a scientific and technological interest. Whenever they can, the Bolsheviks are attempting to bring science close to the people. They organize special exhibitions to show the people how indispensable science is for the social and economic reorganization of the land and how the scientists are working in a completely practical way with the workers in the factories and with the peasants in the fields.

The people watch these exhibitions and discover how science is a necessity in the life of man. They learn what the quantitative and qualitative values of Russian goods were before and what happened after science studied and perfected the process of their production. For the first time, these thick-brained peasants understand that science is not a fruitless and abstract theory nor is the learned man a useless maniac in an office. He is now a priceless leader and co-worker with the laborer.

The attempt of science to come into close contact with the immediate and practical necessities of the land is one of the outstanding undertakings in the Soviet Union. Science must become an instrument of the proletariat, a weapon also for the final victory. It is therefore necessary that all of its theories and research have an immediate and practical purpose: They must raise the level of production and, at the same time, raise the intellectual capacity of the people so that the proletariat can establish itself among enlightened human masses.

Science has always stood as a weapon for the ruling class. In the beginning of man's development, magicians and priests had certain scientific notions—how the stars moved and consequently how to have a calendar for time, how to treat certain illnesses, how to till the land better, how to fashion stronger weapons. Knowledge about these things was kept secret and was used to control and terrorize the people.

Today science is an instrument of the ruling class in the capitalist countries. Of course it is no longer a secret thing; on the contrary, there is a tendency in civilized countries to popularize scientific ideas; but in actuality, science still remains a privilege of a certain social class: the wealthy. Why?

There are many reasons: Science is sold like merchandise at the universities and the polytechnic institutions, and it is very expensive for the poor. If someone from the people manages after many struggles to go through higher technical learning and to excel in his field, he is forced, if he wishes to live and to thrive as a scientist, to enter the service of the ruling class, and to serve, even though he is a man of the people, its interests. That is why all the scientists that constitute the staff of the economic, social and intellectual community of a land are out of necessity instruments of the bourgeoisie. All of science, consciously or not, works to benefit and strengthen the bourgeoisie.

The time has come in Russia for science to enter the service of the ruling class (the proletariat), organizing the social and economic life of the people on a new and wider foundation. Since the final purpose of the dictatorship of the proletariat is to wipe out the class structure, it must create a new science that will organize and reconcile presently conflicting scientific goals and bring, as it will in society, a harmony to science.

To actualize this lofty purpose, science must first become accessible to all. How? Certainly it will not happen with a skimpy and necessarily superficial scientific popularization. The capitalist class pushes such propaganda because it is in its interest to give technical skills to workers, to make them more productive and profitable servants to its aims. Beyond this immediate practical necessity, the education of the people is not in the interest of capitalism. For people to become truly enlightened, the method of teaching must be simplified, and more options must be given to the nation if it is to equip itself scientifically. The large masses must be enlightened, not just the exceptional individuals. All of the people, trained scientifically, must work together to find solutions for the enormous economic and technical problems of contemporary life.

Two new educational organizations are playing a significant role in a gigantic and enlightening propaganda in Soviet Russia: the Club (the recreation hall) in the cities and the reading room in the villages.

Every factory, jail, barracks, and all the schools, the hospitals, the ships, have their own recreation halls. Here the illiterate learn to read and write. There are lectures and discussions. One reads loudly and the others listen and evaluate. There are cultural programs, celebrations, festivals. The recreation hall is a political, social and spiritual institute where the citizen improves culturally and learns what his rights and responsibilities are.

Each recreation hall has its reading room and library. It can also have its musical ensemble in one area, and every so often it presents a film or a theatrical work. In the beginning, traveling professional actors played in the various halls, but later the workers and then the peasants slowly began to take part in staged scenes, and with the astonishing ability that the Russian has for mime, acting and dance, you could often feel in their amateur skits a true artistic joy.

In the small factories, on small ships and in other small organizations, where it is not possible to have a recreation hall, there is the Red Corner, a room with Red flags and communist slogans on its walls—and always with the portrait of Lenin. In the Red Corner, the comrades gather. They read newspapers and books, they discuss, they listen to the conversations of their friends, and they drink tea.

"A new sower strides over the fields—a new seed of wheat he scatters into the furrows . . ." Something new is germinating in the rich fields of Russia. If this sowing holds fast for ten or twenty years, then, as Lenin said, "The world-wide victory is certain, even if the proletariat beyond our boundaries does not take a revolutionary position."

For enlightenment has an explosive power, and when it bursts in its own house, it gives light, whether it wishes to or not, to the house of its neighbor. And truly, if someone asked me what thing in Russia made the deepest impression upon me and gave me the most solid hopes, I would answer unhesitatingly: the holy frenzy of its leaders to enlighten the dark, all-powerful masses.

Pastor Karl Vogel was right. When he returned from his Soviet journey, he summed up his experiences with these simple, moving words: "What I saw in Russia made me regain my faith in mankind, a faith that I had lost."

■ RELIGION

■ HERE IN THE SOVIET UNION, one very often finds the figures of the saints in the streets, in the hollow spaces in walls, or simply hanging on the doors of churches. They are neglected: Their clothes are shabby and dirty; their beards, unvarnished and unkempt. People have stopped nourishing them with prayers and offerings.

I know a wooden angel who came unscrewed from the door of a church in a main street in Moscow. Someone had nailed him there to guard the entrance. Now he hangs there, with one wing down like a wounded bird. And a tin Saint Nicholas at a certain crossroads in Moscow has also become unhinged and now hangs precariously above the frozen sidewalk. When the wind blows, he squeaks and yells like a loose shop sign. No one cares enough to hold him by the legs and steady him or at least take him down altogether so that he will not continue to be tormented.

The saints are hungry in Russia. The angels suffer pain as they hang between sky and earth. God wanders through the streets—homeless, unemployed, persecuted—like a bourgeois.

Each Sunday in the grand outdoor bazaars of Smolensk Boulevard, where everyone sells whatever he has that is old or useless, or whatever hunger forces him to put on the market, you meet crowds of old women carrying icons— Holy Virgins and Christs, richly framed with silver crowns— and they sell them together with old metal things and cracked teacups. I observed people buying incomprehensively useless old objects: a crushed hat, a broken denture, a watch without its inner springs, a part of a quilt, but I rarely saw them buy the saintly figures. One Sunday I stood for a long time next to a pale old woman who was selling a ruddy Holy Virgin that she held in her arms. No one came near her, nor did anyone mock her or cross himself. People were simply indifferent. They saw nothing that they needed here and moved on.

I spoke to the pale old woman: "The Holy Virgins don't sell anymore, *mamochka?*"

And she, serene under her snow-covered kerchief, answered, "What can we do, my son? Patience. They'll buy her because she has a nice frame."

They will buy her, I thought, and in the frame they will place an icon of Lenin. The frame remains—the heart of man. Only the image changes.

The day before yesterday, a Christian holiday, I visited the new Moscow Cathedral next to the river. The immense church, the pride of Tsarist Russia, was empty, unlighted and unheated. Rows of multicolored saints, with the golden halos and the victorious crowns of martyrdom on their heads, shivered in the barren winter half-light like a herd in the cold. A well-nourished old noblewoman who huddled on a bench near the entrance did not manage to warm this holy flock of saints with her breath that moved into the frozen air like smoke.

I remembered one of the truly astonishing writers that Russia had produced: Vassilii Vasilevich Rozanov—free from any idea and yet possessed by all ideas, abrupt and yet gentle, and always alone. "I feel," he said, "the emptiness and silence around me with such intensity that I can hardly believe or acknowledge the fact that other people exist in the world."

An inconsistent genius, he writes articles with liberty-loving enthusiasm, and on the same day, and with a different name, he produces articles that are violently anti-freedom in their fanaticism. When the Russian Revolution burst forth, he attacked with equal fury the "totally corrupt" Tsarism and the "debased" Revolution. He extols the God of life and fecundity. He deifies movement and energy while he wallows in laziness at home. He drinks tea incessantly, and when he goes outside, he scavenges for cigarette butts and says, "I am not searching for the truth; I want my peace of mind."

No one wrote so boldly and so shamelessly about his inner thoughts. "I feel literature," he said, "as if I were touching my trousers." He looks at his incoherent works and mocks himself: "*Scattered Beams. Sand. Rocks. Ditches. What are they for? Are they constructing a road? No, they are the work of Rozanov, of Vasilii Vasilievich Rozanov.*"

I thought of him today in this frozen church because no one hated the religion of Christ as he did. For him God is the god of the living, not of the dead. Death is the "final cold." We must defeat Christ; that is, original sin; that is, the cold; that is, death. Because Christ = cold = death. To conquer Christ, there is only one way: to become children; to deify life, the fertility of the earth, the sun. We must oppose the Christian equation with another: God = sun = newborn child.

I went back and forth hurriedly in this majestic church to warm myself a little. Christ, I thought, is not cold. He ended up cold, frozen because our hearts turned to ice. The gentle Savior is not fragrant anymore like apple and honey, as the poet Esenin assures us. He has the odor of a devastated and empty house, of earth.

Suddenly, while I was pondering how the deepest yearnings of man in every epoch become incarnated into a new myth with such infallible skill and how this myth moves in the vanguard, giving man the courage to ascend, I heard from on high, in a corner of the church, the chanting of the sweetest male and female voices. After some searching, I found a circular marble staircase. As I climbed and climbed, the chanting got more and more powerful. I followed a passageway with paintings of the saints on its walls, and I climbed a new stairway. Before me in the darkness, I could distinguish several old men and women with heavy shawls, gasping for breath as they moved upward.

I reached the summit of this second staircase, and I found myself in a warm corner, in a gilded chapel with lighted candles and with kneeling men and women. The altar was filled with deacons, priests and bishops dressed in gold, wrapped in silk from head to toe and glowing under the heavy silver votive lamps like peacocks.

I shall never forget the warmth, the sweetness, the fragrance of wax, frankincense and naphthalene that I found in that corner. The elderly men, with their sideburns and shabby fur coats, looked like former nobles or the doorkeepers of noble estates; the women, their hair covered by kerchiefs, appeared ready to faint because of their rising euphoria. With his beautifully combed golden hair, his sensual lips, his richly decorated chest, his gold and silver legs, his human hands, eyes and heart—Christ gleamed rosy-cheeked and contented on the iconostasis.

I stood erect in the midst of these kneeling old people, and I thought how different and yet how movingly similar are the beginning and the decline. What a heartrending farewell this gathering seemed to me, just as if friends were seeing off a loved one who was leaving, never to return.

With such bitterness and pathos, the last of the faithful separate from the familiar and loved image of their God, but without any cries. And again the first of the new believers who embody a new yearning for man fall upon and destroy without mercy the old, no longer potent—and for this reason false—idols.

In their speeches, newspapers, books, schools and in all the information they disseminate to awaken the people, the Bolsheviks mercilessly attack not only Christianity but every other religion as well. And yet they have not closed the churches where there are sufficient believers to maintain them. Nor do they prohibit worship. They strive to enlighten the people so that they will make their own choice. Opposite the famous miracle-working icon of the Virgin of Iversk at the entrance to the Kremlin's Red Square, the Bolsheviks have engraved Karl Marx's phrase in large capital letters on the stones of the facing wall: "Religion is the opiate of the masses." On one side the Virgin, and on the other, Karl Marx. You choose and take what you want.

In the schools, however, not only have they abolished courses on religion, but they have systematically and fanatically taught the child that God and the devil are the inventions of the priests and that man is the offspring of the earth and in the earth he begins and ends his life. This materialistic worldview is taught, beginning at the elementary school level. In no way is permission granted for books with a religious inclination to be published. There are also specially designed museums which portray how organic creatures developed according to Darwinian theory and how man, in the course of eons, evolved from the apes.

The Bolsheviks eliminated the old religious models and created new ones. Slowly a new communist ritual is being crystallized, which sanctifies the great moments of human life with new rituals. Frequently when a child is born, a group of workers is often the godfather. They give these Red infants new names: *Ninel* (an anagram for Lenin), *Trud* (Labor), *Profsoiuz* (Trade Union), *Kim* (Communist Youth). They give the newborn child a diploma on which these words are beautifully written in red ink:

> We do not bless you in the name of the cross, the sign of ignorance and slavery, but in the name of the Red flag of labor and struggle. May you equally love workers in all lands and of all races and colors.

Hate with equal passion the kings, bankers, industrialists and priests in all the world. Be a faithful follower of Lenin and hold high and steadfast the flag of science, and always remain a defender of the Third Internationale.

There are special periodicals on atheism, whose purpose is to enlighten the muzhik who clings to his old faith. When I went to visit the director of the weekly satirical review, *The Atheist,* I found the spacious offices filled with editorial writers (men and women), scholars, scientists, theologians and humorists bent over their desks and, with a religious zeal, writing satirical articles in popular form attacking religion.

An unattractive young woman with red hair, her cigarette sticking to her lips, proudly showed me the various volumes of the periodical. I took one and leafed through it: It was filled with caricatures, drunken monks, saints dancing in taverns, vulgar jokes, scandalous anecdotes and crude science.

"Above all," I said to her, "I like your fanaticism and your faith against faith. Isn't this a new religion itself?"

The young woman exhaled the smoke through her nostrils.

"Wait for the director," she said and left.

I waited. I looked around me. The walls were covered with caricatures: priests whose triple bellies were held up by fat angels, a gross, stupefied god with sideburns, monks and nuns riding on he-goats.

In a little while the director, lean, ascetic and red-bearded, entered. His face dripped poison.

I had armed my mind with many questions. I wanted to start a debate supporting God in this center of atheism. I was prepared to do battle for the sake of a fallen feudal lord. But as soon as I saw the leader of atheism, I froze. I already knew all of his "scientific" arguments; I unmistakably fathomed the hissing lips and the sarcastic voice rising from a poisonous, venomous throat.

He looked at me in a way that asked what I wanted.

"Nothing," I answered to his silent question. "I just wanted to see you. I have done so, and now I'm leaving."

He saw me to the door of his office, rubbing his hands. At the threshold, he tried to smile, but his lips, unaccustomed to laughter, pulled back like those of a dog that is ready to bite.

"Are you one of us?" he asked.

"And that means?"

"Against God?"

"What does one mean by God?" I snapped, unnerved. "By the devil? What is the difference? I don't understand."

He pushed me gently and closed the door.

As I walked in the street, I chuckled over his sudden anger. Slowly things settled in my mind, and I saw that all of these energetic disciples of materialism give heavy-handed answers to eternal questions with a naive certainty. And they are attempting, as in every religion, to propagate these answers and make them intelligible to the people. In the Soviet Union today, there is a fanatical, mystically passionate and dogmatic religion: atheism. Cruel, merciless, equipped with an army of millions, it holds millions of children in its hands and shapes them as it wishes. It is all-powerful. It too has its bible: Marx's great *Das Kapital*; it has its great prophet, Lenin; it has its fanatical apostles who travel to many nations, preaching the new good tidings; it has its martyrs, its heroes, its dogmas, its Fathers, its apologists, its scholiasts, its preachers; it has its synods, its heretics and its excommunications; above all, it has the belief that it holds the truth and that it is giving the definitive answer to the problems of life.

We who are alive at this time need, in consequence, to

make a supreme intellectual effort to understand this contemporary and awesome moment in which a new religion is being born.

Without abrupt shocks, the old religion is withering. It still has its priests, its golden vestments, its churches, its sweet, deep-sounding bells, its chantings, but the vital sap has run out and the tree is wilting. In Russia, the old religion and its monasteries are still there. Its most famous one, the Troitskii, is outside of Moscow.

One day the director of the Museum of Hagiography, the compassionate former noble Ivan Aleksandrovich Anisimov, happily informed me: "We have a little sunshine. Shall we go on a little excursion to the Troitskii Monastery? Do you like icons? There you will see the masterpiece of our great iconographer, Andrei Rublev: the Holy Trinity."

During those days I observed the Bolsheviks as they worked with an all-consuming patience and love. They collect icons from all of Russia. They remove all the new layers of paint that have disfigured them. They have established special centers where, in order to find the original image, workers strive with a truly religious attention to scrape off the colors that were applied one after another.

I was moved as I watched this labor for many hours. One icon had been painted repeatedly during different time periods, and it was necessary to scrape off ten, and on occasion twelve, layers to find the first, the oldest and almost always the most beautiful painting. The day before yesterday, I went to one of these restoration workshops where they were working on a gigantic, heavily painted Virgin of the nineteenth century. In one corner of the work, they had removed thirteen layers of paint and had revealed an angel of the thirteenth century of indescribable beauty. It had the austere sweetness of the Byzantine prototype and, at the same time, the violent and

mysterious passion of the Slav. Three skillful craftsmen
with their very fine tools were working very slowly to free
the original icon. They estimated that in six months the
complete Virgin would be delivered.

With this method, the icon worshipper Anisimov had
saved the most beautiful Holy Virgin that exists in the
world. In 1157, Prince Andrei Bogoliubskii had brought it
from Byzantium to the city of Vladimir; from there it was
transported to one of the Kremlin's churches in Moscow in
1355. For centuries, it had been smothered by smoke,
candles and new paint. Now restored, she glows, the pin-
nacle of sacred painting, in the museum. She is all sadness,
tenderness and nobility. Her large almond eyes look down
upon the world in despair, but with infinite love and sorrow,
just as if the world were her son, being crucified.

Whatever the Bolsheviks are doing for the icons, they are
doing the same thing for the old historical monasteries and
palaces. They carefully remove the most recent layers of
paint, the heavy-handed and distasteful ornamentation, and
then the buildings appear in their original forms. They
frequently turn them into museums, decorating them with
furniture, icons, carpets and books of the same period.

"Shall we go?" again, Ivan Aleksandrovich Anisimov
asked me.

We set out. Leaning outward, we look out the window of
the train and see the snow-covered and sun-drenched plain.
We pass a thick forest of firs. They stand motionless, these
proud trees, covered with crystals. It is all a mystery. My
African eyes are still unable to get accustomed to it and be
satisfied by this hyperborean miracle. My courteous companion smiles in his contentment. I hear him talk about
Russian iconography and everthing in this fairy-tale, arctic
land seems like a dream.

"Our first great painter came to us from your country.
Theofanis the Cretan. He filled the churches of Novgorod

with his wild, creative breath. His prophets are an all-inflamed and inspiring passion; his Holy Virgins, severe, without tenderness, like powerful forces of nature.

"From the strong root of Theofanis the Cretan sprang the more supple shoot: Andrei Rublev with his more human and milder configurations of smiling, robust angels and his serene, blond-bearded Russian Christs.

"And later in the sixteenth century, Dionysios appeared, a tender and sweet artist filled with femininity and grace. Like Giotto in the Arena of Padua, he shut himself up at Saint Ferapont and began to cover the walls of the church with the calm, multicolored visions of his soul."

We reached the monastery, which appeared in the snow with its green domes. We stepped down from the train. In red, green and yellow, village women moved about the snow, and behind them followed lumbering muzhiks, wrapped in their sheepskins. There was a bazaar on this day in the monastery's courtyard, and the muzhiks had come from the neighboring villages to trade their goods.

We stepped over the large threshold and entered the monastery. We opened the door of the church in the middle of the courtyard. All at once, Rublev's Holy Trinity gleamed opposite us on the iconostasis. Three serene angels, with their curly hair tied with wide ribbons, were enthroned at a table and were turning to one another as if in conversation. I stood, overwhelmed. In front of me again I had the deep, simple, unadorned and immortal soul of man. For the first time, the Holy Trinity revealed itself to me in such a human, that is to say divine, way. This Trinity was warm, one of our own, blood from our blood—no longer a part of the unapproachable sky, but belonging to this humble, green earth.

We slowly meandered, and I greedily devoured all of these treasures: icons that were all brilliance and color—such are these northern thirsty-for-light paintings—Oriental

textiles, precious crosses, royal dalmatics of pearl, manuscripts with vivid miniatures, censers, heavy miters, silver
baptismal fonts. From a distant world that had sunk and
drowned, these small shining remnants were all that was
left, unclaimed by death.

We entered the heated cell of the director of the
monastery, which was filled with books.

The director was a kind man, a wise hermit of learning.
All of his life was love and work. From his youth, he dedicated himself to this area, this small yet infinite part of the
monastery. He wrote books about the Troitskii, directly
supervised the deliverance of the charming Renaissance
building from earlier tasteless repairs, scraped off the
Tsarist gold, which had been smeared on the iconostasis,
so that the original many-colored flowers appeared once
again on wood. For years, he shuffled his feet among the
remnants of faith, communicating with them. It is for this
reason that he looked pale and serene, could laugh so
easily, and could jump up like a child when he received us
in his cell.

"Welcome," he said, tightly clasping my hands. "Welcome from Greece, the land of my beloved sage."

"Which wise man?" I said with a smile. "Of those, we
had quite a production."

"The great benefactor of Russia, Maximos the Greek. He
was born in Arta in 1480, studied in Paris, Venice and
Florence and finally found refuge in the monastery of
Vatopedi on the Holy Mountain.* An exceptional per-
sonage: wise, daring and saintly. The Grand Duke of Moscow wrote to the ecumenical patriarch in Constantinople:
'Send me a wise Greek to enlighten my people!' And the
patriarch sent him Maximos. He came here and, after being
received with many honors, began to classify manuscripts

---

* Mount Athos, in Greece.

that had been brought to us by Byzantine refugees, to translate new works and to correct old translations. 'Only one thing,' he proclaimed, 'can save Russia: education. Not a narrow education that understands only the letter of learning, but a broad one that can perceive the spirit of the holy scriptures.' This great man of wisdom, who was not afraid, expressed his opinions boldly, set many hearts on fire and enlightened many minds; the best Russians of his time were his students. May God protect Greece! Welcome!"

As he spoke, he placed his hand on an imposing samovar, which shone like an altar in the corner of the cell. We were cold, hungry and thirsty, and as soon as I saw the massive samovar, I remembered the primitive gods of the North, those chiseled in stone—short and big bellied. They sit good-naturedly like owls, and they delight human beings.

Tea. Butter. Caviar. Smoked fish. We ate and drank. Our tongues became free. We talked about the Holy Mountain, Mystras, Daphni, Saint Luke's monastery in Phocis, and the eyes of my two elderly companions became misty as they spoke with nostalgia about Byzantine Greece.

Later at nightfall a tall man dressed like a muzhik, who labored in the workshops that restored the icons, accompanied us as we returned to the railroad station. He held a large lantern so that we would not lose our way in the snow.

He spoke perfect French: "I made three trips to Greece. But at that time I was only concerned with ancient Greece. I went to Sparta, but I did not condescend to take the two steps and go up to Mystras. Now I'd like to go to your country again to see Christian Greece only. But I can't. How can I travel now? I deserve my punishment."

He smiled bitterly. In the unsteady light of the lantern, I discerned his noble bearing, his long, blond beard, his delicate hands.

"It is thus," I answered, "that those who evolve and push

forward are always punished. Had you allowed yourself to remain fixed in your old ideas and loves, you would not have your present sadness. We always pay dearly for every good we receive."

And he answered. "It is just. If we don't give with grace, we do not receive with grace."

For a moment his voice disturbed me, but we had arrived at the train and we said farewell to him. As soon as we were alone, Ivan Aleksandrovich turned and said, "He is Count ————, you know. A great noble who oppressed many people in his life. He once had great land estates in the Ukraine. Now . . ."

Then he fell silent.

■ RUSSIAN LITERATURE

■ I TOO HAVE BEEN NOURISHED with the milk—
no, the flame, since it has no milk—of Russian literature.
Certainly the acute pain and passion of the rebellious heroes
in Russian literature have ravished my soul to a greater degree than those in the famous masterpieces of my ancestors.
This absorbing art has its special qualities—mainly, five—
which distinguish it from European works, and these
aspects were the ones that powerfully excited my blood
when I was a young man:

1. Beyond beauty, Russian literature strives to reach religious, ethical and metaphysical goals. The Russian writer
is always shaken by the momentous problem of life and
death. He asks, what is the aim and meaning of life on this
earth, why do we live, work and suffer? The purpose of
the Russian writer is not the free, disinterested game of
art, the lofty and pure joy of poetic creation; his aim is to
find and communicate to his reader a new hierarchy of
values. What are the rights, obligations and hopes of man?
Art becomes a metaphysical quest and an ethical struggle—a didactic proclamation.

2. Russian literature is in its very essence revolutionary. It
wants to awaken and enlighten the people, to lift their spiritual awareness, to instill in them the knowledge of their
rights and the love of freedom. The Russian people are illiterate, sluggish, fatalistic; the abrupt Europeanization of
Russia by Peter the Great has widened the chasm between
the intelligentsia and the masses even more. The literary
artist who had the ability to put his thoughts on paper was a
rare phenomenon, and he felt an obligation to employ this
magical strength, not only to create works of luxuriant

beauty, but also to serve a more immediately pressing purpose: to enlighten his backward people.

The Russian writer was the first to realize that political and economic oppression are the root of social evil. Only when it is eradicated will a people be saved. As soon as the Russian writer reached this certainty, he bravely assumed his responsibility. At that time, there were no free politicians, journalists, sociologists or teachers; the writer replaced all of them. He was the only voice in the vast land of Tsarist Russia that was rising to demand freedom. He alone defended the victimized, the hungry, the enslaved, because he was the only one who dared through the works of his imagination to let his conscience raise its voice. He was the leader and at the same time the spiritual confessor of his people. His readers asked him in their agony: "What shall I do, how will I become enlightened, how shall we free ourselves?"

3. Russian literature has a heroic character, marked by the persecutions of its creators; all of its history is one long uninterrupted and heroic martyrdom. It has had to do battle with all-powerful dark enemies: with tyrannical forces (Tsars, censorship, police); with an educated upper class, which was superficial, indifferent, hedonistic and cowardly; with a large mass of people, which was illiterate and fatalistic.

For this reason, there is no other literature in the world that has so many intellectual heroes and martyrs who die so young, who are tortured, banished, killed or driven to insanity. The Russian writers not only proclaimed the need for the individual to sacrifice himself for the salvation of the whole, but also made themselves the first blood-stained examples.

4. In a very unique way, Russian literature unites the most acute psychological analysis with the most accurate observation and description of external reality. Never before

has a literature probed so deeply into the dark cellars of the human soul, often with a pathological sensitivity but always with a warm, human compassion. At the same time, the outer world was never portrayed with such vivid accuracy. Pure idealism and realism merged into one.

This is why Russian literature, which is so deeply rooted in the Russian landscape, has very quickly gone beyond its local boundaries and has become universal.

5. Russian literature is not bound by a long and burdensome tradition. And thus, youthful as it is, it is not obligated to turn its head back nostalgically to worship the past. It does not have great predecessors that it must ridiculously imitate, nor does it need to reject the past entirely and lose its roots. It looks ahead. It is free. There are no obstacles in its way in finding new forms and boldly opening new roads.

As a result, it can throw itself uncompromisingly into radical theories. It can neglect form and sacrifice architectural symmetry to content. It still lacks balance and moderation, fruits of long experience; it has all the virtues of youth but is at the same time susceptible to all of its errors.

No literature has affected man so intensely within such a short time frame, and so deeply and richly, as the Russian. It helped us to understand reality in greater depth, to dig more deeply and more fearfully into the darkness of our souls. It freed us from the romantic and classical molds, from the asphyxiating themes on the self or adultery, and it taught us to see our inner and outer world with new eyes.

After setting out for Russia, and throughout my journey, I contemplated with reverence the bloody line that the Logos had engraved upon the oppressed, martyred empire of the Tsars. Amid barbarism and tyranny and under the whip, the Word, bloodied and immortal, advanced like the mysterious and invincible angel of the heroic ballad of Kiev. The seven victorious leaders would return on their horses to sing in their drunkenness: "Even if our enemy comes down upon us from the sky, we will defeat him!"

They had barely finished their boastful words when an angel appeared. "Come. Let us wrestle," he said. "It doesn't matter that you are seven and I am one."

One of the wild leaders, Alësha Popovich, fell upon him and with his sword cut his body in two from the head down. But he suddenly saw not one but two angels in front of him. Each half became a complete angel. Then Dobrynia attacked the two angels and divided them into four pieces. And behold, four angels came into being. Ilia Muromets divided them, and they became eight. And the miracle proceeded and the angels multiplied; the eight became sixteen, thirty-two, sixty-four, one hundred twenty-eight, thousands . . .

Like this angel, such was the Russian Logos.

For centuries tyranny struck it, cutting it to pieces, but it kept growing and spreading. In the last years of Peter the Great's reign, the intellectual pioneers were pulling ahead, numerous rich souls, all fire and vehemence that are born with every Renaissance; Tatishchev with his wild drunken revels—engineer, naturalist, painter, philosopher—became the first historian of Russia; the aristocratic Kantemir, the admirer of French literature, became the first poet of the new age. He undertook to write a giant epic, *The Motherland,* but he could not manage it, and then decided to write satire. "I write satires," he said, "so that I won't put the reader to sleep. In this way I will leap to victory like a general." He used his boldness and cleverness to combat the ignorance and wretchedness of the Russian people, the cruelty and narrow-mindedness of the nobles, the insatiable greed of the priests, the bribed judges, the shameless flatterers.

Trediakovskii, a supreme molder of language and professor at the Academy of Saint Petersburg, entertained noblemen together with the jesters in the Tsarist court. One day the Minister ordered that he be whipped and thrown in jail. In the morning, he was to have ready an appropriate poem for a court celebration. With his back still swollen from the whip, and dying from hunger and terror, this martyred Renaissance figure dressed the next day in the uniform of a clown and delivered the mirthful song that he wrote as he wept during the night. A mediocre poet but a master of language. Up until his time, the Russian language was a disorderly mixture of odd elements: folk idioms, archaic church language, an abundance of French, Polish, German and Latin words. Trediakovskii strove to purify the language, to give it a uniform Russian character. At the same time, he created a new verse, better suited to the new living language. And finally, he lovingly studied the folk songs that had been scorned until now.

The innovators multiply. There is Sumarokov, the father of the Russian theater. His works are slavish imitations of foreign models, but his heroes are genuine Russians. He speaks with affectation, but he proclaims liberal ideas for political, ethnic and social reform. Somewhere he writes with great emotion about the migrating bird who returns from foreign lands, where they do not sell humans like oxen and where the sons do not lose their fathers' property at cards. Still the bird joyfully returns to prepare its nest in the branches of an old Russian oak. Such birds were the Russian writers.

Finally, there is the greatest talent of the Russian Renaissance: Lomonosov. He was a naturalist, historian, linguist, chemist, "the first Russian University," as Pushkin called him. Independently of Benjamin Franklin, he discovered the electrical nature of lightning and was the first to explain the vegetal essence of pit coal and amber. At the same time, he was the first to set down the rules of the new Russian language and create models in poetry and prose. Along with his dream for Russia to free herself of the intellectual yoke of

Europe and create her own pure Russian achievements in science and art, he had, inflamed by his ardent patriotism and indomitable pride, an unshakable faith in the Russian soul. Possessing the gigantic body of an athlete, he began to drink, and his ideological quarrels with his opponents descended to physical battles. He wrote countless odes, but without poetic breath. Pushkin was right when he said: "Lomonosov is the first Russian University, but at this university, the professor of poetry is a good employee, not a national poet."

A polytropic mind, a protean and fighting temperament, a sage and a daring pioneer—Lomonosov is the greatest figure of the Russian Renaissance. He belongs to an age of intemperate enthusiasm, in which new roads open, large passions burst forth and the mind hurls itself tirelessly and fearlessly into all the branches of human knowledge with a childishly optimistic naivete and frequent leaps of the spirit.

And the Tsarina, Catherine the Great, must also be placed among the figures of the Renaissance. One of her eulogists speaks correctly: "Peter the Great gave Russia bodily form; Catherine gave breath to the soul in it." And actually this astonishing woman aspired to take a step beyond her great predecessor. She wanted not only to bring Russia a technical and scientific civilization, but also to civilize the Russian soul with philosophy, literature and fine art. Trained in philosophy and literature and a student of the French Encyclopedists, she corresponded regularly with the most famous writers, philosophers and poets of her time. She also wrote tragedies, comedies with Russian themes, as well as fables, short stories, philosophical and pedagogical studies.

The intellectuals took courage, published newspapers and periodicals, wrote books, in which they proclaimed their liberal political and social ideals. But the French Revolution burst forth, and the Tsarina, frightened, immediately became rigid and autocratic. She began to tyrannize and exile every freedom-loving spirit. The martyrdom of the Russian Word started anew.

Novikov, the bold illuminator of the people, is condemned to prison for fifteen years. Radishchev, the author of the famous *Journey from Saint Petersburg to Moscow*, in which he described with hair-raising honesty the suffering of the people under the rule of the wealthy nobles, is sentenced to exile for ten years in far-off Siberia. Another innovator, the great comic poet Fonvizin, is merciless in his attacks upon the nobility in his comedy, *The Minor*. The heroine in this work, the shrew Prostakova, treats her serfs worse than animals. She is illiterate and cynical. At one time she hears the word "geography," and asks how this art can be put to use. "Whenever you travel in a certain place, you will know where you are," someone explains to her. But Prostakova answers contemptuously, "But why then do we have coachmen? That is their job. No! It's a disgrace for the nobility to study such skills. All the nobleman has to say is: Coachman, drive me here or there!" This comedy has a huge success, but the lover of the Tsarina, Potemkin, sends him this message: "Write no more or die!" The poet understands, and from that moment never writes again. He gives himself to drinking and women, and at the end loses himself in religious mysticism.

The Word is strangled even more mercilessly by Catherine's successor, Paul. No one dares to raise his voice and speak of his pain or his hopes; every free conscience is stifled; poetry becomes silent or degrades itself in flattery; only obsequious civil servants write poetry or prose in order to praise the Tsar.

And yet a secret fermentation continues; reperssion expands, and yet at the same time, so does the yearning for a future freedom. Chaos. The young aristocrats are educated, superficial, confused; the old are uneducated, uncivilized, tyrannical and fanatically attached to their patrimony; the masses are steeped in ignorance and Asiatic fatalism. But the seed has fallen into the fertile Russian earth. In the damp darkness, it thrives and prepares to burst with its first shoots. Those few swallows, the Renaissance Russians, did not of course bring the spring, but neither would they have come if spring had not been on the way.

The news that the liberal dreamer and mystic Alexander I had ascended to the Tsarist throne blew across Russia like the breath of spring. Possessed by his belief in his mission, this Tsar desired to free Russia and all of Europe, first from Napoleon and then from political slavery. Did he not give his word at Madame de Stael's salon in Paris that he would soon free the serfs and give the fields to those who work the Russian land?

When he took the throne, he immediately abolished the secret chancellorship, forbade tortures, established new schools, reorganized the administration, cleaned up corruption in the judicial branch, granted freedoms to the press and listened favorably to the economic theories of Adam Smith.

The liberty-loving intellectuals again took courage. The world of letters came to life again as a French pseudoclassicism receded and a romanticism pouring out of Germany and England took possession of Russia. The abstract classical terms, Humanity, Beauty, Liberty, Idea, which had become lifeless commonplaces, now took on a new life. they became an ardent, passionate experience for man. The old pseudoclassical canons that did not allow the heart to sing in the first person were abolished, and the poet now confessed his individual passions, his joys and his sorrows, without the need to shroud them in lifeless mythological allegories. His heroes were no longer soulless symbols. They were humans of flesh and bone—the poet himself crying out.

Together with the soul, the Russian language gained its freedom. Until then, writers believed that the command "Write as you speak" could only be applied to comedy. But now a young author who was also a historian, Karamzin, revealed that even in a work of lofty creativity the spoken language has the power to express the noblest feelings and the highest ideas. Many of his contemporaries fiercely attacked these linguistic innovations, but the new writers supported this enlightened pioneer, and, as it always happens, they were victorious after a violent struggle.

The father of Russian romanticism was Zhukovskii, the son of a wealthy landowner and a Turkish slave. A calm and gentle person, he felt a nostalgia for a certain undefined supraterrestrial existence. This world, he claimed, was merely an antechamber in which we are confined. Let us wait for the liberator, death, with endurance and humility. He shifted the hopes of this life to the next world, and he unprotestingly abandoned this vain existence to the Tsarist and ecclesiastical tyranny to enjoy.

And thus a new ideal, an unbridled romanticism that was as false as lifeless classicism, became a part of Russian literature: medieval legends, chivalric adventures, anemic love affairs, troubadours and ladies in turrets, phantoms that did not have the slightest concern with Russian history or its soul. Russian literature did not become free with romanticism; it merely changed its mode of imprisonment.

But the most energetic of the young intellectuals suffocated within this spiritual slavery and were stifled within a political bondage as well. As soon as the liberty-loving Tsar defeated Napoleon, he too became a defender of tyranny. The young formed secret societies; agitation constantly increased. The writers, who could no longer express themselves openly, either joined political conspiracies or created allegorical songs. A fable by Krylov, "The Cat and the

Nightingale," made a shattering impression. Behind its clear symbol, you perceive the tragic Russian reality—young poets dying in the claws of tyranny before they can proclaim their song:

A cat holds a nightingale in its claws and speaks to it in a sweet voice: "I have heard that no one sings as sweetly as you. I don't want to eat you. If you sing and I am pleased, I shall set you free. Because, you know, I too am crazy about music." But the ill-fated nightingale cannot sing while in the claws of the cat. It loses its voice and makes a few desperate sounds. The cat is disappointed. "Is this your famous song? My kitten sings better than you do. Let me try your flesh. Perhaps that will be more tasty." And it eats the nightingale.

And the poet adds bitterly: "Would you permit me to entrust something to you, but entirely between us? You sing very badly when you are clawed by the nails of the cat."

Two superb nightingales who were destroyed by the claws of the cat were Pushkin and Lermontov.

"Eto Bog" (He is God). This is the way the Russians, young and old, Bolsheviks and expatriates, speak about Pushkin. He opened the two great paths for Russian realism and idealism. He went beyond narrow pseudoclassical models and boasting romanticism and gave an incomparable and magical grace to language and verse. Every day he matured and went ahead. A few days before he was killed, he wrote to a friend: "I feel now that my soul has broadened so that I can at last create."

But he does not have the chance. At thirty-eight he is killed in a duel, and a young man, Lermontov, immediately steps forward and, with bitter verses that are filled with indignation, says farewell to the great soul that has been lost to the world:

> *The poet died, obedient to honor.*
> *He fell slandered by men.*

The proud head bowed.
His shining genius went out like a candle;
The triumphant crown has withered,
And you, the greedy flock who wander around the throne,
Hangmen of freedom, genius and fame,
Hide yourselves under the shadow of the law.
But God's justice exists—
There is a dread tribunal
That waits and cannot be bought with gold.
It knows only too well the thoughts and the deeds.
You begin your slanders again but in vain—
With all of your unclean black blood
You will never wash away
The poet's honorable blood!

Similarly tragic was Lermontov's fate; he was killed at the even younger age of twenty-seven. He managed, however, to reveal his strength through his passionate songs, filled with satire, pain and love of freedom. He was accused of being slavishly attached to the poetic chariot of Byron. And he answered:

No, I'm not Byron. I am another, a still unknown, chosen child of the Muse, persecuted by society, but with a Russian soul. I began at a younger age and I will finish young. I shall not create great works. In the depths of my soul, just as in the ocean, lie my shattered hopes. O dark ocean, who is able to penetrate your dark mysteries? Who can transmit my thought to the masses? Either I or God. No one else!

■ TOLSTOI AND
DOSTOEVSKII

■ ABOVE ALL, TWO RUSSIAN DRAGONS seized us during the fabulous years of our youth: Tolstoi And Dostoevskii. these two stood as our great Fathers.

One day in a hotel in Lucerne, Switzerland, a poor singer stood in front of tables where richly dressed ladies and well-nourished gentlemen were dining, and began to sing with great sweetness. When he finished, he stretched out his hand, but no one gave him alms. This everyday incident would have been forgotten had it not been for the presence of a merciless eye that witnessed and seized it: the eye of Tolstoi.

Suddenly an awesome flame filled this wild soul with light, and he saw the truth: All of the famed European civilization steeped in its scientific and industrial progress remained hard and inhuman. Wealth is concentrated in the few, and the masses are lashed by poverty and ignorance. Love in man is absent, and in the depths of our culture lurk barbarism, egotism and the manic thirst for gold! And for the first time, Tolstoi asked this question: "Is it possible that this egotistical society that calls itself civilized destroys the instinctive bent of man to help his fellow man? Is this then the justice for whose sake so much blood was shed and so many inhuman acts were committed?

Deeply troubled, Tolstoi returned to Russia. An idea slowly was born within him. "If you want to uplift the masses, you must first begin with the children of the masses. Open a school and educate them." He opened a school with his own pedagogical system. But again he was disturbed and hesitant. "I don't feel that my soul is pure. It seems to me that I'm corrupting the spirit of these peasant children."

His body grew tired; his soul, embittered. He abandoned everything and escaped to the steppes, to the Bashkirs, to nourish himself with *kumys,* the fermented milk of mares, in order to live the simple, primitive life.

He returned from the steppes rejuvenated. He married, calmed down, and for twenty years lived happily in Iasnaya Poliana, writing his most admired works. The poet Fet saw Tolstoi's wife during that time and described her as the ideal companion: "Completely dressed in white with a bunch of keys at her waist, she is unsophisticated, cheerful and continually pregnant."

Tolstoi was happy. He wrote to Fet: "I've become a new man. I am up to my ears in happiness. There is a joyful spirit in my home, in my fields and in all my varied efforts, visible and invisible! I have beehives, sheep and orchards of fruit-bearing trees." He continually bought more land, purchased a hundred mares and produced *kumys.* He raised hogs and rooted himself more deeply and broadly into the Russian soil like a legendary patriarch.

But little by little two awesome questions began to awaken within him and to take head: "Why?" "To what end?" As he confessed himself, it was as if he had been walking for years and then suddenly found himself on the brink of the abyss. He wanted to kill himself. So that he would not hang himself, he removed the rope that was in his room and no longer hunted, so that he would not turn his weapon toward his heart and take his life.

Where did Tolstoi's agony come from? How did he fall from such a height of patriarchal happiness into such despair and turmoil? Tolstoi, entering into old age, began to confront with terror the fated fruit of life—death. Horrified, he sensed that his body and strength were failing. He described how he looked at himself in the mirror and saw his arms grow thin, his hair turn gray and his teeth fall out of his mouth.

With the aging of his body, he sensed an agony in his soul

as well. For Tolstoi the body and soul were an unbreakable whole. Life now seemed incoherent, painful, meaningless: "All of our actions, our intellectual concerns, our arts and sciences, I now saw in a completely different light. All of these things were Sybaritic games without meaning. I began to look at myself with disgust and to perceive the truth."

He no longer had the strength to strangle the dark voices that were tearing apart his inner being. He wanted to renounce everything and flee. "I am a humble parasite, a miserable worm that nibbles at the tree. There is only one salvation: to abandon everything—family, property, glory—and to live freely within the chaste commandments of Christ."

From that moment, the antinomy of his life kept growing. His ideal now, and his only duty, was to a simple existence, isolation and absolute freedom. But because of his weakness and cowardice, he lived the exact opposite life in the midst of his rich patriarchal home and his large and hostile family, which supervised and enslaved him. And from all of Russia and from distant lands, his admirers came to pay homage to him.

He now hated and condemned himself because he preached a way of life that he did not live. Struggling to find some kind of compromise, he did, but it was a cowardly and convenient one, and he knew it; he renounced his property, but transferred it to his family; he wore a simple peasant shirt and worked barefoot in the fields, but at night returned to his fine home and his admirers who stood in a row in his yard, beholding him proudly. He did not eat meat, but his frocked servants served him choice foods, prepared in accordance with very fine and varied vegetarian recipes.

In this way, Tolstoi struggled to reconcile the will of God with the wishes of his wife, Countess Sofia Andreevna, but deep inside he felt cowardly and immoral: "The comfort of an honorable and well-endowed family that requires it to spend for its pleasure what would feed hundreds of starving individuals who are its neighbors is more immoral than the most hideous orgies."

He hated and scorned art because he loved it so much. He turned to more simple people—to the muzhiks, to the poor and illiterate, to the monks—and from their simple mouths he hoped for an answer to his inner agony. He found it: We must return to our first pure and simple Christian societies. Life must be simplified. The road toward the ideal is difficult, and we must continually struggle with perseverance. We must suffer. Whatever prevents us from reaching this ideal—property, church, nation, wars—we must avoid and condemn, not with force, but with a passive and firm resistance. Not to resist evil with force is the central ethical teaching of Tolstoi.

In vain, Turgenev wrote to him from his deathbed: "O my friend, return to literature. Doesn't this gift also come to us from the same divine spring? How happy I would be if I learned that you listened to my pleading! O my friend, great writer of the Russian land, listen to my entreaty!"

Tolstoi did not listen. His moral struggle only deepened. The individuals who came to pay homage to him considered him a saint, but he shouted: "I devoured the labors of the peasants, I was cruel to the muzhiks; I stole, told lies and committed adultery. I killed. There is no criminal act that I did not commit."

He could not restrain himself any longer. On the night of October 28, 1910, he made a decision and left his house. But it was too late. He was eighty-two and could not withstand the hardships of an escape in winter. At the little station of Astapovo, he fell ill, and on the 7th of November, "the living conscience of Russia" vanished.

In this way died the greatest of writers, "the elephant of the Russian land." He was not able to reach supreme harmony. Until the last moment, he struggled to overcome something dark and invincible within him. He wanted to love and sacrifice himself to mankind, yet throughout his life he remained egotistical, proud, friendless and totally alone. He yearned to find a faith to give him the strength to conquer the fear of death. He never found a belief that transforms life and transubstantiates our deeds and thoughts to absolute simplicity. He said it himself: "I am a bird that fell from its nest and, lying on its back, cries in the midst of the tall grass."

Alongside the gigantic and epic personality of Tolstoi rises the tragic mask of Dostoevskii. They both sought beyond phenomena to find and formulate "God," but they took completely different roads in their quests.

Tolstoi was aristocratic and wealthy, possessed of prodigious health and rooted in the Russian earth like an oak. Dostoevskii was a petit bourgeois. All of his life, he suffered from poverty, hunger and illness. His nervous system was injured by every breath of his soul, a neuropathic proletarian of the metropolis.

The eye of Tolstoi saw the external world with astonishing clarity. He enjoyed the body with an astonishing love and acuteness. Dostoevskii hated the body, which he saw as a dark, satanic obstacle. With one leap he could plumb the depths of the human soul.

In Tolstoi, calm logic ruled supreme. He was a realist who knew what he wanted. He endeavored to impose a stern architecture upon his art, his method of ethical search and his life as well. Life for Tolstoi was a problem that he tried to solve with logic. In Dostoevskii, the dark heart, the mystical turmoil and chaos ruled. He was a suffering visionary. His works were disorderly and uneven; his inner and outer life, lightning bolts and darkness. For Dostoevskii, life and the soul of man were a frightening enigma, a gloomy journey filled with a mystery that logic could never unravel.

Only the heart could perceive it through love.

For Tolstoi, pain was the road that leads us to salvation. For Dostoevskii, pain and life, pain and love, were one. Suffering is the salvation.

Tolstoi's inner dramatic struggle between the moralist and artist, which so troubled him in the last years of his life, was absent in Dostoevskii. He did not feel any contradiction between his artistic and his ethical mission; for him, poetic creation, that is to say, the attempt to enter the depths of the human soul and express it in artistic works, was the supreme duty.

Dostoevskii's heroes are not in conflict with the institutions around them. They do not renounce state, church, country; on the contrary, they recognize their despotic powers and seek to find their deeper meanings. His heroes do not become calm when they come in contact with the earth, the muzhik, nature. The only atmosphere in whilch they can move and breathe—one that is dirty, tumultuous, stormy and full of cries—is in the large city, that complex satanic invention where the souls of men are damned. Unlike Tolstoi's wealthy landlords, princes, princesses or muzhiks, Dostoevskii's heroes are proletarian intellectuals who stalk the sidewalks of the great city and stagger on the brink of murder, madness and starvation. The chaos of the soul; this is the spiritual crucible in which Dostoevskii immerses himself and toils.

He rarely speaks about nature, and yet in his few descriptions, you sense a deep feeling and a discriminating and mystical love of the land, the wind, the tree. Unlike Tolstoi, he does not describe the "carnal body" of Russia, filled with blood, mud and smells; he concentrates on the mystical body, which is consumed from heel to crown by the flame of the soul.

The central hero in all of Dostoevskii's work is the humble, scorned, half-mad individual who lives his pain not only with bravery, but with enthusiasm and gratitude. Man's duty, and at the same time his happiness, is this: to love mankind, to feel its pain and to sacrifice himself. This love gives Dostoevskii's hero a sixth sense—an ability to comprehend another's pain, to share it in order to comfort him. He yearns, like Christ, to be crucified, to take all the sins of the world upon himself and save mankind.

Dostoevskii's heroes are possessed by dark powers, by "demons" with whom they struggle throughout their lives. Atheists, nihilists, sensualists, criminals—all of them immersed in their damnation with a powerful passion and a Luciferian grandeur. You sense that the soul of Dostoevskii himself is struggling within his heroes and is damned with them. It becomes the soul of man and that of the entire universe. Paradise exists, but to reach it you must pass through all of hell.

Whom does God save? Only the person who feels humility and love inside himself. These two flames can be kindled in the soul of the atheist and the criminal. To be an ardent soul, a passionate body—this is what is absolutely essential for salvation. The cold, the calculating, the complacent— those who have solved their problems and no longer sense any dread within them—can never be saved.

Nothing fills Dostoevskii with so much contempt as the sociologists who, proceeding from a logical basis, promise justice and happiness to mankind. He hates the socialists and liberals who seek to bring equality and to entangle the masses in political action. He defends the church because it gives form to the obscure awareness of God and is a supporter of the monarchy, not that of Nicholas of course, but the old Russian one in which the monarch was the Father of the people.

Fanatical in his pan-Slavism, he wants to remain a Russian or, as he put it, a man. The Russian lives with everything and in everything. Because he is one with whatever is human and does not discriminate because of nationality, race or country, the Russian has the feeling of the "pan-human."

Dostoevskii has an unshakable belief that Russia is destined "from above" to save the world. He sees Europe as a cemetery, where all the mighty souls have perished, and only the soulless, the practical, the self-interested "grocers," prevail. It is in Russia that the first cry of a resurrection will burst forth. Dostoevskii often compares Russia with the woman in Revelation whom the sun falls upon and impregnates. The son that Russia will give birth to is the new Word that will save the world.

The "devil"—sin, sensuality, passion—in Tolstoi's works is simple, physiological and not essentially dangerous. The strong man can struggle with and conquer him. But for Dostoevskii this devil is a dark, invincible and mysterious force, fused not only with our body but with our soul as well. Perhaps even one with God. Harmony is a necessity of human logic, but God is beyond logic, beyond harmony. Perhaps the most profound distinction one can make between Tolstoi and Dostoevskii is this: Tolstoi was a prophet of such a harmony; Dostoevskii, of such a God.

■ RED LITERATURE

■ DURING MY ENTIRE JOURNEY, I had in mind the red line that the heroic martyrs of the Logos had engraved on the Russian soil. And I impatiently yearned to get to know the new, fortunate and free writers created by the Revolution. How do they now perceive the Russian world? How do they harvest the rich, blood-nourished crops seeded by their forerunners?

But as soon as I stepped on the Soviet soil and began to experience the toilsome, practical preoccupations that possess a completely new kind of young people, I had no desire to get to know intellectuals. When you see the contemporary mold of the new Russian up close—worker, teacher, scientist or clerk—you flee from making acquaintance, even though you may want to, with those who battle with the pen.

At an earlier time, before this tempest of creative energy burst forth, the poets and writers who strove to formulate in words the yearning of mankind for freedom were the only intellectual leaders who could exist. Their words were filled with thoughts and action, and in their time they blossomed quietly, slowly in the hearts of enslaved Russia. These words were the only missiles that the Tsarist regime would tolerate—because in fact it did not realize that they were potentially explosive weapons.

When the words became flesh—they became revolution, war, slaughter, famine and an ever-present embattled reality—the mission of those who wrote novels and songs came to an end, and the intellectuals out of necessity ceased to be the vanguard. They got out of the way so that the words they had sown in the Russian soil would grow in their new embodiments: Red soldiers, workers committed to the struggle, enlightened muzhiks.

Many of the intellectuals were frightened and fled. They denied and cursed the harvest of their seed. Fantasizing in their well-intentioned souls that the salvation they had yearned for would come without blood, crimes and violence, they imagined the Idea as if she were the "Beautiful Lady" about whom Alexander Blok sings beginning in 1905 in his *Verses About the Beautiful Lady*. Before she arrives, the lover is enveloped in dreams of her expectancy. In the morning mist, he hears her voice, listens for her footsteps Her "all-virginal mystery," her "queenly purity," become more tangible as her "inevitable finality draws near." And suddenly there she is. She has "descended" to the earth. The Beautiful Lady takes on the earthly form of a woman. Her appearance and style of dress are transformed. She talks, walks in the streets of the large city and gives herself shamelessly to men.

Such too is the Revolution. And the poet, the naive lover, now starts his satire. In his new song, "The Unexpected Joy," Blok satirizes and degrades himself for having been so naive, pure and ridiculous. The blood that he wanted to shed for the Beautiful Lady was nothing but "lemonade"; his helmet was made of cardboard, his sword of wood. The poet mocks everything he had once worshiped: The ideal landscapes now become the muddy roads of the city, the filthy rooms, the restaurants filled with drunks and whores. The Beautiful Lady is no longer the heavenly Dulcinea that the lover had shaped in his imagination. She is a dark, heavily-perfumed, vulgar and licentious trollop. Her voice is hoarse. She laughs without shame, deserts the poet who has loved her so much and pursues someone with a "beaver fur hat on his head."

Tired and disgusted, the poet, without hope now, accepts his fate with indifference. His tone becomes all the more dry and cynical:

> *Night. Street. Lamplight. Pharmacy.*
> *Ignorant and drab people.*
> *Even if you live another quarter of a century,*
> *Nothing will change.*
> *Salvation does not exist.*
> *If you die, all will begin again*
> *And will become what they were before.*
> *The night, the icy shiver of the channel,*
> *The pharmacy, the street, the lamplight.*

Like Blok, many other Russian intellectuals saw the Beautiful Lady, their Idea, take on flesh, and they went into shock. They had seen her one way in their minds, but she came down to earth in another form—like a revolution, all blood and mud. Her finicky lovers went into a panic and fled, or they pined away in their sorrow and succumbed.

However, others who were stronger and more realistic were able to endure, to set aside the frightful details—that is what details always are—in order to see the full cycle. With joyful cries they greeted the embodiment of their Idea; they sang dithyrambs to the Revolution and to Lenin; others harshly chronicled, without any romantic disillusionment, the martyrdom and heroism during the first muddy and bloody years of the Revolution.

But joy or pain cannot be the inexhaustible source of art, and the retelling of the past becomes tiresome. It seems superfluous and quickly ceases to concern individuals who are impatiently and painfully looking ahead and who are struggling to find an exit for today and tomorrow. Truly in Russia you sense that all of the Spirit has pulled away from words and has concentrated into action.

The intellectuals also mobilize themselves in the huge recruitment camp. From individuals of action, they receive instructions or commands about what to write and how to write it, giving them a specific and objective purpose, as if for battalions preparing an assault. This responsibility endangers their lives, and what is worse, their art. These are the perilous transitional years of the dictatorship of the proletariat when the freedom of the Logos must be submissive to necessity.

Thus, given to more immediate and pressing concerns, I fled from the company of intellectuals. One day, however, I received an invitation and could no longer escape. The wife of Lunacharskii, along with several literary figures, was awaiting me in her home in the Kremlin.

I proceed to the huge guard with Tatar features and I explain to him that Madame Lunacharskii is expecting me. The guard telephones. Permission arrives; the heavy door of the Kremlin opens, and I enter the awesome snow-covered fortress.

In the central yard, guards stand motionless, wrapped in their long overcoats and looking like massive statues carved out of snow. All around, the renowned churches with their all-golden domes. At the edge of the yard, the awesome church bell, the largest in the world. It has a height of eight meters and weighs two hundred tons. It has fallen down and one side has sunk in the dirt. From the battlements, I can see the holy city from a distance as she spreads out in the snows. Above her hangs an intense red sun without rays like a fiery globe.

I enter the vast Tsarist palace whose inhabitants today are the commissars of the people. An old lady suddenly appears from a corridor and directs me. We pass large deserted and icy rooms. Suddenly a small door opens and a blonde, energetic woman with short hair gives me a cheerful look and asks, "Are you the Greek?"

"Yes."

"I am Lunacharskii's wife, Anna Aleksandrova. Please come in."

A small warm room with heavy sofas. A desk piled with books and papers. Above on the wall, the famous painting: Whistler's *Mother*. Opposite, the *Mona Lisa*.

Five or six writers with shaved heads in working blouses, wearing high boots like captains. Animated discussion begins. Here, after a few moments with the Russians, you often feel an inner ease in a warm and cordial atmosphere. They live the pan-human unity very deeply and are able to recognize a brother much more quickly than other peoples.

I, the insatiable one, asked questions. And they, with a ready, heavy-handed and certain answer, responded.

A young poet, short, plump and with still furry cheeks, spoke more loudly than the others.

"Karl Marx," he shouted. "In our literary sector, too, Karl Marx is the chief. The old ideals have fallen. Pushkin, Tolstoi, Dostoevskii—they no longer can answer our urgent contemporary concerns. No one believes that, with the emancipation of the serfs, the Russian problem can be solved. Nor with the re-energized *mir* and *artel** can Russia be saved. Nor with pan-Slavism or the light of the West. Nothing. All the ideals have failed.

"One hope only: to overthrow the status quo by force. But that revolt will not be carried out by peasants. They are always conservative, glued to the earth. Only the workers can start a revolution. And only one prophet has proclaimed the certain road to our salvation: Karl Marx.

"Karl Marx saved us from fruitless laments and utopian

---

* *Mir:* peace; *artel:* small guild of artisans.

dreams of the previous generation. In addition to hope, he gave us the scientific belief that our struggle, in keeping with unshakable historical laws, would out of necessity end in victory.

"This promising breath that rushed forward to destroy old forms—economic, social and political—influenced our literature as well. Our writers accepted this new inspiration and undertook to tear down the old artificial forms by renewing their verse techniques and wiping out the academic establishment. They did not manage, however, to understand scientific materialism very deeply and to subject their thought to certain molds. They wished to keep their creative freedom intact—and they got trapped.

"Moving away from the road of Karl Marx, they reached strange conclusions: Visible reality, they said, is a prison. And not only Russian reality, as the previous generation believed, but every reality. Yet they thought they could crush the doors and free themselves. Visible reality, they believed, was a simple symbolic representation of a higher invisible reality, which the writer has a mission to reveal to mankind. And thus came to be born among us, a few years before the Revolution, that sour, juiceless and seedless fruit: symbolism.

"This world, they whispered, is a forest of symbols, and we promenade and sing in this forest. We are free. We depend only upon the Eternal. And what is this renowned Eternal? Each person finds it within himself. And thus each worshiped his ego, the source and center of the universe. 'I am alone,' shouts Balmont, who is one of them. 'I am alone in the silence of night.' Let us leave him, shouting alone in the nightly silence."

The young man broke into laughter. He filled his teacup and began to sip loudly, like a strong, thirsty animal.

"You are unjust. You are unjust, Ivan Dimitrievich," responded Madame Lunacharskii, who was also laughing.

"You forget that our major symbolists performed their duty and opened vast doors for the spirit in Russia. You forget the sensitive Annenskii, who worked our language as no one had and enriched every material thing that he touched with a fine aura of invisible presences. You are unfair to Balmont, who worshiped, as no one did, the beauty of each passing moment. Possessed by a burning Dionysianism, he strove to merge with the eternal elements—the sea, the earth, the air. How magical was his verse technique, his internal rhymes, his play of sounds, his divine rhythm, his colors! He is the one who so ardently praises what we are today, and what you especially, Ivan Dimitrievich, love: the strong, rich personality, within which good and evil move with equal power. If one of these two sources of strength dries up— either the good or the bad—the soul is impoverished. Balmont deifies each moment of life by giving it the intensity of eternity, since he believes it to be unique and irreplaceable. The purpose of art, he postulates, is to save these moments by giving them the most consummate form. You also forget the difficult, profound and hermitlike Ivanov, who proclaims that the Old Testament is not the Hebrew one but the Dionysian religion of the ancient Greeks. You forget Briusov, who is all will and discipline, and who does not view poetry as inspiration or a divine gift. For him poetry is the result of systematic labor, a human victory. 'Go ahead, dream, my faithful ox!' The poet, proclaims this giant pioneer of ours, must sacrifice everything for his craft. His highest work brings him to a conflagration as he moves upward, 'bleeding in the name of the lyre and of verse,' hoping to create perhaps 'seven or eight lines' and thus save himself. Don't forget, Ivan Dimitrievich, that Briusov appealed with prophetic strength to the 'future Huns,' who will pitch their tents among the ruins of today's industrial civilization. All these symbolists that you scorn completed their duty in heroic fashion; they broke open doors to help us, their children and their grandchildren, to enter. Don't be unjust and don't mock!"

"I am unjust," Ivan Dimitrievich answered quietly, "because I am young and I don't have the time to do fine sifting and minute examining. I'm in a hurry."

Lunacharskaia turned and looked at me, smiling.

"Don't pay attention to the young," she said. "They are harsh. They are in a hurry. They are looking ahead, and they are right. But symbolism in Russia was beneficial; it widened the narrow boundaries of realism, forced the poet to deepen his soul so that he would not servilely mirror the outside world. He made clear the inner harmony of the world, finding metaphors and resemblances that until now had remained hidden. At the same time, it gave amazing flexibility to language and unsurpassed musicality to verse."

"And Soviet literature?" I asked impatiently.

"You are in a hurry too," she said. "Soviet literature at this moment? But art needs physical and spiritual time, so that the passions can subside and the facts can attain some distance. We have to get away from the whirlwind. Don't forget that most of the new artists who write today held rifles for many years before they picked up the pen. Suffering a great deal from hunger and cold, they saw and learned in three or four years what they could not do in a lifetime in other times. Every new figure who writes in Russia today has had such a rich and painful experience that his spirit and his creation cannot have any relationship with his contemporaries in the rest of the world. The Russian Revolution and the victory of the proletariat forced poets and prose writers to come down from the 'ivory tower' and to merge with the people. They were not to engage in small talk, wretched erotic adventures or endless, turbid internal monologues. Now they were to express the large movements and needs of the masses, the struggle for a new social symbiosis, more honorable and just.

"You should have lived here during the Revolution to see and suffer what we did in order for you to understand. In the early years of the Revolution, writers not only did not have time, there was no paper and ink for writing, no print shops for publishing. For this reason, they recited their poems in barracks, military camps, clubs, public demonstrations. These poems, of course, had a completely revolutionary content: hatred against worldwide capitalism and Russian reactionaries, joy for a redeemed Russia, faith that the whole world would be liberated. Their expressive means were simple and striking, so that the masses could understand. In frozen buildings, in snow-covered squares of cities and towns and out in the camps, thousands of hungry, ragged people listened enthusiastically to their verses, their eyes filled with flames.

"In Moscow the futurists are dominant, aspiring to tear down the past and create a new world from the foundation. Our great poet Maiakovskii shouts to the Red Guard:

> *You pinned the Whites to the walls and killed them,*
> *But why forget Raphael? —*
> *Fire, fire, in the museums!*
> *Why don't you pounce upon Pushkin?*

"In Saint Petersburg, however, the poets still sensed the worth of tradition and form; they loved balance and meter. This perception prevailed as soon as the revolutionary fever subsided. A new life: abundant paper, unprecedented publishing activity, thousands of books in millions of copies, newspapers and periodicals. Art, which had mobilized to serve the Revolution, demobilizes. The old writers recover from their original shock and begin to find strength. The newborn post-revolutionary literature begins to stammer.

"Literary writers begin to separate into three categories:

"1. Followers of the right: These are not revolutionaries; their souls remain outside the new cosmogony. They simply recognize the huge spiritual rebirth in Russia, traveling with the revolutionaries on their right, on the margin. This is how one of them, Sapenko, expresses the creed of his group:

> I am not a communist, nor a socialist. I am not a monarchist. I am a Russian. I don't have a political program. Many condemn me for this reason. What innocence, they say, does this man cling to after three revolutions? But such is my naivete and it gives me great joy. I don't hate anyone. That is my ideology.

"Such a follower of the right is our major poet, Nikolai Alekseevich Kluiev: 'I don't belong to the Russians who make swords and cannons but to the golden underground vein that creates holy icons and songs.' Kluiev loves and praises holy Russia with a mystical passion; he sings hymns to God and the mystery of the world and the Russian soil, scorning the large city, 'the daughter of rock and iron.' In the beginning he greeted the Revolution with enthusiasm, hoping to see the emancipation of the muzhiks. He dreams about an ocean of wheat fields from Lake Baikal to the warm Crimean Sea, and he greets the 'Tsar of the wheat,' his crown made from wheat stalks. He compares Lenin with the 'red bull of the mating tale,' with a 'paradise of mountain cedars where the sun is relentless like a warrior.' 'May this bloodied name of Lenin,' he cries, 'spread over the earth like the tail of a peacock!' But Kluiev cannot endure the new, harsh features of the Revolution; he quickly becomes disenchanted and again steeps himself in his mystical visions.

"2. Followers of the left: These accept the Revolution

with all their souls, but they maintain a certain independence, giving an important significance to form and not completely submitting their art to the proletarian ideology. These followers on the left played a very active role in the war and in the Revolution as soldiers, officers, propagandists. They endangered their lives every day; they created history. Babel fought in the South, on the Rumanian front and in the North, against the rebel Iudenich; he worked in Cheka* and for the soviet of Odessa; he was a reporter in Saint Petersburg and in Tbilisi. Another one, Vsevolod Ivanov, beginning as a working printer, became a fakir, a wrestler, an actor; he fought bravely as a soldier, and on two occasions was almost executed.

"Many young people who never dreamed they would become writers lived many years in war, hunger and danger. They didn't have time—or paper and ink—to write. They simply put together revolutionary songs which they recited in the army. In prose, Pilniak was the first writer with courage enough to portray the Revolution as it was, without ideology or romanticism. He describes the horror of anarchy and the dark instincts that awaken: hunger, erotic passion, the necessity to survive by killing. Tragic, hair-raising depictions: In a village, there exists neither food nor clothing, only coffins. People trample each other to buy them first because they too will soon be gone.

"In all of his writings Pilniak strives to find and depict the eternal face of Russia that looms behind the ephemeral ones: the muzhik, the Bolshevik, the Tsarist, the intellectual.

"Superior and richer than Pilniak is Vsevolod Ivanov. He too experienced all the terrifying spectacles of the Revolution in Siberia and the Far East: the vast roads, thousands of frozen corpses, the village scenes of horror and fear—and he struggles to give them form in his descriptions, restraining

---

* Extraordinary committee (for internal security).

his lyricism with difficulty. The steppe is a 'rosy blue animal'; the muzhiks, 'heavy, drenched in sweat, glowing in their new Sunday shirts.' He creates strong descriptions of man with all of his instincts, appetites, vulgar illnesses, and his animal sexual urges.

"Lydia Seifullina comes from Siberia; she describes the Revolution in a spasmodic manner, with a brazen rawness and an uncompromising realism. Her writing is filled with obscene curses, rapes, repulsive details and naturalistic heavy-handedness.

"Babel, a better artist, allowed all of his raw remembrances to crystallize within him and began to write at a later time with simplicity, composure and a condensed strength. He depicts his subject with exactness, simplifying his wealth. Having learned from the war how simple life and death are, he strives to impart this essential characteristic of reality to his art.

"But all these works are hurried, piecemeal, fragments, you would say, from an unfinished epic. 'Life is vast,' writes Seifullina. 'Many volumes are needed to describe it. Everything whirls around us. We don't have time to write. It's better to create fragments.'

"But several writers already begin to undertake works of greater scope. In his *Years and Cities,* Konstantin Fedin strives to describe the crucial period of revolutionary and post-revolutionary Russia and Germany. With a unique impartiality for a young Russian writer, he creates living types: workers, muzhiks, communists, reactionaries, Junkers . . . In the same fashion, Leonid Leonov struggles to embody in his novels the components of the new life in Russia. Following the Russian tradition more faithfully, he describes his heroes through a fine psychological analysis. Numerous characters, disorder, obscurity—but the writer's strength is often manifest.

"3. Proletarians: These writers have completely subjected

their art to the proletarian Idea. Indifferent to beauty and form, they are concerned only with content, their technique having only one purpose: to propagandize the ideology of the proletariat. Most of these writers have also returned from the various fronts of war, and their eyes have overflowed with bloody and dark pictures. Their memories burst forth, rushing to be dressed in words. The tone, out of necessity, is quick, cinematic, violent; their themes have nothing to do with symbols, idyllic adventures or the boredom of life. These young writers saw a great deal. They killed, were in danger of being killed; they went hungry, experienced the most primitive pain, enjoyed the most primitive joys. They lived, and they loved life. They sensed deeply that the existing reality is not a fantasy or a symbol but a horrifying, bloody truth, and it must become better. Life is not monotonous and melancholy as in the time of Chekhov; it is filled with diversity, fever and ascending intensity. Endless flow and action. As soon as the soul begins to grasp it, life has already changed and moved further ahead. It is natural, therefore, that the literary tone of the new writers will follow this endless flow and diversity: it becomes quick, feverish, impatient, running pantingly behind life to catch up with it.

"Certainly we should not expect masterpieces from our newborn Red literature at this time. I said it is still very early. Our Red art is still performing its propagandistic service: the communists are pure ideologues and fearless heroes; the reactionaries, brutal and dishonorable scoundrels. From this one-sided distortion of life, masterpieces do not come forth. But the day will come. The fever will go down, the mind will clear, necessity will lighten, and then the Russian soul will again create major works of art. We ask only for time. Nothing else."

"I agree with Trotskii," shouted a pock-marked young man as he jumped to his feet. "We should not expect miracles from proletarian literature. The dictatorship of the proletariat is temporary. How long will it last? A few decades. Never centuries. Will we have time during that interval to create proletarian art? I doubt it very much. The decades during the transitory period from the tyranny of capitalism to communism are crucial, filled as they will be with deadly, fierce strife, and struggle will be our major preoccupation. Our main strength will be devoted to defense and then to attack until we finally win—and the dictatorship of the proletariat will then relinquish its place to an integral communism. Because finally, what does victory of the proletariat mean? The disappearance of the dictatorship of the proletariat and its replacement by communism. After the victory, whatever works are created will not be proletarian. They will be communistic. That is my opinion; forgive me. We are not now creating art; we are making propaganda."

Protests. Shouts. A violent discussion breaks out. In this atmosphere that Lunacharskii lives in, the communist Idea is not inflexible and dogmatic. Of course these Russians have a firm belief in Marx's teachings, but they give it a very wide, open-minded meaning, and disagreement is not looked upon as a betrayal or an insult.

From all of these conflicting opinions, I was able to crystallize these conclusions about contemporary Russian literature:

The new Russian writers did not come out of universities or prestigious homes. They studied in the very superior schools of hunger, danger and revolution. They lived among peasants, soldiers and workers, not like different men who condescend to study the people, but like soldiers, peasants and workers, without realizing that one day they would become writers.

Russian reality has taken on a deeper, richer content that even the old masters of realism could never have imagined.

Life and death, idea and hunger, dream and everyday society concerns, have meshed together tightly, becoming a unified and diverse reality, which surpasses in richness all imagination and every symbol.

It is not surprising that the content of Russian literature has changed. The old themes—complaints, laments, boredom, interminable psychological discourses, hysterics and decadent sensuality—have disappeared. New tragic and compact themes filled with action are now dominant: war, death threats, merciless class struggles, attempts to formulate in works of art the new communist dream of the world.

Literary technique also has changed. There is the major influence of the cinema: Scenes quickly and spasmodically follow one upon the other; the texts often have gaps and suggested meanings, so that the reader can no longer read and passively accept. He has to work along with the writer toward completion.

The influence of foreign literature has lessened because: Contemporary life in Russia is infinitely more interesting to a writer than any aspect of life in Europe; most of the new writers have been in battlefields and have not had time to learn foreign languages; there has already been established a strong Russian literary tradition that the new writers can use for support; and no major literary movement exists today to inspire the Russian intellectuals. On the contrary, they expect each new idea to spring from the regenerated Russia.

Literature no longer plays the leading role it played in the Tsarist period, when the writer was the only relatively free voice that expressed society's concern—the only sociologist, political analyst, journalist, teacher, moral and spiritual guide of Russia.

The situation today is radically different. In the vanguard, in the most dangerous front of Russian struggle, it is the people of action who are in battle: politicians, soldiers, economists, engineers, scientists.

In this new and embattled society, literature is striving to open new roads, to find a tone that is more harsh and varied in order to be able to mirror contemporary life faithfully. It is trying to give beauty a new face, one that is different— more tragic, simpler and more human.

It was late at night when I left. As she said good-bye, Lunacharskaia brought all the conflicting opinions into harmony with these words of her beloved poet, Kluiev:

> *Let us unite, brothers, in the blazing marriage*
> *Of the heart of the people and the strong wind of October,*
> *And let's leave Turgenev on the shelf*
> *To shed paper tears*
> *Over the palaces of nobles.*

I had drunk the sweet wine of poetry during the long night. When I reached home, I opened a book of the angry Maiakovskii, and with a strong voice, I read his flaming words:

> *Listen, scoundrels!*
> *Nailed by these words of mine, be silent.*
> *Listen to these howls of the wolf*
> *That don't resemble a song.*
>
> *Strike the fattest one,*
> *The baldest one;*
> *Grab him by the collar*
> *And push him*
> *Into the mud and the accounts!*
> *"Committee to aid the hungry!"*
> *Look behind these naked numbers;*
>
> *A gust of wind*
> *So strong and so very sweet—*

Wraps in snow
Thousands,
Millions of rooftops.

Even the crows are disappearing.
Because they smell—
There, it is arriving—
Sweet and sickening
The smell of the son, father,
Mother,
And daughter they are roasting.
Whose turn is it now? No help!
Lost in the snows—
Yes, and no help whatsoever!

No help!
Even the mud in the road—
We eat.
In ten provinces
Count the graves.
Twenty million—
Twenty—
Die!
And all alone, a hoarse cry
With curses.
With her snow-covered hair
That the wind tears,
The Earth sings a dirge.

Bread,
A little bread,
A little more!
The city stretches out its worker's hand.
A little bread! A little bread!
The radios howl on all the frontiers

And they answer,
A pile of idiocies,
The newspapers.
London.
Official luncheon
In the presence of the King and Queen
Where they mock what isn't gold.

May you be damned!
Let fall upon your crowned heads
From the colonies
The wild ones,
The cannibals.
May your kingdom burn
In the fire of rebellion,
May your capitals burn to their foundations!
The successors to the throne, the princesses, should cook their
*   food*
In their crowns instead of casseroles.

Paris.
Parliament in session.
Exhibition on hunger
By Fridtjof Nansen.

They listen smiling.
As if they hear a nightingale,
As if they listen to a tenor,
The song in fashion.

May you be damned!
May you never again
Hear the human voice.
Proletariat of France—
Eh!—

Seized in the noose
Thousands of necks!

Washington.
The owners of estates
Having eaten a belly full
Having drunk as much they could—

Bring cranes
To lift up their bellies—
They throw whatever remains of the fine flour into the sea.
They stoke their factories with wheat.

May you be damned!
May your roads flood—
Blood—
North and South of America.
May they find whatever softness you possess—
Your bellies—
And use them to play football!

Berlin.
The emigres come to life—
Their gangs are overjoyed.
In Berlin,
He twirls his mustache,
Struts and preens himself,
The Russian soldier.

May you be damned!
Out!
Out for eternity.
May the world spit upon you—
Judases!
Forests of Russia—

Gather together and pick your tallest trees;
Hang the bodies of the emigres.
Let them sway—
Darkly—
Eternally
In the sky.

May you be damned!
May each bite you eat
Burn your belly.
Your bloody beefsteak—
May it become a knife
And rip your intestines!
Damned
In all eternity—
Those who turned away their full mouths
From the Volga!

▪ RED ART

▪ WHAT IS THE PLACE of art in Soviet reality? In the economic, social and political areas, the Revolution angrily wiped out everything that had its roots in the bourgeois class. But did it act with the same relentless fanaticism with regard to the old works of art? And, in a more general sense, what is the Soviet conception of art? What are the new horizons that the new worldview opens up with respect to beauty, and how are the fine arts used for the spiritual ennoblement and the aesthetic education of the people?

During the first months of the Revolution, works of art were in grave danger. And this, not only because the frenzied muzhiks were looting the houses of the aristocracy, which often contained precious artistic treasures, but also because many fanatical and uneducated workers vehemently proclaimed that the old bourgeois art must disappear in order for the proletarian civilization to flourish freely. "Better to have a poor civilization of our own that a rich foreign one."

But the Soviet government set itself against this surge of vandalism. It made an effort to save all the works of art left by the bourgeois culture and to gather all the private collections into museums for the people's enjoyment. Its program included restoring the monasteries, the churches and the palaces of the aristocracy to their original architectural forms. At the same time the government undertook to aid artists in their search to find and realize the new revolutionary aesthetic forms, and it put the great masses of the people in direct contact with art.

In this period of violence, carrying out such a complex

program presented immense difficulties. There was no money and no competent technical personnel. All the attention and all the strength of the new Russia were devoted to military and economic problems.

And yet this task of protecting art amounted to a remarkable achievement. Within a few months, all the private collections, the churches, monasteries and objects of worship that had historical or artistic value, as well as the private mansions and Tsarist palaces with their treasures, were catalogued and placed under state protection. Old museums were enriched, and hundreds of new ones were founded; and from the most remote points of Russia the common people came, as if on a pilgrimage, to see and feel works of art that until this time only the privileged few had seen and enjoyed.

Simultaneously the new Soviet Russia struggles to create a new art: Schools of fine arts are established for workers and peasants for the teaching of painting, music and theater arts.

The Bolsheviks hate the old bourgeois way of life and struggle to express their own proletarian emotions with new forms. New visions rise in their minds: scenes from the Revolution, the terrible years of famine, the Red Army— barefoot, hungry and victorious; and then later, the daring new quests through which our epoch with its swift, spasmodic rhythm can find its expression.

The old, renowned craft industry of the Kustari takes on a new vitality and discovers its subject matter. In their huts the Kustari, men and women, fashion their famous handicrafts: laces, embroideries, woven fabrics, pottery, statuettes, toy dolls, paintings, carved and painted woodcraft. But the new communist motifs are now dominant: the Revolution, the worker, the Red soldier, the Soviet life, the youth scouts, Lenin . . .

I often admire a miniature by Golikov, the former icon

painter, that I bought at the Nizhnii Novgorod bazaar. On a tiny box, lacquered in black, he has painted a farmer plowing. The horse is gigantic, supernatural, in stunning red; its mane a dense cluster of flames, its head like a rising sun. Behind the horse, the farmer, himself red like the horse, bends toward the earth, driving the plowshare into the soil with a religious concentration. The old icon painter has retained his mystical soul, but he gives new content to his burning emotions. Following the rhythm of his times and his people, he paints one of the holy icons of the new religion, based on the three eternal motifs: man, animal, soil.

All the new Russian artisans and artists are inspired by the new communist themes. Art, they declare, must not simply create beauty; it must order life. Today's artistic beauty must express contemporary life faithfully. Art and the machine must come to harmony with one another. The ideal of the Soviet artist is to express the different forms and needs of our industrial age.

But it is difficult to attain this ideal. The technical artistry of the machine is in its essence different from the creative breath of the artist. Yet the Soviet government, by establishing new art schools and applying new teaching methods, endeavors to mold a new kind of artist capable of uniting creative inspiration with mechanical skills so that the creator—neither a slave of the industrial order nor a rebel against it—remains a co-worker and friend.

This cooperative effort is most clear in architecture. Before the Revolution, Russian architects imitated different existing styles—baroque, Gothic, neoclassical, neoromantic. The spirit of the Revolution swept up all these artificial deviations from a more authentic art. The Russians now dig into their souls while intensely living the historical moment through which we are passing. They struggle to find the most true and complete forms for an architecture that corresponds to contemporary economic, social and aesthetic demands. No more superfluous decorations. The new architecture must be un-adorned like logic. Factories, ministerial buildings, railroad stations, housing developments for workers, schools, hospitals, theaters, new cities—all must be strictly harmonized with the new materials of cement, iron, glass. Grace stripped of ornaments, functional adaptation, solidity—these are the characteristics of new Russian construction.

The same kind of alliance between art and machine is sought by the daring stage director Meierkhold in his Moscow theater. His staging is bare, like the logic of a perfect piece of machinery. The same is true of the mode of acting: quick, spasmodic, dry, without lyricism.

The Russians are by nature dancers and mimes; they have gusto and the power to act out, to represent. They can quickly move to Dionysian intoxication, communing easily with other souls, becoming one with them. This is why the Russian theater is surely the best in the world.

"Shall we go to Meierkhold's tonight?" my young Russian friend suggests. "They are playing the *D.E.*"

"The *D.E.*?"

"*The Destruction of Europe. D.E.* for short."

"Let's go," I answered. "I like the title."

Outside it is snowing. The leafless poplars along the way are covered with crystal. Sleds are gliding on the icy streets; the sweet melancholy sound of their bells falls to a hush outside the snow-covered theater.

The entrance is crowded. Women are arriving hurriedly—some tall and lithe like Scythian Amazons and others, massive matrons from the North with wide hips. The men take off their sheepskin coats and wool caps, revealing long, tightly-belted smocks and shaven heads. None of the women is richly dressed. The aristocratic ladies with their diamonds and pearls have gone. Some of them have managed to take their jewelry with them and are selling it piece by piece to survive in exile; others did not have time and abandoned it in Russia where it now graces the treasures in museums. The dandies with their spats, monocles and patent-leather shoes have also left.

My friend and I pace in the corridors of the theater, waiting for the performance to begin. Students and workers of both sexes, shop clerks with their full shirts, high boots and leather belts. All of them are young, and you rarely see an aged person.

"What happened to the old people?" I ask my friend.

"They have gone away or died. Or they are sitting in their homes mumbling," he answered. And a moment later: "The theater audience here tonight puzzles you, eh? A large British mission that came to observe the new Russia asked a famous Tsarist dancer, who did not leave to go abroad but stayed to dance in front of Bolshevik workers, what she thought of her new audience. And the renowned dancer answered, 'Certainly the jewelry and the expensive fineries are missing. But I feel that these workers come to see and enjoy my art. And even though I'm getting along in years, I feel a responsibility, and I strive to dance better than before in front of this new audience.'"

The air smells of leather boots and the cheap tobacco that men and women smoke incessantly. Many pull apples from their pockets; they rub them on their coats and devour them, peel and all. Others look at their watches impatiently and endlessly munch on sunflower seeds.

The young pace back and forth. Their eyes are glittering, their pointed cheekbones sending out lightning flashes underneath imperial chandeliers. Nowhere have I seen youth so silent and fiery as these Slavic youths that have begun to descend from the Russian steppes. And like their ancestors—hunters and archers—they place their flat palms above their eyes to block the sun's glare, and they scan the horizon toward Europe. Their eyes shine like the eyes of snakes, filled with a dangerous charm.

The Slavic women similarly cast a dangerous spell. They often have gray-green eyes, square solid chins and large hips that remind me of a wooden Gothic Virgin I had seen in Ulm, who sat holding a brood of newborn children in her lap.

All the strong smells around me, the din, the snow dimly shining through the windows, the neighing horses outside, the excited and severe women who pace back and forth, the men with their belts and boots—all this gives me the feeling that I am breathing the air of a snow-covered, wild military camp.

The bell suddenly rings; men and women quickly throw away their cigarettes, hurriedly swallow the last bites of their apples and stuff the sunflower seeds into their pockets. The curtain opens. Not a trace of decoration on the stage, no painted panels, no cardboards, only some movable screens that represent walls. These screens open, close and shift to form rooms. The floor revolves as furniture and actors arrive upon it.

A bare stage without the slightest emotional tone. In earlier times the painter dominated the staging of plays. When the Russian theater began to tour Europe, Western eyes were dazzled and intoxicated by the stunning colors. The famous Russian directors—Benois, Bakst, Galovin, Korovin—flooded the stage with fantastic colors to the point at which the work and the actors paled in such excessive glitter.

The Soviet stage abolishes painted scenery. The theater according to Bolshevik directors does not exist for the playwright or the director; it is created for the actor. In the simplest framework and within three bare dimensions, the actor moves and manifests himself. Everything else is romantic extravagance.

Meierkhold is the most fanatical of all these innovators.

His scenery consists of moving platforms, scaffolding and ropes; he has trained his actors to jump and climb like circus acrobats. And he recreates and arbitrarily transforms the theater piece to suit his own staging conception for his actors.

The dynamism that erupts on the stage during the performance of *The Destruction of Europe* is indescribable, something that is rushed, high-strung and technically flawless. The comic mingles with the tragic in a new way, as though man were a puppet or a performer executing a dangerous leaping act. It is the panting, tempestuous contemporary life that has no time for monologues or for the stringing up of beautiful, impassioned speeches. This kind of life—raw, bitter and savage—can be expressed only with this kind of rhythm, only on this kind of stage.

At first you are surprised. Where is the tragic grandeur that the old masterpieces had us accustomed to? Gradually, however, the energy, the storminess and the contemporary truth sweep over you, and you feel that this whirlwind is the true rhythm of your soul. And this stagecraft of machines, scaffolding and metal structures—without beauty, perhaps, but not without its own grandeur—is the only framework for an industrial and merciless age. The metal, the wood and the machinery that Meierkhold uses so daringly are, whether we like it or not, whether they possess any beauty or not, the bars of our prison.

I return to my room at midnight. Snow-filled streets, women on street corners selling cigarettes, apples and caviar sandwiches. Through a window, I discern two pale, withered Chinese men bending over an ironing board. An old Chinese woman sitting on a primitive sofa is delousing herself.

Two youthful tramps, in their picturesque rags and their tall, dirty sheepskin caps, are still searching outside the restaurants. They roll on the snow, laughing and disappearing like Shakespearean demons, all gusto and wretchedness. A thousand times I have stood and marveled at the young tramps of the Revolution as they embraced the heaters at restaurant entrances to warm themselves. In the underground restrooms, they sit contentedly around the heat of the fires. When the cold is severe, they light fires on the streets; they jump and dance around them, their stiffened limbs glowing underneath their colorful rags. By dawn they are asleep inside train stations, in crates, underneath the covered entrances of large homes, wherever they can hole up. In people's demonstrations, in military parades, in grand funerals, in Red holiday celebrations, they are the first and the best in their loyalty. And at the end of the day, when city workers get off work and rush to the big restaurants to eat, the youthful vagabonds stand at the entrances eyeing them with sardonic and hostile glances.

The central streets are flooded with light. Here and there a night watchman stands motionless in the middle of a street. The frozen river glows beneath the moon. Thousands of crows are sleeping in the snow-covered trees; once in a while in the midst of their slumber they let out a hoarse cry, as if they were dreaming.

Two well-nourished, perfumed and uneasy men with spats and heavy fur coats walk hurriedly along the walls. I glance behind them. No one is chasing them. Yet their walk is troubled. They seem confused, as if they did not feel well. They cannot breathe comfortably; there is something disturbing in the air for them. Soviet Russia, like a cat, plays with these well-bred mice; she does not eat them but scratches them a bit with her claws and then immediately pretends to be indifferent, closing her eyes as though asleep. But the well-fed mice are not feeling well.

The same manner of walking, though a bit more relaxed

and a little more shifty, characterizes another group in today's Russia: the clergy. Occasionally you meet a priest who is somewhat stooped. As he walks his gray hair falls over his shoulders, his hands hang awkwardly at his sides, and his eyes have a paternal, vacuous and frightened look. The priests are not feeling well either. One of them was telling me the other day, "Go away? Leave, you say? Where can we go? We are staying right here."

And his "here" was as if he were saying: in the mousetrap.

■ THE THEATER

■ THE SNOW IN THE STREETS is knee-high; the sidewalks, a frozen crystal. A woman slips and falls; a dog sniffs her and goes off. The proud *izvozchiki*, the coachmen, with their thick peasant beards and their green fur-bordered felt caps, perch high on their benches, erect and motionless like Asian noblemen. They no longer cross themselves as they pass the churches. Inside themselves, they must be cursing the incomprehensible mania of humans to overthrow the nobility, the men and women who would not deign to set foot on the ground and who made their rounds in troikas and paid generously. The world has become cheap, has declined; and all trudge in the mud or climb into those terribly crowded, accursed trams.

Carts are passing by, loaded with lumber and flour. The horses, heavy and still untamed, neigh, shake their heads under their harnesses and immerse their legs deep in the snow. The drivers, wrapped in sheepskins, shout wildly as if they were still in the desolate steppes. They are also walking heavily like their horses. In the streets of a Western city, this primitive procession of carts, loaded with flour and lumber, would be out of place; but here, under the red turrets and the embrasures of the Kremlin, all this activity harmonizes perfectly with the wild, multicolored, warlike soul of Moscow.

Flocks of crows are flying from tree to tree and from roof to roof; from the edges of the tiles they shake little balls of frozen snow on the passersby below. The crow, which so often appears in the pages of Russian literature, is truly the dominant bird of the Russian sky. I first saw crows, thousands of them, in Odessa; later I enjoyed them as they flew

173

over the black-soiled fields of the Ukraine, and now in Moscow, I marvel at them as they swarm in groups, sitting on the double-headed bronze eagles that are still gazing above the towers of the Kremlin toward East and West.

Women pass by on the sidewalks—massive, powerful, and from a primitive race, a wild one like the Russian horses that are all endurance and fertility. They are women who have not had their fill yet of eating, working and giving birth. The other ones, the delicate aristocrats who were full of fatigue, boredom and intellect, have gone, have become expatriates, and as the Russian poet says: "May they be accursed!"

A former aristocrat stands at a street corner, his fur well worn, his cap frayed. He stretches one hand out conspicuously and begs. No one pays attention to him. His face is very gentle and sweet; his rosy skin still glows with its left-over fat. He greets every passerby with a slight bow and is silent.

A little farther, an old muzhik sits cross-legged on the snow-covered sidewalk. With a little bag open before him, he sings a sorrowful, monotonous, desperate song. It's as if the vast frozen steppe of Russia were crying out. In the many-colored, multi-souled harmony of Moscow, all these sounds—the faint sighs, the neighing of horses, the songs—are so well harmonized that you do not think of individual suffering; instead you enjoy every cry, every sound, as a necessary part of a symphony.

Underneath the red-gray sky, I stand this afternoon and enjoy the renowned Saint Basil's Cathedral. Ivan the Terrible had it built and, as it was finished, had the eyes of the architect gouged out so that he would not be able to design another like it in the world.

In front of the Parthenon my heart does not leap with emotion; only my mind, after long contemplation and intellectual play, understands and is then possessed by a serene, cold admiration that befits that structure. But here in front of this barbaric church, my heart soars and screeches like a hawk. The cathedral appears to me like an immense haughty cactus, its tentacled branches blooming in green, red and yellow. With its Oriental domes that twist like turbans, it resembles a gathering of emirs. This Oriental richness and gentleness and, at the same time, heroic surge to controvert logic are indescribable.

The people who envisaged and afterward built this cathedral with all its stone, wood and colors, and the Emperor who loved it so much, belong to a race that has nothing in common with the geometric simplicity of Greece or the sober, practical ordering of Europe. How will today's pioneering leaders of Russia, fascinated with technology, be able to fit this wild Asiatic soul into a Western mold?

A platoon of Red soldiers marches across Red Square. They move with wide steps; their ankle-length gray coats sweep the ground, flapping in the frozen air like wings. Here is the answer! The mind hesitates, eternally suspended between Yes and No. It calculates and weighs accurately, attempting to order with mathematical precision all possibilities before making a decision. It searches, endlessly counting the sand particles of our inner sea. But action bursts; it opens the way, following an obscure but certain impulse of the soul, contemptuously leaving behind the Hamlet-mind reciting its monologues.

The store windows glitter. A few fabrics, fewer jewelry pieces and hardly any adornments. Only two items are displayed in abundance: food and books. This is the constant phenomenon that follows every revolution: hunger. The dual hunger of body and mind. The new class rose to power led by that powerful Amazon—hunger. Here in Russia, you must see the male and female workers and the people, how they eat and with what appetite they open books; with what exhilaration do they give themselves to satisfying these two equally fundamental needs. Bread and spirit find once again their original mystic unity.

The feeling that I am living in Byzantium, the great crucible of East and West, takes hold of my mind again. Different streams of blood rush in the purple winepress of Moscow, mixing and fermenting like must. A turbid Dionysian whirlwind stirs the air all around me. When, after how many generations, will this boiling must turn into pure wine?

Night was falling. A fiery serpent uncoiled in front of a cinema entrance—an advertisement. I remembered that the director of Kamernyi Theater, the celebrated Tairov, was expecting me, and I hurried on.

A friend had laughed earlier in the day when I told him that I would be seeing Tairov: "It's not worth your while. Tairov has grown fat."

I found him at his office just before his new review, *Ziroflé-Girofla*, was to start. He was indeed fat, but elegant and content.

"I saw your *Salomé* in Berlin, before the Revolution," I said to him. "And the other day, I saw it here for a second time. It was the same. The Revolution did not incite you to change your orientation, to leave behind your marvelous earlier achievements?"

"Didn't you like it?"

"Not much. When the Berliners were applauding enthusiastically, do you recall the few whistles and boos in the theater? That was me with some friends—Jewish, Polish, and Russian women. Sorry."

This satisfied artist, with his finely combed, parted hair and his round cheeks, was getting on my nerves. He smiled affably: "So you have come to the enemy camp tonight to see his forces and how he deploys them?"

"No. I have come to the camp of a comrade to see how he goes to battle in his sector. And I would like to know this from the good fighter: What is the influence of the cosmogonic event, the Revolution, on your art?"

"Its influence is great. I am at a critical point in my artistic development. I am looking for something more quick, more truthful and more dynamic, something that matches our contemporary soul. Not a narrow realism, nor a cloud-bound romanticism. Something new, a synthesis or whatever you want to call it, a neorealism perhaps. I do not reject romanticism, providing that it is a healthy romanticism."

"Goethe defined romanticism as a sickness. What content do you give to the word "romanticism"? Or do you mean that you accept not only the realistic presentation of the world of the five senses but also the invisible, indefinable inner world?"

"Exactly. To express the essence."

"But this is the same as what classicism accepts, if we define as classical the simple expression of the essence. What is the difference then between classicism and a healthy, as you call it, romanticism? Or is it perhaps necessary to rid ourselves of all these overused words? And then perhaps we'll be able to see that the synthesis you seek is not the blending of different complex sophistic definitions but only a simple action like love, a direct mode of contact?"

Tairov thought for a little while and then: "I think the bell has rung, and you will miss the beginning, which is the best part of the work."

The next evening I went to the Jewish theater. After the inert atmosphere in the theater of the man who grew fat, who tired in conversation and could not go forward, I wanted to breathe a more turbulent Jewish air.

The performance had started. Simple expressionistic

scenery, rough shadows, severe lights, colorful rags for costumes. The eyes, the lips, the entire mask of the face of the actor, are coarsely painted like the dance masks of primitives. There is no artificial attempt to remain faithful to a so-called realism. For example, instead of a real hanging lamp, there is a roughly cut cardboard in the shape of a lamp; instead of reading a real newspaper, the actors hold a piece of wrapping paper; instead of writing with pencil and paper, the actor makes a quick motion in the air over his palm . . .

The actors move spasmodically like intoxicated, nervous robots. You feel that the soul is an explosive power that bursts violently and deforms the body. Here in the Jewish theater, you enter the realm of vertigo. You sense that art is not a tidy, sober representation of life but a sacred drunkenness, a heroic exodus from time and space.

You are not interested in the words that are spoken, nor do you pay much attention to the plot; these play a secondary role. The emotion rises from the rhythm that possesses all these players with their rags, cries and grimaces. Here you begin to guess what must have been the essence—the music and the dance—of ancient tragedy. Such rhythm must have stirred and crushed the dry shells of words, which are what is left from the ancient tragedians. In Meierkhold's theater you experience logical, uncompromising art at its most extreme irrational consequence; in the Jewish theater, intoxication is the starting point, one which is also uncompromising but which, because of its powerful soulfulness, rises to the level of a heightened Logos.

But of all the joys that the Russian theater gave me, the newest and the most unexpected was my pleasure at the Blue Blouse. For a moment it seemed as though the sacred Dionysian chariot of Thespis, with all its coarse jokes, barbaric lamentation and primitive force, was passing before me. Another god, the proletariat, is torn to pieces and suffers. And all the people—his limbs—sit below on the coarse seats and suffer with him. The god is resurrected; he rises all-powerful and kills his enemies; and the people too gain strength and their hearts rejoice. From the eternal passion of the god in his new contemporary mask, this humble proletarian theater gives birth to the new tragedy.

The Blue Blouse is a little proletarian theater, simple, unpolished and awkward. It is the most authentic theater-child of the Revolution. Here the actors are workers who attended the Soviet fine arts schools. The staging is simple, as in the time of Shakespeare: A sword in the middle of the stage means an officer, a rifle means a soldier, a tree stands for the forest, a chimney for a factory . . . These plays are written and staged by workers; they contain strikingly dramatic moments and coarse humor; scenes change quickly and haphazardly; there is no strict unity among them, but a kind of cinematograhic and impatient rhythm. All the political events, national and international, that are connected with Soviet Russia unfold before the audience at a fast pace. The actors of the Blue Blouse are simultaneously singers, dancers and acrobats; they play harmonicas, and they struggle by every means to maintain a wakeful and stirring attention in the masses.

Today there are thousands of Blue Blouses in Russia, traveling workers' companies that play in reading rooms, labor halls, prisons, military camps, people's restaurants and festivals. As in a more primitive age, the audiences follow the performances with intense agony, with curses and wild laughter. It is with difficulty that the audiences restrain themselves from jumping on the stage to participate in wiping out the bourgeois masters and liberating the oppressed.

Most of the staged works have no exceptional literary value: Their aim is not to create beauty but to be proponents of revolutionary social ideas. Today's proletarian writers cannot, naturally, escape their everyday problems and rise toward the spheres of a selfless, tranquil art. Not do they want to. Art, they proclaim, is itself a weapon in the hands of the proletariat. They do not create art for art's sake; they do not care about perfection of form. They proclaim ideas with one purpose only: to awake and enlighten the masses. Neither the writers and actors nor the audiences care about pure beauty. They have faith in an idea and then struggle for a new order in the world. An internal and external danger hangs frighteningly over their lives and does not allow them to abandon themselves to pure play. And now that they are many in this gathering place of comrades, united as one soul by the same longings, they delight in seeing their ideas on the stage triumphing over their enemies.

A new faith is born and, as it always happens, art, like all other manifestations of the individual and collective life, serves with blind and joyful obedience the new utopia of man.

In the pre-revolutionary years of oppression and suffering, all those who had creative powers wrote and lightened their burden with words and symbols; they sought escape in the work of art. But today the time of realization has come; all the strong souls of Russia, who in former times would have turned toward theory and art to breathe while in slavery, now burst out into action. They have become commissars, generals, economists, scientists, pilots, teachers . . . They no longer dream; they are building the palace of their freedom.

Later, after the terrible turmoil subsides, and when the new reality establishes itself and the threatening danger passes on, the creative Russian souls will again be able to distance themselves from immediate practical action to create works of disinterested art. Then they will have the ease and freedom that are necessary for creation and at the same time the right to consider art as the highest form of play.

The new culture, created during so many bloody struggles, will find its true art only after its stability and balance are achieved.

■ THE RED PRESS

■ IN THE HANDS OF THE BOLSHEVIKS, the press was a most valuable and effective means of enlightenment. Here too, as in all segments of political and social life, the collective good became the supreme measuring standard. And something as powerful as the press could not be left uncontrolled. So it was necessary to place the press under a discipline of military strictness in order to submit it to the new order and to ensure its contribution to the final victory. Was the Revolution good or bad? Such questions which lead to endless discussions were considered both dangerous and useless. To move forward on the road that was opened with faith, with thoughtfulness and with intense, disciplined cooperation—this was the only way to realize the salvation of Russia and provide a model for the rest of the world.

This is why the Bolsheviks, as soon as they rose to power, closed down all reactionary publications. The revolutionary government immediately began to print and disseminate free newspapers and periodicals which, in all tonal ranges and with tireless repetition, declared daily war against every bourgeois idea, attacking every old superstition and emphatically extolling the great virtues of communism.

After so many years of oppression under the Tsars, the people were uneducated. The muzhik was a dark, powerful animal; he did not clearly understand much of what was happening around him. It was necessary to tell him, again and again, the same refrain with simple phrases, with broad assurances, with patience and wisdom, so that he would know it by heart. In this manner, little by little, the muzhik too would be able to believe in the new order and become himself, consciously and freely, a co-worker in the new society.

"Even if we had nothing except the newspapers," Lenin used to say, "we would be able to uproot all the superstitions of the masses." And he correctly added: "If we waited for the majority of the people to become educated through an evolutionary process, even five hundred years would not be enough time."

For these reasons, the Bolsheviks gave paramount significance to the organization and propagandistic function of the daily press. The purpose of the newspaper is not simply to print the news of the day or to serve special economic or political interests; its mission is to traverse the vast land from one end to the other and to instill the new gospel into the people's souls.

The newspapers are printed in millions of copies for all segments of the population and for all the ethnic groups of Russia. And everything, written with unique skill, is based on the three great principles of mass psychology: the simple striking phrase, the endless repetition of the same arguments and the assurance to the reader, since you believe it yourself, that the communist idea is the only true one, which will rapidly conquer the world.

All those who are capable work together with apostolic zeal in this mission of an enlightening propaganda through the power of the press. People's commissars, political leaders, higher and lower public officials, workers and farmers, men and women—all become journalists and endeavor to their utmost capacity, each in the area he knows best, to educate the masses. They often analyze each aspect of communism—political, social, economic—with the patience and concentration on detail characteristic of the scholar. This is why the Soviet newspapers have something monotonous, heavy and bookish about them; they are completely different from the usual bourgeois newspapers, because their purpose is not to entertain or to exploit their readers, but to enlighten them. The Soviet newspaper centralizes activities and functions as teacher, book, public speaker and catechist. Social scandals, hair-raising crimes in all their gruesome details, titillating erotic sections, are nonexistent in the Soviet press. Everything in the Soviet newspaper serves a higher, unvarying, enlightening purpose.

A remarkably close bond is created between the reading public and the newspapers. In them, workers and peasants from all over Russia express their opinions about all matters of general interest or they freely criticize practices in their local areas. In this way the newspaper becomes a living organism, continuously receiving and assimilating new elements; and this lessens the risk that, in the context of the strict limits of communist discipline, newspapers may become soulless and pedantic.

One of the most original journalistic developments in the new Russia is the *Wall Newspaper*. In every factory, workers' training school, prison, military camp and school of any type, one sees newspapers edited by local committees and put on walls. Some are dailies; others, weeklies or monthlies. Sometimes they are printed; on other occasions they are typed or handwritten. They are always a single sheet, very often illustrated with caricatures and affixed on a bulletin board at the entrance or in the meeting hall of buildings.

In every work unit or institution, a committee is elected for a period of three or six months to gather news and other important pieces of information regarding the group; it writes articles and takes care of the printing. The *Wall Newspaper* checks into things, asks questions, arrives at conclusions, "enlightens."

The *Wall Newspaper* came into being in a simple and most natural way. Because of the shortage of paper at the outbreak of the Revolution, the official news agency would print the most important news on pieces of paper and send them to various factories. There the workers would post them on walls and would add, on a scrap of paper or even on a cigarette pack, their opinions or other news they had come upon; or they would scribble on walls with charcoal or pencil. In time this habitual practice became a necessity and the *Wall Newspaper*, more systematically handled, came into being.

Those peasants or workers who show exceptional talent in editing a newspaper are sent, at their group's or factory's expense, to study journalism at special schools. Through this process of continual selection, the journalistic corps constantly renews itself directly from the ranks of the people and from all professions and vocations—from the best elements of the proletarian body. I'll never forget the young editor of a *Wall Newspaper* in a refuge for young vagabonds.

"We have," the director of the group told me, "a committee overseeing health and nutrition. Before eating, the children stand in line, and the committee members inspect their hands for cleanliness. Each morning they supervise their bathing, the combing of their hair and the brushing of their teeth. Then we have special committees of boys to supervise the reading room, gymnastic programs, musical activities and the *Wall Newspapers*. If you like, I'll introduce you to a young fellow journalist, a ten-year-old boy from Kharkov who puts together our monthly newspaper almost single-handedly."

He called a boy and sent him to fetch the very young editor. In a few moments a small rosy-cheeked boy, wearing a red tie, came before us. He was snub-nosed with sparkling blue eyes. We greeted each other with an air of seriousness, and then we started our conversation.

"What is the goal of your paper, dear colleague?" I asked him.

"To enlighten all the comrades of our school!"

"What does 'to enlighten' mean exactly?"

"To be clean, to tell the truth, to love Lenin."

He came to the point with a few words. His mind worked simply and with certainty. His eyes were full of curiosity. He began to interview me much before I realized it. He asked me if we have *Wall Newspapers*, youth scouts and Lenin in Greece as well and if priests and kings still survive in my land. He had taken a little notebook out of his pocket and was making notes. I sketched a *foustanella** for him and drew a *tsarouhi*.** He gestured good-bye and dashed off.

The director was laughing. "He ran to write a new article for our *Wall Newspaper* on the young of Greece," he told me.

In the evening of the same day I was talking with a journalist about freedom of the press. He answered me with precision and passion: "It was necessary to do one of two things. Either to start discussions—and you know that Russians go on talking interminably—or to get to work. To do both together would have been impossible. We know all the traditional slogans: 'freedom of the individual,' 'The truth emerges from discussion,' and all that. But we have new teachings and new commandments: 'If your fellow man doesn't want to be saved by gentle means, do it by force,' 'If personal freedom stands as an obstacle to the liberation of the whole social body, strangle it,' 'From action, from ceaseless struggle against difficulties, from long, persevering obedience, truth is created.'

"Truth for us is not an abstract notion which can be grasped by our minds through discussion; it is not something

---

* *Foustanella:* a short pleated skirt, part of the national costume of men in Greece.

***Tsarouhi:* a shoe of the same costume, a clog, curved at the point and ending in a pompon-shaped tassel.

ready and finished outside ourselves waiting for us to find it; truth is a balance achieved through our everyday struggles with reality. It is not revealed; it is discovered, created.

"That is why we have set out to find the truth through action, not with debates and sophistic acrobatics of the mind. We have chosen to rid ourselves of those interminable quarrels of an uncontrolled press and to go forward with obedient discipline to the end of the road we have taken. These are difficult times. Our enemies are many and well organized; our entire strength must by necessity be mobilized without delay and concentrated behind our new Idea. We have opened a new road and we assume responsibility for it. The battle has begun. How can we be victorious? There is only one way: for all of us to work together in the same direction. Neither right nor left but straight ahead. At the end of each road, victory always awaits."

He spoke to me, and I looked at him with admiration but without indulgence. Men like him are rigid because they have faith; unfree now because they are creating a new liberty; without morality because they are shaping a new morality. Hard like steel. Two verses of Nikolai Tikhonov come to my mind: "They should forge nails from such men; nowhere then in the world would harder nails exist."

■ THE 7TH OF NOVEMBER/ STALIN AND TROTSKII

■ ONE OF THE MOST LUMINOUS DAYS of my life. Perhaps the most beautiful. For years I have struggled to comprehend certain fundamental concepts, but only today, suddenly and without any effort on my part, were all their meanings radiating light within me. And above all, this truth: Whoever comes from a Western culture, with its age-old metaphysical questions and refined intellectual reservations, can understand absolutely nothing of the cosmogonic turmoil in today's Russia, regardless of whether it is attractive or hateful to him.

To the refined bourgeois mind, most elements of Soviet ideology today seem to be made of rough-hewn parts of a system; many theories are seen only as rules for action— simplistic slogans for the masses. A sober, sensible intellectual of the West would be terrified contemplating what bloody adventures the cry of Russia might lead us into. But fortunately life does not heed the sensible bourgeois mind, and that is why it can forge ahead; that is why we have surged beyond the plant to the animal, and from the animal to the human being. And now from the enslaved human being, we are evolving into the free one. A new world is being begotten again with all the blood of birth.

It is the eve of the great day: The Russian Revolution is celebrating the anniversary of its bloody arrival. The Revolution is still like a young girl, daring in her newly-won emancipation, playing on sidewalks and disturbing the neighbors. From across the earth, pilgrims have come bearing gifts. In other epochs and with the same anxiety and excitement, the dark races of the Middle East must have arrived at Mecca; the silent swarms of the yellow races, at Benares. The earth centers have shifted. Today friends and enemies across the earth have their eyes, filled with fear or hope, fixed on the Red crib of the Kremlin.

Yesterday as we walked in Red Square watching the feverish preparations for the celebrations, a Spanish poet said to me, "I had redeemed myself; I had left behind me the old seductive sirens: religion, fatherland, art. I was free, living in a hut perched on an Andalusian summit. From there I watched the fields and people below. But suddenly a new song struck my ears. I turned toward the North, listened, and then my freedom could no longer contain me. So I came here pursuing the alluring new song of the Abyss. The Siren now sits in this northern land, in this expanse of snow; she has green eyes and a Slavic voice full of passion— her breasts are covered with blood."

I watch imposing women in the streets, holding in their arms red stars made of fabric with which to decorate their doors. Children are pasting red ribbons with black letters across the vast walls: "Proletarians of the world, unite!" From a corner of the street, two platoons of Red soldiers spring forward. The passersby scatter to the sides, out of the way. A woman carrying a basketful of apples shrieks in alarm; the apples spill in all directions. A joyful shiver spreads across my spine as I see the red apples scatter on the snow. And I do not know why a vision flashes through my mind that the Russians have pillaged a great city: Berlin, New York or Paris.

Everywhere around us workers are hanging or pasting multicolored signs. From a rosy flush of dawning flames, a crimson hammer and sickle are rising. Lenin stands erect; he raises his hand, and peasants and workers, as in Michelangelo's *Last Judgment,* rise up from the soil, blackened masses full of mud, stretching their arms toward the light. Far off, a soldier with a red star on his forehead places his outstretched palm above his eyes to screen the sun and stares searchingly toward the horizon.

With its manifesto at every street corner, "To all workers, peasants, Red soldiers of Soviet Russia, to all proletarians, to all the oppressed of the earth," official Soviet Russia gives a report on what has been accomplished so far and what great and difficult tasks remain to be done: "We must build a new and powerful industry to transform our agrarian land through electricity and cooperatives; we must free ourselves of the merchants, the kulaks, and rid ourselves of bureaucracy, illiteracy, alcoholism and ignorance. Comrades, we are only at the beginning."

We are only at the beginning. Yet—so certainly and with such huge strides does their faith advance inside them—in their minds they have already arrived at the end of their march in victory. Nikolai Gumiliov, the wild poet who died so young, has sung:

Victory, glory, bravery—
pale words forgotten by men—
resound in the soul like a thunderbolt of bronze—
like the voice of the Lord in the desert.

Daybreak. I am leaning out my window. The electric lights are still on. Hammers and sickles glow in the dim dawn. Red signs still engrave the dark, as I struggle to make out the vanishing words: "Proletarians . . . seven-hour day . . . Lenin . . . world revolution . . ."

I dress quickly. In the hotel corridors and staircases I come across the invited guests from all over the world: workers and intellectuals. I meet the Japanese architects and their proletarian poet, Akita; the representatives of Persia and Afghanistan, two imams from Arabia, three Hindu students and two charming workers from Thailand wearing orange shawls; on the upper floors, the blond and svelte

Westerners, the wheat-dark Italians, the Spaniards with their stern faces under their berets; on the second floor, two gigantic Mongolians and three gaunt Chinese generals with eyes full of slyness. We all greet each other with quick gestures. All faces glitter; I see in their glances the dangerous seething of the earth.

We are all hurrying to catch the beginning of the ceremonies. Extreme cold under a gray sky. Nostrils, mouths and overcoats are steaming. On one side, at Lenin's tomb, the dignitaries; next to them on the platform, the foreign guests. A dull noise rises from the multitude. The streets are flowing with people like rivers, a cataclysm of the masses. Underneath you hear the ground rumbling as in an earthquake. At the far end of the square the Cathedral of Saint Basil, the beloved of Ivan the Terrible, with its multicolored domes, an unbelievable phantom wrapped in thick fog.

All around, on the red walls of the Kremlin, signs calling the peoples of the world to unite like brothers; slogans for the new life, numbers, statistics, diagrams—this has been accomplished so far; that remains to be done in the coming years; so many illiterates have known the light; this is how production rises and hope increases.

In Soviet Russia the life rhythm is impetuous; time here has taken on its true, profound meaning. It is a priceless substance that is dense and irreplaceable. Whether you are saved or lost depends on whether you use it wisely or foolishly. The Russians feel they have no time to lose; if they do not manage to organize themselves quickly, to catch up with or surpass their enemies, they are lost. Here you often sense the panting breath of the Idea, the ardent impatience; the urge to build factories, schools and homes, to educate the peasants, to turn natural resources into energy, to join rivers, to drill new oil wells. Industrial progress in Soviet Russia is not a matter of greed or luxury; it is a matter of life or death. Survival depends on the intensification of production, on austere vigilance over consumption, on systematic and determined struggle.

In the dim morning light, I gaze at the golden domes of the Kremlin, the red walls, the violent slogans, the stirring masses. And in front of Lenin's monument, erect, solidly built and with his Mongolian helmet: Stalin. Little by little I begin to understand: All this is a great preparation for an all-consuming struggle; the entire land of Russia is a fully mobilized camp, no longer the land of the dispossessed and the weak. Power is shifting toward the victims of injustice. The world is changing masters.

Suddenly the trumpets sound and the parade—or rather the charge—of the Red Army begins. Wave after wave of soldiers break ranks in front of the Lenin Monument; then they scatter and disappear and new waves energetically follow: the infantry, artillery, the sailors of the Baltic and Black seas, the airmen, the parachutists, the Moscow Guard, the GPU,* workers with leather shirts and short-butted guns, women workers with red kerchiefs and guns on their shoulders. The cavalry charges next: Circassians, Kazakhs, Caucasians, Mongolians. Their leader moves ahead, sword raised in the the air. The entire cavalry follows, galloping, a sea of ethnic costumes, bayonets and multicolored banners. Leading them is an honorary battalion of old veterans with white beards.

After the armed forces follows the astonishing and interminable parade of the peoples of the Republics, all passing in front of Lenin. From the other three sides of the immense square, three deep red rivers of humanity pour forward: the October Children, the Pioneers, the Komsomols, the representatives of different factories, men and women

---

* State Political Office, predecessor of the KGB.

workers, the awkward muddy-bearded muzhiks. Here are all the ethnic groups of Russia and the entire earth: blacks from Central Africa, Asians with multicolored costumes on camels, Chinese holding over their heads an immense dark green dragon of cardboard and cloth that opens and closes its jaws. On a huge truck, a gigantic globe encircled with chains. A Pioneer strikes the chains with a hammer and smashes them. Crowded on trucks in an endless column, the disabled veterans of wars shout excitedly, brandishing their crutches triumphantly in the air.

Suddenly the sun bursts through the fog, and the faces of the multitudes shine, their eyes sparkling. The huge square shakes with hurrahs and the heavy pacing of the crowds. In front of me, the two Thai women grasp their orange shawls and wave them in the air like flames.

Hours pass. The streets keep pouring crowds into the square. A group of workers are carrying a model of their factory made of lumber, metal and glass, with reverence, as though they held the holy sepulcher. Farmers pass, waving their shining sickles over their heads. Further back, others raise up large wood or paper caricatures, satirizing the bourgeois class. Others carry simply made statues resembling primitive African masks.

What makes the deepest impression on me, however, is not the array of satirical cartoons but those who carry them: peasant faces, some ecstatic and others somber, which look as if they were kneaded from heavy Russian mud, slaves who are still terrified in their struggle to become free and who can not break loose from their primordial numbness. A tall, wiry, russet-bearded peasant is holding a grotesquely comical effigy of a former landlord. Looking at it, you can not hold back your laughter. But the peasant who holds it, turning right and left to be seen by everyone, bows most somberly, as if he were holding a sacred liturgical banner, or carrying a dead lion in his arms. But he is trembling a little as if he can not quite believe that the lion is really dead. Yet this peasant has made the wooden statue himself; he has sculpted it in his hut, has painted it black, red and green, and has brought it, wrapped in heavy blankets, for Lenin to see and to laugh at. But his body is not yet synchronized with his soul; for, while his soul laughs sarcastically at his old master, his body sees him and shivers.

My eyes watch the terrible sight insatiably, until everything becomes blurred and I no longer see anything. Against my wishes, my "child's tears" then run down my eyes.

Deep into the night, the three inexhaustible red rivers pass in front of Lenin and salute him like worshiping pilgrims. The riders have dismounted all around the Kremlin; their horses are neighing. The Kazakhs and the Caucasians take to singing and dancing. Beside me a flame-bearded Norwegian is weeping; others laugh, and two old peasants stand gaping, their eyes filled with armies, workers and horses. Balalaikas and bronze flutes, Gypsies dancing in the mud. Rosy-cheeked Germans are struggling to communicate with the swarthy horsemen of Azerbaizhan. They ask them what they earn, how much they eat, if they still remember the Tsar. But the slender Orientals with their flaming eyes do not understand; motionless, they look at the shaven Western faces and twirl their mustaches.

Suddenly a shout rends the air and disturbs the grand procession. From a balcony across the square, a violent soul belonging to the opposition rears up and shouts. To this impatient soul, all these triumphant celebrations seem to be a deceptive mask that covers the black face of truth. It is the cry of Trotskii, an explosion of fiery lava that has not yet frozen and become a set crust of earth; it is still boiling with a restless revolutionary rage, unable to accept the settling and narrowing reality that is being shaped. His fire wants to blow up the crust made of Kulaks, merchants and bureaucrats, who are gaining strength each day and who will attempt to asphyxiate the rebellious flame of the Revolution.

Today in all of Russia two powerful personalities stand in opposition to one another: Stalin and Trotskii. Both of them have set the same goal for their lives: the triumph of the communist Idea. But they are separated by the tactics that each of them employs in order to arrive at the goal. More simply, it is their temperaments that separate them.

What is Stalin's personality? Lenin, in his famous testament, judges the character of the future dictator of Russia harshly: "Stalin is rash and this defect makes him unbearable as general secretary of the Party. For this reason I propose the comrades replace him with someone more mannerly, more tolerant, more flexible, one who can treat his comrades less arbitrarily."

And Stalin one day, when speaking to the general assembly of the Party, responded: "Yes, comrades, I acknowledge that I am abrupt, but only toward those who harm the Party. Many times I asked to resign; but they themselves— Trotskii, Kamenev, Zinoviev—insisted that I remain. What was my duty? I never left my post in the battle, wherever I was placed. It isn't in my character to quit."

A Greek merchant, who had known Stalin when he was still a worker in Tbilisi, related to me a truly revealing event in the life of this powerful leader. The Tsarist police had captured Stalin and several of his comrades as conspirators. All of them were condemned to torture. The Tsarist soldiers lined up, each holding a whip with studs. One by one the comrades passed in front of them, and each soldier whipped each one with all his might. Most of them collapsed midway through the line of soldiers; some died before coming to its end. When Stalin's turn came, he bent to the ground, cut a blade of grass and put it between his teeth. He then proceeded slowly and quietly to pass in front of each soldier who waited with the whip. Blood streamed from his entire body but he went on, unbending, with his heavy peasant step. He stood before the last soldier, took the leaf of grass out from between his teeth and showed it to him. "Take it," he said, "to remember me by. And look. I didn't bite it in the least."

Stalin is such a man. His name describes him: steel. Slowly, quietly, he moves forward like a peasant to achieve his goals. He does not shout, does not hurry, does not get excited. He advances confidently and pitilessly, like a force of nature. He has the patience of the farmer and of the earth because he knows this simple, ancient truth: Victorious is he who outlasts his adversary, even by a quarter of an hour.

But the fiery and stubborn makeup of Trotskii cannot accept such a pace. He is in a hurry. Stalin is the earth; he is the flame.

"Where are we heading?" he asked that day from the balcony, in his wild and passionate voice. "Stalin is pushing us fast toward the right, from the proletariat to the bourgeoisie, from the simple militant communist to the career communist, from the poor peasant to the rich kulak. Stalin is betraying the Idea!"

The voice of Trotskii was swallowed up that day by violent interruptions, by abuse and laughter. But now and then the hoarse voice of the great communist prevailed over the din. Unconnected phrases were heard amid the shouts. "Today's regime becomes an obstacle to the vanguard of the international proletariat . . . bureaucracy is omnipotent . . . lowly tyrants . . . nouveaux riche proprietors . . . class . . . privileged intellectuals . . . treason! Treason!"

Who is right in this clash of titans, a clash that will sooner or later have its consequences in the entire world? Stalin or Trotskii? Both combatants are powerful men: Stalin, obstinate, cunning, a Georgian full of passion who seizes his adversary like an iron vice; Trotskii, swift in his motions, with all the great passions of the Jew, a wild soul that strikes like lightning and illuminates the solid, vigorous, steady body of Stalin.

During one of the last days of his life, December 29, 1922, Lenin wrote in his political testament: "What interests me is that the Party is not split. This depends above all on Stalin and Trotskii; on these two depends the unity or the dissolution of the Party. Comrade Stalin, as soon as he became general secretary, concentrated in his hands a vast power, and I am not certain that he will always use it wisely. Comrade Trotskii, on the other hand, distinguishes himself with his exceptional abilities. But he has an exaggerated confidence in himself, and he gives excessive importance to the administrative aspects of every question. These characteristic differences between the two most important members of the Central Committee could, if the Party does not take timely measures, cause its disunity."

Yet, as it happens with all living organisms, the antagonism between Stalin and Trotskii could have a beneficial outcome. If the ways of Trotskii prevail, there would be a great danger of quickly angering the peasants, who would then resort again to passive resistance, an effective yet very destructive tactic. And this might lead to a dangerous flaring up of the revolutionary forces in every bourgeois society, with the real possibility that Russia might, in spite of her unpreparedness, throw herself into a global military adventure, more demanding than her present resources would permit. If, on the other hand, Stalin's policies prevail, another danger could manifest itself: The kulaks would gain time to strengthen themselves for a takeover of the agrarian segment of the land, while the *nepman* would become dominant in the urban areas. And then it would be too late for Stalin to bring them in line with the communist Idea.

Now, because of their mutual opposition and their severe criticism of one another, the leaders of the two extremes interact, and they push reality toward a sensible yet daring direction. The violence of Trotskii's ways is transmitted from afar. It is not actually dangerous, and it may even be beneficial for the official Soviet course of development that is being slowed down by *nepman*, the bureaucrats and the kulaks.

■ LENIN

■ IN THE IMMENSITY OF RED SQUARE the wooden*
mausoleum of Lenin, simple, serene, perfectly balanced,
rises, covered with snow. From its dark, low entrance to the
opposite end of the square I see a dense line of men, women
and children, who have been standing there four abreast.
Immobile since daybreak, they wait. They have come from
every quarter of Moscow, from every province of Russia,
from every land on earth to see and pay homage to the Red
Tsar who lies below the earth, looking almost alive.

I approach, take my place in line and wait. In the sparse
light of dawn, I make out the features and expressions of a
vast diversity of ecstatic and patient faces. Tatars smelling
like buffaloes, peasant women with prominent bellies,
Americans with heavy jaws, sickly looking Chinese, tall German youths and peasants of the Caucasus with towering
sheepskins on their heads.

No one makes a sound. In the snow and frost they are
waiting with mystical anticipation, their eyes fixed on the
"holy sepulcher" before them. I turn in my mind the entire
life of this new "Father" of Russia, and slowly murmur to
myself the verses of the poet Nikolai Kluiev:

> *Lenin! mystical paradise of cedars*
> *where even the sun is an ardent combatant.*
> *Ah! that this blood-dripping name*
> *could open up like a peacock's tail!*

Suddenly a massive block, which until now stood quietly

---

* The mausoleum of Lenin has since been rebuilt in feldspar and granite.

like a statue of snow, sways at the mausoleum entrance. The Red Guard stirs to open the gate. And as if with the same motion, the massive front of the procession moves like a gentle wave. Heads rise, and those in the beginning of the line cross the threshold and vanish inside. Those behind me push me gently; I inch gingerly forward. My turn comes and I enter the dark corridor. Feet advance searchingly, go down steps through subterranean passages and go up steps again. Warm air, the walls phosphorescent red. You inhale the breath of other human beings; you hear the shuffling of feet on steps.

Suddenly the dim, sheepish faces of the two muzhiks in front of me light up as if a mysterious subterranean sun had descended upon them. I stretch my neck: Below, deep in the heart of the earth, the great crystal that covers the embalmed body of the new messiah. Inside it, a luminous reflection: the pale, bald cranium of Lenin.

Covered from the waist down with the Red flag, he lies in his gray worker's smock, looking as if he were alive. His right hand is a clenched fish; his left, stretched across his chest. His rosy face with its vivid blond goatee is smiling, a calm satisfaction in his austere and yet very tender countenance.

The Russian throngs watch ecstatically. A few years earlier, before this new savior arrived, they had marveled at the rosy, fair face of Jesus in front of the holy altars of churches with the exact same mystical glance. The eyes of the muzhiks, as they watched this "Red Christ," revealed the eternal struggle of fighting man more clearly than all the theories of the mind. The essence remains the same; only the names change.

Those who have faith feel the same way that believers perennially feel, regardless of what they worship: Their souls are regenerated, the entire world is reborn for them. Their desire reaches the goal, becomes fulfillment; their strength multiplies. This is the awesome secret of every faith—today, of the communist faith.

Moved like the muzhiks, I watch this shining, clear cranium, as his entire life flashes through my mind with lightning speed. The "Red Tsar" struggled, suffered exile, poverty, betrayals and slander. His convictions and his obstinance terrified his most trusted friends, and many abandoned him. Now, under this high-arched cranium, around these small, extinguished eyes, Russia—with its villages and cities, its mountains, its snow-covered steppes and great rivers—cries for help.

Because he was the strongest and consequently the most responsible soul in Russia, he believed that the motherland called him and placed on his shoulders the responsibility to save her. She had shaped him with her struggles and her hopes, had made him the most powerful spirit in order to assign to him at the critical moment the most difficult mission. And so Lenin, like the heroes of legend, started out from the humble worker's house in Zurich, where he lived alone for years in poverty and exile. His simple Swiss landlord, the cobbler, said to him, "Where are you going, Ilich? It's the beginning of the month and you have paid the rent in advance. Do you think I'll return a portion of it to you if you leave early?"

"It doesn't matter, it doesn't matter," Lenin would reply, smiling.

"But where are you going, Ilich?" the simple cobbler would ask again. "Do you think that in Russia you will find a room to stay in?"

And Lenin would answer, "How do I know if I'll find one? I don't know, but I must go!"

He traversed Switzerland and Germany, arrived at the Russian border, entered the boundless, completely armed Tsarist empire. Wearing his worker's cap and worn clothes, he stood for a moment and stared at the vast fields before him. What was the goal of this short, laconic, poorly dressed voyager with the small, penetrating eyes? To overthrow the great empire, to take possession of all the houses, the factories, the land of Russia; to chase away the Tsar, the Tsarina and their children; to expel the military lords, the bureaucrats, the nobles, the bourgeoisie and the clergy; and to give dictatorial powers to the wretched and famished proletariat.

"Megalomania! Madness!" cry the sensible who believe that reason—that miserly, virtuous old maid—governs the world. But within a few months, this poorly dressed simple man will take possession of Russia, will enter the palace of the dancer Tshcheshinskaia, mistress of the Tsar, and from her balcony will address the proletarian multitudes: "History has chosen this palace to become its workshop, and from these chambers that symbolize the old, corrupt Russia, history charges out to destroy the tyrants. This palace of the imperial whore is now swarmed by the smoke-smeared workers of the factories. Soldiers run here on foot from the trenches, their warped bodies covered with lice, to proclaim the new gospel!"

Private property, commerce and money are abolished. Banks, factories, mines, all urban and agricultural property, are confiscated to belong to all. Monarchy, aristocracy, bourgeoisie, legal and social inequality between men and women, religion, clergy, suppression of nonwhite nationalities, Tsarist army and police, courts, educational system, are all wiped out within ten weeks.

A pitiless flame, a simple, fecund faith in the omnipotence of the Idea, always characterizes the beginning of all revolutions. The new breath blows spontaneously, chaotically, irresistibly, not knowing the limits of human malleability and endurance. It does not as yet have experience; nothing burdens it, not even good sense, believing as it does, in the delirium of its initial strength, that it can destroy and rebuild the world in three days.

An Idea was entrenched in the mind of Lenin; and the world had to take the road opened by this Idea. One can disagree with the means employed or with the final goal, but no one can deny the power of the soul, the ascetic purity, the audacity and sharpness of this mind. Lenin has been compared with Genghis Khan and with Peter the Great. But such comparisons are always superficial and at this point premature. We do not as yet have the necessary distance of time to see the entire picture and to judge the tree by its fruit. But one truth will remain unshakable throughout history: This poor and simple man, who after the day's toil now sleeps the serene sleep of the just, came upon the earth and fulfilled his duty.

When I came out of the mausoleum, which was beneath the snow-covered walls of the Kremlin where they are now beginning to bury the great comrades of Lenin, I walked for hours with a Russian friend and listened to him speak with all the ardor of his youth about this great soul of his people: "Lenin is a password; he has already lost his human dimension and is entering the domain of legend. The children born in the years of the Revolution are called 'children of Lenin.' The mysterious visitor who comes on New Year's, loaded with gifts to distribute among children, is no longer Saint Nicholas or Saint Basil. It's Lenin. Every woman of the people, who has a deep need within her to pray to a superhuman power seeking its protection, slowly replaces in her simple heart and imagination the beloved old icons with the already legendary, saintly face of Lenin. And every evening she lights a candle before him.

"In the most remote villages of Russia, from the frozen shores of the Arctic Ocean to the tropical villages of Central Asia, the simple peasants, fishermen, women—talking, weeping, laughing as always in their long night vigils—continually create the portrait of Lenin. The women embroider him in multicolored silks, the men carve him in wood, the children erect him in snow in the middle of their villages—and the other day, a group of Moslems from Turkestan brought Lenin to Moscow in a mosaic made of wheat. All of Russia, bending over the soil, resurrects him with her warm, omnipotent breath.

"Lenin for all of us, educated and illiterate, has become a signal. The great strengths that were sleeping in us have awakened. The Russian national type has already begun to change. What does this mean? To liberate the forces that Tsarism kept enslaved inside us. Lenin, of course, did not create new energies; he only awakened the dormant ones; he liberated those in chains. For us Marxists, the great man is not an independent new personality who stands over the people who bore him; instead he consciously embodies the strengths and desires of his people and of his time. Whatever the people incoherently cry out, he utters in coherent speech. And as soon as it is articulated, it cannot be lost. It becomes a signal.

"We have given a new social image to the world; we have created a new, higher type of human community. Now either we or the bourgeoisie must disappear from the world. Two such realities cannot coexist for very long. They will wrestle each other like queens in a beehive; and the one will devour the other."

"Who will devour the other?"

"You saw the little children of Russia, the October or Lenin Children. You saw the Pioneers and the Komsomols—the flame, the life, the faith—when they parade in the streets, when they play or work, and when and how they respond to your questions. This entire new generation possesses a flame that surely must fill the bourgeoisie with fear. And not only a flame, but it also knows, and this is the most important thing, where to turn its flame and what to burn!"

My friend became silent for a moment. He looked around the walls at the graves of the first martyrs and at the constantly renewing procession of pilgrims that descended into the earth to see Lenin for a moment. For an instant his face melted in concentrated communion and love; then his lips moved again: "A pure, uncut crystal, his mind. He knew the where, the when, the how—infallibly. He was able to see with unimaginable clarity events as they were, neither worse nor better, but *as they were*. He brought together all factors and with mathematical precision found the unique moment for action. A few days before the outbreak of the Revolution, he was saying to his comrades who were impatient and to those who were hesitating and wanted to postpone it: 'To give the signal for the Revolution on the 6th of November is too early, on the 8th is too late; it must be given on the 7th of November.'

"Such was Lenin. Trotskii a flame, Stalin the soil, Lenin the light."

Listening to the young Russian, I held my head high as though listening to a distant rush of breath from the steppes. An eastern wind struck and burned my temples. And I heard, passing like the march of the Red Army, the heavy cadence of Alexander Blok's terrifying words:

You are millions; we are the innumerable children of the steppes. Try to march against us! Yes, we are the Scythians. Yes, we are the Asians with open, insatiable, slant-cut eyes. To us belong the centuries, to us this hour! Ah, old Europe! Rack your brain and seek like a new Oedipus to solve the riddle of the Sphinx! Russia is the Sphinx; tortured, dripping with blood, she charges, filled with blood and hate, against the aged world!

■ DIALOGUES

■ AND TOMORROW?

Leningrad. I pass through the city streets in a troika. Heavy sleet is falling; a din is rising from the Neva. Near a bridge I dimly discern a large statue.

"Comrade, coachman," I shout, "whose statue is that?"

The coachman, with his heavy cowhide coat, his green cap and ruddy hair, stretches a huge hand toward the statue: "Yesterday it was Catherine the Great. Today it is Lassalle, I think."

"And tomorrow?" I ask.

He shrugged his shoulders. *"Tchort znaet,"* he replied. (The devil knows.)

■ FATHER AND SON

The father was a little merchant, a peddler; he was still able to make a living near the great cooperatives; but as a merchant, he could not vote, had no rights of any kind, and his ten-year-old son, a Pioneer with his red tie, scorned him.

His little store was near my hotel in Moscow. Occasionally I bought butter, smoked fish or black caviar from him. One day I found him in tears.

"What's the matter, Ilia Ivanovich?" I asked.

"I can't anymore, *Gospodin* (Sir). I can't anymore. I'll go away. I'll kill myself. Life is unbearable at my home. Every noon, every evening, fights. As we sit at the table, my son rises from his chair, and instead of crossing himself like a human being, you know what he says? He looks at me with hate in his eyes and shouts, '*Doloi spekuliatsiia!* Down with profit making! Your days are numbered.' I can't bear it anymore, *Gospodin.* I can't!"

■ THE PRIEST

He is one of the more educated clergymen of the old "holy Russia." Well fed and greasy, his cheeks still reflect the gastronomic splendor of the old days. The walls, tables, curtains and pillowcases in his room are covered with icons, lithographs and embroideries of beautifully painted, well-combed Christs. Everything is nauseating. The Madonnas over his bed are weeping; two heavy furs are hanging from hooks on the door. The air smells of butter, borscht and incense; the samovar is steaming; its vapors cloud the atmosphere in the saint-laden room.

"The Church has gone through much more inhuman persecutions," he tells me, lifting his fat, hairy hands toward the samovar, "but it has always come through victoriously."

"Are you making an effort to make the Church compatible with today's realities? The times have changed, *mon père.*"

"Of course we do! Yes, we work with apostolic zeal. We have founded an association of the best ladies. I interpret the gospel and we find work for poor women, who do embroidering, underclothes and lingerie. Every Sunday we all drink tea together."

"I mean an internal attempt to regenerate the Church, to give a new contemporary interpretation to its dogma, to give religion a new form so that today's tortured man can understand and love."

He was offended. He took in a deep breath and exhaled violently, like a whale, before replying, "The Church has no need to evolve, to change. It does not follow the fashions of man. No! The people must adjust to the Church, not the Church to the people. The things of which you speak, forgive me, are the theories of Marx, the Anti-Christ."

He took the cover off the samovar, and the fragrance of tea rose toward the well-fed Christs. The priest calmed down, licked his gluttonous lips and, turning his head ceremoniously toward the door, "Anniutochka," he said in an overly sweet voice, "bring the teacups, my little girl. And bread and butter and smoked fish and a little caviar. Bless you."

■ An Old Nobleman

He invited me to his home where he still retained a small collection of fine china. I had met him at the local Farfornyi Museum. The Reds had taken away his villa and placed him and his old spinster sister in a hallway with two tiny rooms. The rest of the grand old building was occupied by workers' families with a swarm of children who were ruining the floors and the walls. When he passed through the hallway, they would pull his old nobleman's smoking jacket and shout, "Uncle Museum, Uncle Museum!" But the old nobleman suffered all of it quietly and fatalistically. He held the tails of his smoking jacket and slipped through the courtyard of his home like a thief. Sometimes, in order to get on their good side and reduce their ridicule, he would take sunflower seeds from the pocket of his smoking jacket and hand them out.

He told me his story quietly, simply, as though narrating a fairy tale, and he invited me to go to his house in the afternoon to show me what was left of his porcelain collection.

Since there wasn't enough space to lay it out, his piled-up furniture filled the hallway. He was selling it little by little, clandestinely. We sat on the high ancestral chairs, drinking tea in mismatched cups and talking. His sister passed through without making a sound and vanished like a ghost. I looked at the fallen aristocrat with respect, sympathy and, at the same time, great attention, as though looking at the painting of a famous artist. His skin was silken, his clothing worn but clean, his voice gentle and velvety like a caress. He lowered his voice even more, stretched his neck, his breath touching me: "Write that we're in hell now. They took our homes and our precious collections. There is no freedom. Shout it! Tell the truth to the world! Look where we have fallen! We're governed by workers, porters, muzhiks, uneducated people who cannot tell the difference between a vase of the Ming dynasty and one of the Sung!"

"Why aren't you more fair?" I said to him. "You enjoyed things. You sat at the table for centuries—you ate, drank, vomited, ate again. Let others eat now. Replacing those who have sat at the table—that is the law of history. Look back: One class rises, becomes rich, eats and drinks—creates. With time it grows fat, gets tired and declines. Another class, oppressed and hungry, charges forth, and the same cycle begins—struggle, victory, creation, decline.

"In your position I would take my hat off without undignified whinings, regret or sorrow, and politely—with a light irony, if you wish (because I can see from afar that the new lords will also fall someday)—I would greet the hungry newcomers and exit from the dining room. A dining table. That's what I call being in power."

The old nobleman looked at me, terrified. He attempted to rise from his aristocratic chair but sat again; he swallowed two or three times, trying to loosen the collar that was choking him. "I thought you were with us," he murmured.

"I am with the human being," I replied, "with him who rushes to sit at the table and with him who has overeaten, has been humbled and is departing. I suffer with mankind; I observe the entire march, uphill and downhill, with awe; and I strive to be careful not to let my individual interests obscure my judgment."

"Perhaps because," replied the old lord, his lips pinched with irony, "you do not have an ancestral heritage; you don't have palaces and privileges that you would be sorry to abandon."

"Precisely. Because I have no chains. If I owned these delicate porcelain pieces that you showed me this evening, how could I have understood a new Idea?"

■ THE SMILE

The young professor of sociology at the Communist University of Moscow analyzes in a clear and confident manner all the economic factors present in ancient Greek society and proves that the smile of the caryatids on the Acropolis of Athens has its origins in economic causes.

The audience, orthodox Marxists, accepts this wise explanation without hesitation and bursts into applause.

I smile, and the young professor, unnerved, turns to me: "Why are you smiling?"

"I assure you, comrade Professor," I reply, "my smile is not the result of economic causes."

■ DISCUSSION WITH A LEADER

Yesterday I met by chance with one of the intellectual Bolshevik leaders. Discussion began. I made notes of our conversation from what I could remember. He declared, "As we succeed in the material world, we are able, by isolating the constantly repeated elements, to find the laws that govern physical phenomena, and submit them gradually to their laws; and every human being who is not unbalanced accepts them as he accepts natural laws, without opposition."

"But I have an objection," I replied. "Do you recognize that there are limits to the human intellect and consequently to scientific investigation? Can science judge with infallible authority not only the relationships that exist among phenomena but also, behind phenomena, that which the philosophers call Being?

"There are no limits to science; science—and only science—can, with absolute authority, pass judgment on everything. It establishes laws with no possibility of error."

"So the social laws and the physical laws possess the same exactitude?"

"Yes, the same."

"We can foresee an eclipse of the sun with split-second accuracy. But can we, with the same precision, predict what the Russian reality will be three years from now?"

"Not yet. Sociology, or better still, social physics, is still in its infancy. We have just gotten rid of theology and metaphysics and barely entered a path of the positivist examination of life. We have just begun to apply to social studies the empirical method used by the physical sciences: observation, analysis, comparison, induction; and so, little by little, social science, like mechanics or astronomy, will discover the infallible laws that govern social phenomena."

"I do not agree. Social phenomena do not unfold, like the physical ones, in linear time. They cannot be measured, like space, or gathered and expressed in a mathematical formula. Such phenomena of life unfold and mature within a nonlinear psychological time, which cannot be condensed and measured without distortion. Nor can it be expressed within a formula like simple quantitative, colorless, odorless uniform space. Time is an ever-evolving creative force—a perpetual maturation. That is its essence. It is not a composite of elements, all of which pre-exist and, with the passage of time, simply merge mechanically into predictable new combinations. Time is a continuous emergence of unexpected elements—in one word, creation. In this domain there can be no predictions since law means repetition—the same causes produce the same results. And the essence of life, its qualitative difference from matter, is precisely the creative act. And what is creation? For something new to be born which is not contained in existing elements. Never, in any circumstances, can the same identical causes recur; consequently the same results can never be expected or predicted. And since the phenomena of life cannot be summed up into laws, science, which is a system of laws, cannot by nature exist for social phenomena."

"I admit," the Russian replied, "that the social sciences are not as exact as the physical. We cannot predict a revolution with the same accuracy that we foresee an eclipse of the sun. But the social sciences explain the past, reveal a basic rhythm in every age; they follow a luminous thread in the obscure labyrinth of history. And they are not lost following it. And so learning about the evolution of a people, we are able, more securely than with any other method of the human mind, to predict and formulate the future."

"I accept this," I answered. "Social sciences have value only when they search into the past. And why is this so? Because only the past is composed of finished events, which have ceased to live, to flow, to creatively unfold. At the time they were emerging from innumerable factors, only ten, let us say, became operative, and those ten factors created that which we call a historical event. The social sciences struggle to find those ten factors, and as they are found—of course with some approximation always—the social sciences shout triumphantly: 'What happened, happened of necessity. Given those ten factors, only this could have happened.'

"And certainly—as a necessary consequence—only one event could result from those ten existing factors and no other. When among many possibilities certain ones prevail, it is natural to conclude that only these factors were necessary for a historical event to occur. But the problem is not this at all. The problem that interests us—and divides us—is this: Can the social sciences discover which among innumerable factors will prevail in the future to create a historical event?

"Over a frozen lake two children were skating; suddenly one of them became bored and said, 'I'll not go on, I've had enough,' and turned back. The other child went ahead and had barely taken ten steps when the ice cracked. The child drowned. Some years passed; the French Revolution erupted. What would be involved in its unfolding? Infinite—no, not infinite, but numerous probable causes. Suddenly the child who saved himself from drowning while skating—it was Napoleon Bonaparte—intervenes, controverts the logical expectations, brings in the unforeseen. He conquers nations, establishes kingdoms, becomes an emperor.

"But who can support the claim that Napoleon the Great was the only possible outcome of the French Revolution? And that, if he had drowned in the frozen lake, then necessarily—since the same causes bring the same results— another leader identical to the one who had drowned would govern France and the world? What social science could impose laws on life?

"Looking at finished events from our perspective, we can analyze and formulate laws that have a retrospective value only; and we can equate the immobile body of an age with the gigantic breath that gave it life, before the existing possibilities solidified into events. Therefore social science can do only one thing: dissect the past.

"And you cannot in the least support the idea that searching into the past can provide a lesson for the future— to make social sciences a useful guide for our thoughts and actions. Not only can causes not re-emerge identical with those of past epochs and consequently create the same results; this doesn't happen with absolute accuracy even in the physical world, since a small coincidence, a minor event that has depended on unimaginably complicated details, can give a new, unforeseen turn to history.

"And so social science, by projecting itself to the simple folk as possessing the hope of foresight, can become dangerous. Life is so incomparably superior, and so much richer than human logic and fancy, that we can, without being paradoxical, support the idea that social science, as regards foresight, has the following value: that whatever it predicts never happens. A small value indeed, since what we exclude in this way is only one of the innumerable possibilities that struggle to give birth to the future."

"You are ignoring one fact!" retorted the Russian, irritated. "That in spite of all its imperfections, and with all the complexity that I agree exists in the phenomena of life, social science is still able to establish the iron law that governs human societies: the economic causes.

"This is the solid base: The mode of production in material life determines the functioning of the social, political and intellectual life of mankind. Everything—political systems, ideologies, religions, systems of justice, art, morality—is based on these solid foundations, the economic factors. It is therefore certain that, since the human ingredients do not change, economic factors will play this primary role in the future as well. Thus by possessing this fundamental law, we can intervene in social struggles with greater certainty of success. We know now that we must concentrate our greatest attention on the social class that has run its course and must fall, and on the class which, spurred by this social law, must be organized and prepare itself for the assumption of power. And so our intervention, guided by this fundamental social law, is sure and effective."

"In all that you are saying," I replied, "there is a good deal of truth, and I respect that. But you generalize so much; you load your main principle with so many demands that it runs the risk of becoming false. False and dangerous. I will attempt to clarify and justify this thought of mine:

"First of all, the 'law' that you formulate is not absolute. Economic factors are not always the primary forces that mobilize people. Certainly they always play one of the chief roles, because they serve the basic needs of man; but sometimes other factors—religion, race, historical adventures, the appearance of a great personality—dominate and determine the historical evolution of a people.

"How can you explain on the basis of economic factors alone the sudden triumph in the seventh century of an insignificant Arab tribe that up to that time is unknown and wretched? The same economic problems burden this tribe for many centuries. This whole time, it barely manages to survive, pillaging and plundering, living idly, impoverished, bloodthirsty, alcoholic and idolatrous. But suddenly a human being of great personality is born to this race; he declares, amid scorn and danger, that only one God exists, that the soul of man is immortal and that this world and the other—paradise—belong to the faithful.

"He preaches and no one listens. Seven years pass and Mohammed manages to acquire only eleven disciples. His people ridicule him, his life is in danger at every moment; his followers increase, wars begin. The small, unarmed troops of Mohammed are sometimes victorious, sometimes defeated; his mission hangs from a fine thread; the unforeseen at every moment is ready to open a new road in history.

"And behold, a few more years and the desert is filled with mosques; the faithful pour out of Arabia on their horses and conquer the world. Within a short time, they subjugate and regenerate the peoples of a vast region with a new, unimaginable civilization. On the one side, Egypt,

Libya, Tunisia, Algeria, Morocco and Spain, and on the other, Syria, Mesopotamia, Persia, India. What sudden irresistible force spurred them? Certainly not only economic causes, but a deeper force, a richer and more uncontrollable one—faith. The breath of Mohammed.

"What was the essence of Christianity? To organize the slaves, give bread to the hungry, wipe out social and economic inequality upon the earth? Not at all. Christ did not preoccupy himself with economic problems. Do not concern yourselves with what you will eat, what you will drink, what you will wear. Just look at the birds in the sky. Seek one thing only: the kingdom of heaven!

"Certainly the slaves and the hungry distorted, in accordance with their needs and desires, the message of Christ and declared him the leader of the oppressed, who would overthrow the overfed lords and lead the tortured masses to social equality and economic well-being. That is why Christianity spread so quickly. By linking itself to immediate social needs for change, it became a human passion, seeking revenge and the terrestrial kingdom. As was natural, the kingdom of heaven was transported to the earth, for, when an idea touches the masses and stirs them, it takes on an aspect of personal passion and hope for immediate reward.

"In all epochs, with all peoples, the economic factors are among the most powerful motivations in human life, because man always has the need to eat. And a historian can easily, if he wants to relate historical events to a central idea, prove whatever he wishes, leaving some events in the dark while vividly illuminating others. Various possibilities exist: that history is governed by economic causes or by the hand of Divine Providence or by heroes or by racial characteristics or by blind chance.

"But he who studies history with all the impartiality that human nature can muster—what will he see? That all these causes work together on the masses, sometimes one being dominant, sometimes another, sometimes several or even all in unison. But the degree to which each factor contributes is difficult to determine. In normal times, when the masses are not inflamed by a religious faith, the primary role is, I think, played by economic factors."

"This which you just admitted is already very important."

"Not really. For who can guarantee that within the social flock, which only concerns itself with material life, there will not arise at any moment the unforeseen storm that will violently transfer to second place the material needs of man?

"But even in entirely normal times when such a storm does not appear, you can, if you examine more deeply, narrow even further your fundamental social law: Economic factors are not the causes but the results of numerous other factors operative within a certain time, place and people. We must not say: 'Since the economic conditions are such, this will be the evolution of a given people.' Race, fate, climate, wars and invention, among other causes, contribute to create a particular set of economic conditions. The economic aspect is simply the most visible manifestation of more obscure, deeper factors. And if the economic conditions can become effective slogans, they owe this to the fact that behind the economic banners operate hidden forces, which may not have been identified and thus remain unused as slogans for the masses.

"This is true in normal historical circumstances. At other times these obscure forces assume a name and a form that sweep the masses, and then the economic concerns withdraw into secondary positions in the ongoing battles of mankind."

"But," he persisted, "you agree that an economic change will surely bring along numerous other changes—moral and intellectual. Economic factors therefore are not results but causes of change."

"Bring along? Or is it perhaps that these moral and intellectual changes are results of factors that precede economic change, but their manifestations follow the more visible economic change, while the more complex matters—moral change, art, thought—become manifest later. And since economic change manifests itself first, superficial thinking would assign to it the causation of the other changes.

"And I would like to make one more observation: Even the most fanatic Marxists agree that the economic liberation of mankind is not a goal but a means. What does this mean? That there is in man a need more powerful, more profound, and it is for this need that man struggles, whether he knows it or not. It is for this need that he wants to be better fed, and to have more free time after his day of toil. And when they ask you, 'What is this more profound need?' you answer, 'To live like a human being, to have time to educate oneself, to make one's children better, to enjoy life . . .'

"But all these answers are one-sided and vague. They are, of course, correct, sensible, practical, but incapable of sweeping the masses. In order for the masses to be mobilized, to risk their lives and create great events, they need a sacred madness—a faith. That is why I consider all your sociological theories not only intellectually deficient but also practically incapable of creating that which you seek: a new civilization."

"What is missing in them?"

"The myth."

The Russian frowned. "If you remain in Russia," he said, attempting to smile, "and you decide to propagate these ideas, I will give the order to hang you."

"It is the only silencing answer you can give me," I responded, smiling in turn.

I answered him with a chuckle, but deep inside this discussion embittered me. With what sidetrackings, with what struggles, with what narrow-minded, fanatical leaders, the peoples of the earth move toward the future!

All these economic systems, new laws and political changes are utterly incapable of renewing the face of the earth!

Only if there is a transformation of the human heart can this complex reality, with its insoluble problems, become simple. But in order for solutions to become possible, mankind must first immerse itself in blood, in misery, in famine. Such has always been the road to salvation. Only the blood-drenched, famished vitals of man can create the liberating Word.

And this is why no one can deny that these fanatical leaders, without being able to clearly see the entire cyclical process, contribute nevertheless to the plowing of the vitals of man, as they faithfully carry out their harsh, pioneering duty.

■ THE PROPAGANDA
OF THE EAST

■ I left the theater tonight, moved and disturbed. I saw a new work: *Howl, China*. The entire martyrdom of the yellow working class exploded on the stage, the entire inhuman exploitation by the white capitalists.

A small Chinese woman, the pathetic heroine of the work and the only luminous soul among the wretched heaps of the yellow proletariat, moved about like a burning conscience, singing a monotonous, soft and despairing tune. Later, she hanged herself with a slender rope.

The theater was filled with Chinese who were invited this night to see the torments of their land. In the front row sat a young Chinese general with his staff. They had found refuge in Moscow, persecuted by the fascists of their motherland. As the dense Asiatic anthill of the coolies toiled, suffered and died in order to make the Americans and English rich, an air of horror and indignant anger rent the theater. Tonight all these people on the stage cried out, and their shout reached deep within us. A Russian woman worker next to me was weeping. And when the curtain fell, another worker who was unknown to me turned and asked me, "How can your soul bear these injustices any more?"

I didn't say a word. I watched the Chinese with their enigmatic, closed faces as they silently rose together. In the middle advanced the small-framed general, followed by his officers in grand uniforms. Their faces had turned to clay. They bent as they walked, touching one another. I could not see their lips moving, but I heard, as they passed near me, a muffled whir like the droning of passing birds. As they

219

passed, they stared at all of us whites with their stern and merciless Mongolian eyes. And then, all together, they vanished in the snow-covered streets.

They are an indomitable race, their numbers uncountable; and the game of the Bolsheviks seems dangerous to them. They struggle to awaken the masses—hate and vengeance raging inside them. The whole of Asia is stirred by the communist propaganda; its flame spreads across China, India, Persia, Afghanistan, and on to Arabia, Egypt and the northern shores of Africa. Every new fermenting idea is by nature imperialistic. It seeks to displace all other ideas that oppose it—above all, those related to it—to leap across borders and conquer the world. It employs without hesitation all means: violence, gentleness, deceit, virtue, crime, hate, whatever is expedient. It knows that all means become sacred even if they are not, as long as they bring victory.

But the global capitalist order proves itself to be well organized, well armed, ready to throw itself into harsh, desperate struggles in order to retain its privileged position and continue to grow fatter upon the hunger of others. The new Idea encounters great resistance. "Yes, the enemy," Zinoviev cries out, "has gained many positions in the West. But another front remains. It is there that the final assault will take place; and this will decide the battle: the Asian front."

And so the Bolsheviks turned toward the East. Clever, indefatigable, daring, they spread out toward the most remote, primitive villages of the Orient. What do these new missionaries proclaim? They provide very simple notions that even the most simpleminded Asians can comprehend: "The European and American capitalists eat up the fruits of your toil, rob the riches of your lands; they defile your religious traditions, step on your honor and your freedom, treating you like animals. Wake up! Rise! Chase them away! Asia for the Asians! Russia asks for nothing, wants nothing.

She only illuminates and wakes her Asian brothers. Listen to her voice, comrades!"

All of Asia listens with attention, agitated by the new gospel. The Bolshevik apostles, sometimes workers, sometimes small merchants or doctors, pass through villages and cities awakening the vast masses. The name of Lenin, commanding and full of hopes like the name of the Prophet, now resounds within the Moslem hearts of Asia. The Persian poet Mirja Ali Mokrim sings: *"Lenin is not dead—immortal, he lives and reigns among us. The future generations will worship Lenin because his heart suffered for Persia!"*

When Lenin was ill, Tatars, Mongols and Chinese left their villages for a long journey to the Siberian border. They asked, "How is Lenin?" And they stayed there for days to hear a good word, good news to take back to their villages.

In Moscow there is a special university for the Asian peoples. Males and female students come from all over Asia to study, their expenses paid by the Soviets. I went there the day before yesterday. All of the Asian and African peoples— yellow, swarthy, black—send their brightest youths here to learn. What do they study? To become missionaries. All these youths of different colors have one purpose only: to return to their homelands, to awaken their peoples, to organize their hopes and their hates.

A girl from Korea, about fourteen years old, broad-faced, slant-eyed, with glossy black hair, was saying to me, "I like Russia, but I'm in a hurry to return to my homeland."

"Is your land beautiful—the mountains, the rivers, the trees?"

The yellow mask smiled scornfully: "How well you show that you're bourgeois!" she murmured. And then with a messianic fervor, she shrieked as if she were a complete bureau for propaganda, "The beauty of the earth is a luxury that concerns only those who live in comfort. Only they can see and appreciate it. But those who are hungry, those who return exhausted in the evening from the factory or the fields of their landlord, do not have the time or the urge to see if the mountains, the rivers and the trees you ask about are beautiful. Let us first liberate ourselves from oppression, and then we'll look at sunrises and sunsets!"

As I listened to her, the well-nourished poet of India, Tagore, came to mind. As he passed through Germany a few years ago, he wanted to proclaim his serene and beautiful religion to the workers. He invited them to a large hall and stood at the podium in his all-white Hindu tunic, immaculately clean and impressively beautiful with long nails on his aristocratic fingers. He spoke: "When you return in the evening from your day's work, your soul will be uplifted, your toiling will be forgotten; it will be enough to behold the sun's setting and hear the song of birds at dusk!"

But the workers screamed in a rage; they clenched their fists, shouting, "Down! Down!" And Tagore gathered his robes and departed.

At the same university, I asked an Armenian student whom she loved most, Tolstoi or Gorkii. "Gorkii," she replied. "The other one doesn't interest me. Gorkii describes life."

And a tiny hunchbacked Hindu student corrected her: "Our life!"

All faces, intense and fanatical, are glowing. The East, this blazing workshop, is awakening and shouts. I see pinned on a wall the manifesto that was signed at the conference of Baku by representatives from all Asia:

> Rise, Hindus, living skeletons, victims of hunger and
> oppression!
> Rise, villagers of Anatolia!
> Rise, peoples of Arabia and Afghanistan,

lost in the deserts, swept by winds and
separated from the rest of the world by England!
Rise to fight the enemy of humankind—imperialist
   England!

The imperialism of the new Idea denounces British imperialism; both struggle to conquer inexhaustible Asia, filled
with treasures and peoples. And the imperialism of the new
Idea seeks to spread through the entire world to liberate it. It
does not ask the Asians for anything, and this is precisely why
it gets everything, since what its propaganda seeks—the freedom of the Asians from bourgeois capitalism—will be the
most imperialistically productive of all communist advances.

At a meeting in Moscow the other day I remember a
black man with the jaws of a gorilla rising to speak. His
gestures were wild and violent; his bright amber eyes glittered as he repeated the words that had been spoken a thousand times: "proletariat . . . liberty . . . justice . . ." But he
uttered them with such passion that he gave them an incredibly menacing meaning. The white Europeans in the
audience applauded, thinking that the meaning of these
words spoken by the African had the same content given to
them by Europeans. But when he shouted "justice," I saw
scenes of slaughter, looting, gorging and destruction in his
eyes, while in the eyes of the Europeans, concurrent with
the word "justice," I saw well-fed workers and great
metropolitan development. . . .

Complex philosophical and economic theories are crystallized, as is natural for the masses, into a few easily understood slogans: "class struggle—dictatorship of the proletariat—the land for the farmers, the factories for the
workers—religion is the opiate of the people—proletarians
of all nations, unite!" Dangerous, explosive phrases that
have the power, because they are simple and repeated endlessly, to organize the anxieties and desires of the masses

and to open a single definite path for their energies.

These slogans are capable of awakening terrible dark powers even in the most savage of tribes. Will communism be able to illuminate them in time?

At the same congress a Chinese student mounted the podium—a mere youth, wild and at the same time immobile. A tensely wound spring. He held his hands behind his back and crowed, his head high on his long neck like that of a vulture. He recounted the tortures suffered by the Chinese poor who worked for the white capitalists sixteen or eighteen hours a day, who slept inside filthy barracks, heaped like worms, and who died in droves from hunger and tuberculosis. The monosyllabic shouts of the Chinese student penetrated the immense hall like a dirge. A savage monotone, a rending cry.

Suddenly an American professor sitting at my side turned to me, terrified: "I say this to you, and don't forget it: Today there is no greater event in the whole world than this. The Bolsheviks are stirring the whole of China with their propaganda. Five hundred million souls are rising. . . ."

As we were leaving, an exiled Italian journalist approached me. "What do you think?" he asked me, his eyes filled with fear. "You heard? You saw? How does this terrible preparation seem to you?"

"The chronicler of holy Russia, old Nestor, was right," I replied: "'Each nation has its own guardian angel. And the guardian angel of Russia has gigantic wings.'"

■ PANAIT ISTRATI

■ IT WAS IN THIS COMBATIVE ATMOSPHERE of agitation and struggle in banner-decked Moscow that I met Panait Istrati. He was also one of Russia's invited guests for the great festivities celebrating the tenth anniversary of the Revolution. I had not met him before in person. I had only read his tales, full of fire, blood and human cries, and I knew of his heroic, adventure-filled life.

The restless and daring man, George Valsamis, a smuggler from the Greek island of Cephallonia and possessed by an incurable Cephallonian wanderlust, met a strong, beautiful and wise Rumanian in Braila—Zoitsa Istrati. They had a son whom Valsamis, of course, baptised Gerasimos.* But later they gave him an additional name: Panayotakis, Panait.

The father died while Panayotakis was still an infant, and his mother—saintly, tender, hard-working—toiled as a washerwoman to bring up her son. She dreamed that one day she would send him to school and marry him to a fine little woman so that, God willing, he might become a good Rumanian family man. But the wild Cephallonian blood boiled in the veins of the little boy. When he was only twelve years old, he abandoned his mother and began the life of the tramp. He went hungry, got sick, slept in the streets; he stowed away on ships; and on the roads of Egypt, Palestine, Syria, Turkey, Greece, Italy, Switzerland, he hid in the back of wagons and under boxcars. He was burning with an insatiable thirst to live, to see, to experience all the joys and all the bitterness that this earth could give to man. During his

---

* Patron saint of Cephallonia.

225

vagabond days he read Russian literature and heard Eastern stories and the tales of *A Thousand and One Nights* in the coffee shops of the Levant. To earn a crust of bread, he worked as waiter in a cafe, candy-maker's assistant, laborer, mason, ironworker, stevedore, housepainter and, finally, street photographer on the Côte d'Azur in Nice.

One day in January of 1921, he grew weary of his hunger and suffering and decided to put an end to his life. He took a razor and entered the public park of Nice to kill himself. Two years earlier he had written a twenty-page letter to Romain Rolland, in which he told the story of his life, his bitterness, his longing to hear a friendly voice and to shake hands with a sincere human being.

This was Istrati's great passion throughout his life: to find a friend. Even above the love of women or riches or fame, friendship played the dominant role in the life and work of Istrati. He wanted to give himself to a friend who would do the same in return, and they would go together inseparably on the great adventure of life. He often fell into this sweet trap, but his friends betrayed him, and Istrati found himself entirely alone in the human desert. In this despairing condition he wrote to his spiritual father who alone stood upright and pure among the passions that tore and cheapened the whole of Europe. Istrati confessed all of his life to him and asked only for a good word in return. But Romain Rolland did not answer, and Istrati decided to kill himself.

He slit his throat. People gathered around. He was taken to a hospital. He wrestled with death, was saved, and fifteen days later, half-dead and half-healed, he was cast out into the streets again. In his pocket there was a letter he had written to the communist newspaper, *L'Humanité,* in which, hours before his suicide attempt, he saluted the Russian Revolution and the new world that would be born from the current sufferings of Russia. When the letter was found, the French police ordered the hospital to throw out this social rebel.

But in the streets Panait was now a happy man. He had received an answer from Romain Rolland. "I'm not interested," wrote the well fed and pure idealist, "in the fact that you are miserable, but only in the fact that the divine flame of the soul burns inside you. Don't write letters to me anymore. Write books."

Panait was encouraged. A fellow Rumanian, the shoemaker Ionescu, rescued him from the streets in Paris, put him in the basement of his shop, gave him paper, ink and a plate of food. Panait began to write. A few months later, *Kyra Kyralina* emerged, a work filled with passion, a carefree spirit and an unbridled love of life. The saintly prostitute obeys her god by reveling; fulfills her duty by distributing her kisses. A book as warm, throbbing, lively and soft as a human being. Among so many lifeless French romances, *Kyra Kyralina* sprang up like a true cry from a passionate throat. Romain Rolland saluted Istrati: "I read and remain astonished by the bursting of your genius. A fiery wind that blows across the plain. A confession of a new Gorkii of the Balkans."

When I knocked at the door to his room at the Hotel Passage in Moscow, I was happy that I would be seeing a "true human being." I had defeated the mistrust that possessed me every time I met a new person, and I was going to Istrati with true confidence. He was lying in bed ill, but when he saw me, he jumped up and cried out joyfully in Greek, *"Moré, kalós órises! Kalós órises, moré!"* (Hey! Welcome, welcome!)

The first contact, the most crucial, was cordial. Each of us looked at the other, attempting to divine and to sense each other like two great ants that feel one another with their antennae. The face of Istrati was thin, emaciated and deeply furrowed from his many sufferings. His hair, straight, gray and shiny, fell in disorder on his forehead like a child's. His eyes shone, tragic eyes full of guile and sweetness; his lips drooped hedonistically like a goat's. The physiognomy of a tormented and passionate Macedonian *comitadji* (rebel).

"I read your speech at the congress the other day," he blurted out. "I liked it. You really let them have it. The dumb Westerners think that they will be able to stop the war with their pacifistic little pens or, if war breaks out, the workers, supposedly illuminated by their propaganda, will rise and throw their guns away. Nonsense, nonsense! I know the workers well! They will creep into the slaughter and kill. You gave it to them! Whether we want it or not, a new world war will break out, and let's be ready!" He looked me straight in the eye, stretched out his bony hand and grasped my knee. He laughed: "They told me that you're a mystic, but I see that you have your head straight and you never get enough of fresh air. That's not a mystic, eh? How do I know? Ah! Words, words! The hell with them! Give me your hand!"

We clasped hands, laughing. Then he leaped out of bed. There was something absolutely wild about this man. Agile, sharp movements, rapacious eyes, a savage grace. He lit a little alcohol burner and put the coffeepot on. *"Ena metrio!"** he cried out in sing-song like a waiter. He remembered Greece; his Cephallonian blood came to a boiling point, and he began to sing some old songs that he had heard at the tavern of Kyrios Leonidas in the Greek quarter of Braila: "Oh, to be a butterfly, to fly near you . . ." Greece stirred in the depths of his being; his father's spirit rose within him, and he yearned like the prodigal son to return to Greece. With a Cephallonian impetuosity, he abruptly

---

* "Moderate in sweetness and strength," referring to Turkish/Greek coffee.

made a decision: "Hey, give me your hand again! Listen: I'll go back to Greece with you!" He grew tired, coughed, stretched on his bed again, slurping the last drops of his coffee.

We spoke of his work. The main character in all of his works, Adrien Zographi, is Istrati himself. Throughout his life as a tramp, he hears stories of love and freedom, and he retells them. He gives himself entirely to friendships that deceive him and to women who will betray him. In the midst of the cowardice and ignominy of today's life, he longs tremblingly to meet a soul who does not yield, a man who holds his head high, sets all his hopes on fire and turns the entire cycle of his fate into a conflagration. But Adrien is finally defeated because his passions are unbridled; he cannot bring them into a viable rhythm. His desires are undisciplined, his heart rebellious, his mind unable to order chaos.

"You're exactly like your Adrien," I said to him, laughing. "You're not a revolutionary, as you believe, only a man in revolt. The revolutionary has a system of thoughts and order. His actions are coherent, and he can control his heart. You are a rebel. It's very difficult for you to remain faithful to an idea. But now that you have stepped on Russian soil, you must put order in yourself; you must decide, you have responsibility."

"Leave me alone," Istrati shouted, as though I held him by the throat. And immediately, "Are you sure?" he asked in agony.

"I read your last article in *L'Humanité*. You are filled with indignation and disgust. You vow to renounce Western civilization forever, because it rots in injustice and infamy; and you are turning to the new land, to stay and work. I like this."

"Why do you like it? Are you a Marxist yourself?"

"Don't fear," I answered, laughing. "I like this decision

of yours because it's brave. The moment that you begin to reap and eat the fruit that every writer dreams of—fame, riches, women—you spit on them with disgust and leave. You abandon all comfortable security and throw yourself like a vagabond into a new adventure, the unaccommodating reality of Russia. That's why I like you."

Istrati had again sat up on his bed, lighting and putting out cigarettes restlessly; and I was enjoying stirring his blood. I thought that it would do him good.

"The Rumanian Adrien Zographi is dead," I said suddenly in good humor, holding his bony arm tenderly. "The Rumanian Adrien Zographi is dead. Long live the Bolshevik Adrien Zographi! Panait, it's time to get away from the narrow ghettos of Braila where we suffocate and to turn our hero loose on the vast Russian plains! The restlessness and the hope of man have increased; Adrien Zographi must become larger too. The narrow life of the individual must merge with the larger universal rhythm of Russia, which at last is acquiring coherence and faith. The time has come for the superior balance that Adrien sought in vain for so many years, a harmony that will bring together his life force and his wild, conflicting passions to be actualized, because there is now a foundation to build upon, not just the incoherent destiny of a rebellious individual, but the solid mass of a great people shaping its future."

"Enough of that!" shouted Istrati, unnerved. "Enough! What devil brought you? Here in Russia I contemplate the things you tell me day and night, but you don't ask me if I can do them. You shout, 'Jump!' but you don't ask me if I can."

"We'll see. Don't get nervous, Panayotaki," I answered quietly. "Aren't you yourself curious to see whether you can or cannot do it?"

"But this is not a game. How can you talk like that? It is a question of life or death."

"Life and death too are a game," I said and stood up. "A game, and whether we win or lose depends on such a moment."

"Why did you get up?"

"I must leave. I'm afraid I have tired you."

"You're going nowhere! You will stay. We'll eat together, and in the afternoon we'll go somewhere together."

"Where?"

"We'll see Gorkii. He sent me a message that he's expecting me. Today for the first time, I'll see this celebrated 'Istrati of Europe,'" his voice betraying a childlike envy for his great prototype.

He jumped from his bed in one leap, dressed, and we went out. He held me tightly by the arm.

"We'll become friends," he kept saying. "We'll become friends because I already feel the need to give you a punch in the face. You must know this: I cannot feel friendship without blows. We must from time to time get into a fight, break our heads. Do you hear? That's what love is."

We entered a restaurant and sat down. He uncorked a little bottle that was hanging from his neck like an amulet and poured olive oil from it over his food. Then he took out a little box containing pepper from his vest pocket and sprinkled it plentifully into the thick meat soup that they had served us. "Olive oil and pepper!" he said, licking his lips. "Just like in Braila!"

"To our meeting!" I said, lifting my filled glass. "A good merging, as we say in Crete!"

We ate in good spirits. Istrati was gradually remembering his Greek, and each time he resurrected a word, he clapped his hands joyfully like a child. "Welcome, welcome!" he shouted to each new word he remembered. "Welcome!"

First of all he remembered insults, curses, dirty words. He saw my scandalized face and burst into laughter. But he didn't lose his head at all; every once in a while he looked at his watch. Suddenly he sprang up. "It's time," he said. "Let's go."

He called the waiter, bought four bottles of good Armenian wine, stuffed his overcoat pockets with packages of *zakuski* (hors d'oeuvres), filled his cigarette case, and we started out.

Istrati was excited; he was going to see Gorkii for the first time. Surely there would be the expected embraces, the prepared table, tears and laughter, "a recognition of brothers." The smoke-filled room, the cries and cordial salutations— the complete romantic atmosphere that he loved.

"Where is he expecting you?" I asked.

"At Gosizdat." (Government Publishing House)

"Panait," I say to him, "you're moved."

He did not respond. He paced on nervously. There were many people at the vast chambers of Gosizdat, faces from all the races of the Soviet Union. The director was a huge young Tatar with a black beard and languorous eyes, like those of heavy anthropomorphic lions in Oriental tapestries.

We went up a staircase. I looked at my new friend with side glances. I was pleased to watch his tall, lanky body, his overworked laborer's hands, his insatiable eyes.

"Panait," I said with indiscreet insistence, "you're nervous."

"Yes," he said as if bored. "Why do you ask?"

"Can you, now that you will see Gorkii, restrain yourself? Refrain from starting with embraces and shouts?"

"No!" he responded, irritated. "No, I'm not a cold Englishman. I'm a Greek, a Cephallonian! How many times do I have to tell you? I shout, I embrace, I give myself. You can pretend to be an Englishman . . . And to tell you another thing," he added a second later, "I would prefer to be alone. Your company annoys me."

"I know it," I said, laughing. "But I don't want to miss the spectacle: how the universally celebrated Istrati meets the Gorkii of the Balkans."

The teasing words were still hanging on my lips when Gorkii appeared at the top of the staircase, a cigarette stuck on his lips. He was a very tall, thick-boned man with small blue eyes, hollow cheeks, protruding facial bones and sad, restless lips that were incredibly embittered. I had never seen such sorrow on a man's lips. Istrati recognized him as soon as he saw him; he scaled the steps three at a time and grasped his hand.

"Panait Istrati!" he shouted, ready to fall on Gorkii's broad shoulders.

Gorkii quietly stretched out his hand and looked at Istrati attentively; his face did not show the least joy or curiosity. He watched Istrati silently, and then a few moments later he said, "Let's go inside." He led the way with a calm, wide stride; Istrati followed nervously, the necks of the wine bottles and the packages of *zakuski* protruding from the pockets of his overcoat.

We sat in a small office filled with people. Gorkii spoke only Russian. The conversation began with some difficulty. Istrati, embarrassed and emotional, began to speak. I do not remember what he said, but it did not matter. What was important was the fire of his words, the tone of his voice, his expansive gestures and his burning eyes.

Gorkii responded calmly and somberly in a sweet, even voice, continually lighting his Russian cigarettes. He spoke of his childhood, working as a baker in Nizhnii-Novgorod, and about the ardent thirst with which he read books under an oil lamp or in the bright light of the summer moon.

His bitter smile gave his quiet speech a tragic depth. You sensed a man who had suffered much and who was still in agony, a man who had seen such terrible atrocities that neither the grand Soviet celebrations and ovations nor honors and fame could ever erase the constant flow of incurable sorrow that lay behind his blue eyes.

"My greatest teacher," he said, "has been Balzac. Balzac! I remember, when reading his fiction, how I would raise the page toward the light and look at it with astonishment. How can this page embody such life force, such power, I would say. Where is the great secret hidden?"

"And Dostoevskii? And Gogol?" I asked.

"No, no. Of the Russians, only one. Leskov. No one else." He paused for a second. "But above all, life itself. I have suffered much, and I have much loved the human being who suffers. Nothing else." And he became silent, following the blue smoke of his cigarette with his half-closed eyes.

Panait took the bottles out of his pocket and placed them on the table; then he took out the packages one by one, but did not have the courage to open them. He sensed that it was not appropriate, that the atmosphere he wanted had not been created. He expected something else, a different, more fraternal meeting, a chance for the two combatants who had suffered and were triumphant to drink and shout, to say great words, to shed tears of joy, to dance and celebrate their final bloody victory.

But Gorkii was still plunged in his tormented, desperate struggle. He watched the Soviet miracle around him but did not harbor any illusions. His sight remained clear; his glance, penetrating and luminous.

He stood up. Some youths called for him, and he went into in the next room with them. They discussed a new program of propaganda, lectures, tours, a new magazine . . . Istrati and I remained alone. "Panait," I said, "how does the teacher seem to you?"

With a nervous twist he opened a bottle of wine. "We

don't have glasses," he said. "Can you drink from the bottle?"

"I can." I took the bottle. "To your health, Panait," I said. "Each human being is a solitary animal of the desert, the abyss all around each one, and there is no bridge. Do not be bitter, my little Panait. Don't you know how it is?"

"Drink fast," he said irritably, "so that I can drink too. I'm thirsty."

We drank the light and fragrant Armenian *naparauli*. He wiped his lips. "I know it," he said, "but I always forget."

"This is your great value, Panait. If you didn't know it, alas, you would be stupid. If you knew it and didn't forget it, alas, you would be cold and insensitive. While now you're a true human being, warm, contradictory, a bundle of hopes and disappointments and later again new hopes. And so on until death. Reason will never kill your heart."

"Let's go now. We have seen Gorkii. It's finished!" He put the bottles back in his pockets. We gathered up the packets of *zakuski* and left. In the street he said, "He seemed very cold to me. To you?"

"To me, very bitter. Inconsolable. I never expected so much pain. I never saw such a smile, so much more bitter than a desperate cry or a sob or death itself. He had triumphed. He wrote brilliant books, got rich and famous, married a beautiful woman. A princess, I believe. He had children and grandchildren, and finally, the most important thing, he saw his dream come true: the liberation of Russia. And all these things did not lighten his heart."

"He should have shouted, drunk or wept to unburden himself," Panait groaned with indignation.

"There was a Moslem emir," I replied, "who, after his people were killed at war, decreed to his tribe: 'Do not cry, do not shout—do not lessen your pain.' This is the most proud, the most harsh discipline that a man can impose on himself. For this reason I liked Gorkii very much."

Panait didn't say a word. He murmured something angrily and looked at me almost hatefully. And suddenly he grasped my arm, his hand trembling.

■ FROM MOSCOW
TO BATUM

■ A FEW DAYS LATER about twenty of us writers from all over the world decided to leave Moscow and head toward the shores of the Black and Caspian seas. With us was the congenial Japanese poet, Akita, who was always smiling; the wise and impetuous Argentine professor, Quintana; and the Hungarian writer, Holitscher. Istrati and I were by now inseparable.

We left snow-covered Moscow behind us and plunged into the serene plains toward Kharkov. We got to know each other with care and curiosity. We spoke many languages. We strove to divide ourselves into various groups: orthodox Marxists, communist sympathizers, post-communists.

On the second day Panait blurted out, "I'm bored with them! Let's isolate ourselves in a compartment. Only the two of us."

All these intellectuals of the East and the West felt like strangers to us. We circulated among them but could not connect with any of them. To us the Westerners seemed cold, analytical, full of pride for their "civilization"; the Asians, on the other hand, were excessively silent and incomprehensible. And so the two of us remained alone again, two souls born between East and West; one at the delta of the Danube, the other on Crete.

Closed in our compartment, we spoke about Greece and Rumania. Entire hours, during which Istrati talked about his life, seemed to be moments passing with lightning speed. I had never met a man who recounted his life with such fascinating absorption. You heard him and said to yourself, how beautiful and bizarre life is! May his mouth

237

never stop talking! A Near Eastern color to his stories, sensuality, human warmth, love for life, women, the earth and man.

One of Istrati's heroes, Kosmas, would open his arms and the earth would shrink. He spoke to his sensible brother: "Speak, Elias. If you are right, look out!" "You can kill me, Kosmas, but I'm right." "Then get up and turn your back on me!"

Elias got up. Kosmas jumped on him, piggyback, and turned him around in all directions. Sweat dripped from the nose of Elias. No one spoke. Suddenly Elias staggered and fell to the ground. Kosmas left him there, sat cross-legged and smoked while looking at his brother: "Speak now, Elias. I permit you. Speak now, o logic!"

Such are the heroes of Istrati and such is he himself. A demonic fever consumes them. Astride the steed of logic, they wander across the world in their madness. I looked at Istrati and mused, filled with emotion: "How did this multicolored bird—the soul of Istrati—fall into my hands? What happiness is this!" Our humble train compartment was filled with wings.

From time to time I cast a glance out of the window to watch the snow, the frozen rivers, the whitened upright cedars, the smoking *izbas* (peasant huts). But soon I would turn my eyes toward my companion, and once again hang on his every word.

The soul of Istrati is like Princess Scheherazade who, like everyone else, is condemned to die. But before she dies, in order to prolong her life, she begins to tell interminable tales. . . . I sit like the Sultan in *A Thousand and One Nights,* and I listen. Voluptuousness, bitterness, woman, ideas, hunger, revelry—all merge passionately inside this soul that had composed the sacred, tumultuous, carefree, shameless face of Kyra Kyralina: life.

Snow-covered Russia passed by us right and left. The

grains of wheat were stirring and thriving underneath, the wheat that feeds the body and the other wheat that nurtures the soul: Pushkin, Gogol, Tolstoi, Dostoevskii, the great loaves of bread. And now a new harvest from this fecund soil: Lenin, Trotskii, Stalin. A fertile, inexhaustible land, blood-drenched, deeply furrowed, filled with seed.

It was night when we arrived at the great industrial city of Kharkov. We went to the opera. *William Tell* was playing in the Ukrainian language with Ukrainian music. We had Ukrainian food for supper. We listened to joyous Ukrainian drinking songs.

In the morning we toured a giant complex of buildings, an entire city, constructed to house the syndicated workers of Kharkov, the Palace of Labor. Simple, bare, contemporary architecture without adornment of any kind. Everything adapted for the day's necessities without lyricism. The Palace of Labor was naked like the truth, steeped in light. It was comfortable, solid without heaviness, structured entirely in steel, cement and glass. "Such must be our writing style," I thought. "Such must be our lifestyle!"

We departed again by night. Scheherazade resumed her tales. The hours passed. Every so often we opened the door of our compartment and friends entered. Holitzer described his Asian journeys and spoke of Tagore, whom he found surrounded by dark-complexioned, delirious women burning aromatic fragrances at his feet. In a high-pitched, unpleasant voice, a Chinese man spoke in English about the Chinese poor. The Japanese poet, Akita, sat in a corner, silent, smiling, smoking.

Snow-covered mountains appeared in the distance. The plain moved like a wave before us. The snow was now spotty on the ground, and by evening the soil was a bare, dark brown. We spent one more night on the road, and in the light drizzle of the next day, we arrived at the Caspian— dark, odorless, graceless with her muddy waves. Leaning out of the windows, we stared at everything. We were entering the celebrated capital of petroleum, the capital of the Moslem-Soviet republic of Azerbaizhan, Baku.

It was raining, a biting cold. We waded in the mud, inside a forest of drilling towers. The air was greasy, the earth vomited oil. Black-green bogs everywhere. Deep wells, engines pumping the precious dirty liquid from the bowels of the earth, filling thousands of meters of pipes, which start out at the Caspian and reach the Black Sea, from Baku to Batum. Here in this contemporary inferno, blackened workers, oiled like rats, struggled to earn their daily bread, smeared by fumes and petroleum.

Our Western companions, taking out their notebooks to make notations, asked the workers about their daily wages. They were glad that the lot of the worker had improved. I thought about how much industrial civilization has complicated our lives, how ugliness and meaningless toil have become oppressive realities in the contemporary world. Anyone who sees this terrible inferno with flowery optimism is certainly naive. Whoever watches it without indignation is a shameless cynic. He who sees it with anger feels his heart torn with pain and struggles to find some salvation from this hell. How can we make our lives simpler? How can we shift the battlefront? How can we become content without material riches by enriching and disciplining our inner life?

For the evening's entertainment the intellectuals of Azerbaizhan had organized a local concert of Near Eastern music. Mandolins, ouds and lutes. Old men, their faces hidden behind tambourines, singing. Handsome boys with painted eyes and fingernails, swaying their bodies and humming *amanes,* Eastern airs that express the passionate longings of the insatiable heart. Suddenly in this voluptuous air, a girl of about twelve leaped into the dance. She was decked from head to toe with golden trimmings and paillettes; her dark face, her painted hands and her tiny feet were shining. She danced quietly without violent movements, almost as if she were motionless. Her teeth sparkled, white and pointed like those of a small animal.

Dance and the starry heavens, I believe, are the two most sublime spectacles the eyes of man can enjoy. Some years ago, I saw the two great dancers, Sent M'ahesa and Pavlova. Entering into their whirlwind, I felt that the man of clay can transcend the limits of life and death. But this little savage dancer of Baku with her transfigured dance gave me the supreme pleasure, the essence of the dance. The immobile heart in the eye of the storm.

I turned to my side; Istrati was weeping. The Japanese poet, completely pale, was no longer smiling; our Western companions smiled ironically. An abyss separates, I felt once again, the Oriental and the Western soul. When they meet a stranger, the primitive men of Africa don't ask him, "What tribe are you?" but, "How do you dance?" For them dance is the most profound characteristic of a people. Two human beings who similarly become ecstatic or weep when experiencing a dance are brothers; all others are infidels and strangers.

During the rest of the journey, this flaming flower of the land of petroleum danced in my mind; and before I knew it, we had arrived at the capital of Georgia and the city with the most handsome people in the world: Tbilisi.

Full of emotion, I stepped again on the soil that a few years earlier had devoured a beloved friend. The bitter memory of him merged unrequitedly with the women who sat at our table that evening. Ah! The sudden leap among the tables of the most beautiful woman of Tbilisi, Nadia Bahenzhe the dancer. Once again I voluptuously tasted the divine Armenian wine; and we descended into a cellar, three Georgians, Istrati, myself and five women. As three blind musicians joined us with oud, tambourine and flute, I felt the plumed deadly snake of the East winding itself around my chest, licking my ears. Everything—communism, the proletariat, class struggle—instantly sank at that moment into the velvety dark eyes of the primordial serpent.

At daybreak we separated. Istrati and I roamed the streets. The bazaar of Tbilisi was opening. We went to a little *chainaia* and drank tea. Someone lit narghile pipes with Persian tobacco for us, and we serenely resumed our sweet conversation. Our hearts grew lighter. The world became beautiful; Tbilisi, a paradise. On the sidewalk outside, the sun was rising on the mountaintop. Two Moslems, kneeling on straw mats, raised their slim arms toward the heavens. Their gaunt sunburned faces sank toward Mecca.

That evening we left for Batum; the next morning an agitated greenish-blue Black Sea stretched before us. We traversed the public garden with its thick foliage and its broad-leaved banana trees. Soon we stretched out on the sun-drenched shore. A strong wind, the strong smell of brine, the waves galloping like the frothy-mouthed horses of Homer. Akita, blissful and always silent, gathered shells. For the first time the Scandinavian poet opened his mouth to utter an inarticulate cry. All of us, full of happiness, rolled on the pebbly sand.

"Do you know why I am full of joy when I roll on the ground?" Istrati asked me, a diabolic glint in his small brown eyes.

"I know," I answered him, laughing.

"You know?" he shouted, terrified. "Tell me then!"

"Because our journey is over, and soon we will be separated from our companions!"

Istrati leaped toward me and embraced me. "You'll choke me!" I shouted, trying to disentangle myself. But he held me gently in his bony embrace and said tenderly, "You're a devil of a man, you! A devil, and I like you."

The journey was over. Russia, from snow-covered Moscow to the warm sun of Batum, blazed deathless inside of us. It was as though we had journeyed from one end of our souls to the other.

■ CRUCIFIED RUSSIA

■ ONE DAY I WAS LEAVING a communist meeting, together with a European friend. We stepped out into the clean air, breathing deeply. Inside the huge smoke-filled room the workers had harangued endlessly. Inert, sturdy peasants clasped their calloused hands and twirled their fingers as they listened to the interminable speeches. The same key phrases, the same correct, heavy-handed dogma, the same monotonous winding up of the people's souls. For the delicate intellectuals, such endless repetition of so many cliches is unbearable. But history is not made by the delicate; mankind does not go forward led by the highbrowed elite. The masses have a thick skull, and it must be hit and hit again with a persistent and rhythmic force if it is to crack open.

Ah, the Spirit! Always superior to the wretched details that irritate us, it struggles without disgust and with profound reverence to knead the body and mind, to throw into terrible convulsions all this mud we are made of and give it shape! With sleeves rolled up and with broad perspectives that can easily absorb both beauty and ugliness, the Spirit is the kneading worker who bends over a rough-hewn mankind. How many of the masses will be enlightened? How many will escape their private hell? How many will comprehend the universal law and follow it freely? A tiny minority. And yet all of them together, menacing, starving, laughing, become combatants for the light which may never illuminate them.

I turned to my friend, who was sighing. As I laughed, I pressed his shoulder. "Hey, comrade," I shouted, "you seem to be coming out of hell, and you haven't as yet gotten used to the sweet light of earth's purgatory. You are stum-

bling into those who pass by us. What are you thinking?"

"I'm disgusted with human beings! That's what I'm thinking. The Idea deteriorates when it touches them. Inside our mind it rises intact, filled with light and love; but as soon as it descends upon the streets, becomes public, it wears makeup, flirts, plays in the dark, becomes belly and womb. I don't like it."

"What would you like the Idea to be, comrade? A virgin spinster residing in a cobwebbed chamber of your mind? The Idea, you said it right, is like a woman; her belly was created in order to eat; her womb in order to give birth. What could an Idea achieve if it remained inside a wise head? It would wither, go stale and die, sterile and malcontent."

"It's better for it to die pure than to be prostituted going public. I lived with people; I had an Idea and I wanted to turn it into action. I agreed, for its sake, to surrender my most precious possession, my freedom, and I placed myself under the oppressive yoke of the state. For three years I fought against this stupid, inert, bankrupt machine. I struggled to do as much good as I could, but every day I became more and more disappointed; I began to lose my faith in the struggle, in the worth of man.

"The measures and actions that could have saved a number of people moved so slowly, so laboriously, that all these souls that should have been saved were perishing. Perhaps, if I had not attempted their salvation, they would have survived somehow; but now they are lost. Any creative breath was considered rebellious within the stagnant party line. It stirred an inherent evil, which rose against it. When the evil ones, who often hated one another, saw the good, the great enemy in front of them, they banded together and became one like brothers. I observed how an idea was born within me and how it came in contact with those who should carry it out. How they distorted it and cheapened it; how they changed its nature and its purpose! And I was seething with indignation and disgust.

"In time I came to the conclusion that it wasn't the fault of the people but of the state machinery. Many of my young friends had given themselves to the struggle with energy and with high and pure ideals. But slowly the wheel of the great machine ran them over. They fell into compromises, became comfortable, perished.

"At the risk of dying of hunger, I left so that I would not slowly become one of the comfortable without realizing it. Today's state is the great enemy, I argued. It must be wiped out!

"And I went to the workers, not to all of them but to the few—the best—those I had seen who were restless like myself. Like me they were thirsty for light, justice, love. Or so I thought. I gave my entire self in a struggle to organize them, to make our duty clearer and more conscious, to help them rise above small passions and gross desires, to relocate their center of gravity from the belly to their hearts . . . But in vain. They too were condemned by their small human passions. And if they agreed to be organized, they did so in order to charge toward a richer table, where the bourgeoisie feast today, so they too can feast like them. A worship of the belly, the phallus and the womb. They will begin the belly-feast too, I said to myself. They will sing the same songs, and the same stupor will possess them."

"Stupor?"

"Yes, the lethargy that comes after too much eating. The heaviness in the brain and sleepiness." He became silent for a moment, as though unnerved, and then continued: "Eh, comrade, don't you see that before they take power, the masses must be enlightened about why they are struggling and must be made to understand that their ultimate goal is not a material and satiated well-being but a transubstantiation of the food of life into spirit. In their fantasies all these workers of yours keep seeing steaming roast meat and women undressing. How can you expect such people to regenerate the world?"

"And how do you think, my distinguished comrade," I retorted, "the world can be regenerated? With what bait do you think you will excite the masses? Your nerves are very delicate, and you give too much of a Christian value to the purity of the Idea. Go and put on the monk's robes, become an ascetic so you don't have to look at people anymore. Or if you prefer, sit down so that you too can write about an ideal society inhabited, naturally, by people without a belly and without gender, neither male nor female, who are like pawns. And give them as their goal a geometric problem to solve. What are you doing here among the wretched, restless creatures who have a belly, a phallus or a womb?

"In my mind I run over everything you have said. I don't agree with any of it. You want the masses to be educated first, and then, enlightened, they'll rise to fight a revolution. But when did a majority start a revolution? Always the few, organized around an idea or a passion, bring as many others as they can into their ranks with the lure of a sure and quick recompense. They all rise in a frenzy, and fighting begins. Defeated at first, they fight again, are victorious, rise to power. They step upon freedoms, terrorize, commit injustices, until they solidify their authority. When in power they begin to be afraid again. They identify an opposition, but do not consider it dangerous. Freedom returns—blessed be her name—and with it, indefinable as yet but certain the possibilities of the next overthrow of power.

"Blood has always been a necessary initiation. If I had it in my hands to choose the manner in which a new idea could triumph—with blood or with peaceful means—I would choose blood. Not because I am bloodthirsty, but because I know that the more violent the opposition to evil is, the more bloody the struggle, the more powerful is the surge upward, the more stable the victory.

"You see, 'God'—let's give this name to the dark forces—is not a kindly head of family, as we naively have thought. He is cruel; he is not interested in individuals. He kills, gives birth, kills again, gives birth again. He goes forward without consideration for our virtues and desires. You don't like it that way, eh? You would want him to be gentle, with a human face, white robes and clean hands, a kind of wise ruler who holds the scales of justice and distributes the bread and the brains equally and justly among man. But he doesn't check with us. He descends as he pleases, holds on to anything he likes—the belly, the heart, the mind—and stirs humans to revolt.

"The first incarnation of this sacred Spirit is chaos. With time the fever falls, passions abate, the combating forces balance out. The new seed emerges from blood and tears. Eternal happiness, peace, justice? Neither now nor ever, thank God! Injustice again, hunger and misery. A new cry is heard from below, the new army of God, the new oppressed.

"Justice and happiness are a state of slumber, contrary to the high law of life. They're only chimeras, but they push the masses higher, elevating life by stages. Injustice and hunger from time to time destroy the hardening social order; they engender new desires, hates and hopes; they awaken the blood and create new visions. The oppressed then charge out, possessed by the new myth, and struggle to overthrow the oppressors so that they can bring—so they sincerely and naively believe—happiness and justice. And here are the highest moments of man: the moments of surge. Mankind no longer stagnates in the bogs of slavery. Nor does victory and well-being solidify. Man continues to surge upward—and all of life with him."

My friend burst into shouting: "And when man rises to

the top—eats, overeats and declines—other masses, you say, will spring from below. And this eternally? My mind does not accept it. It wants to see an end; to stand and rest there."

"The miserable mind of man gets weary. You are right. It wants to set a goal and reach it, in order to rest. But life is restless, without beginning and end; it always turns on its wheel, the flesh and the spirit of man. The best minds recognize this law and fall terrified into silence. Others attempt to love life with Bacchic intoxication. Still others oppose this terrible law of life and struggle to force it into the mold of their hearts or minds.

"This is how I see the struggle of man, how the cycles of history reveal themselves to me. And this is how we must see today's rise of the proletariat. And we must bend our heads in reverence over Russia, because she is the pioneer in the world today; she opens the way, in the midst of hunger and blood, to bring life higher.

"An apocryphal story in the Bible states that the beloved disciple John, as he was weeping in front of his crucified teacher, saw an astonishing vision: The cross was not of wood but of light; and on the cross, not one man but thousands of men, women and children were groaning and dying. John stood terrified, unable to focus on the face on the immense cross. The innumerable faces kept changing and flowing. Slowly the faces were blurred and all that remained was a great crucified cry.

"Today this vision of John stirs before us. The whole of Russia, millions of men, women and children, are crucified and suffer; they are vanishing, their faces blurred to our vision; you cannot distinguish a particular shape; and from the innumerable deaths only the cry will remain. And thus, comrade, will the world be saved again. And what does it mean, 'saved'? To find a new justification in life because the old has lost its meaning and cannot support the human edifice. A new savior comes; that is, a perfect receptor and at the same time emitter of his age, and he creates a new illusion. And he does not create alone; his heart gathers all the scattered parts of illusion with its anxieties and hopes and embodies in the simple Word the rough, faceless, inarticulate needs of the people.

"And suddenly—it seems sudden, but in fact it takes long, persistent maturing—the Word becomes flesh again and marches on the earth. The forerunners see him and are terrified. The prophets—poets, sages, visionaries—cry out, 'We never wanted slaughter and famine. We sought justice, freedom and love!' They never realized that these three daughters of man—justice, freedom and love—always have their soles, ankles, calves and knees sunk in blood. And the prophets shout and protest and denounce; but the Spirit, superior to the prophets, blows violently upon them; it leaves them behind and proclaims a mobilization across the whole earth.

"The Spirit is greater than the prophets, greater than leaders, greater than Russia."

"But what if this cry of Russia that you describe does not manage to formulate itself into the articulate Word? And not only the cry of Russia, but of the whole earth? It isn't only the Russians and only the workers of the world who struggle; the whole earth is seized by pains like a woman in labor. And if the child that you seek is born, will all these struggles be in vain?"

"When a man on a mountaintop desires with resolve," I answered, "his desire will make a mystical descent and will conquer the cities. Today the sensible, the comfortable, the scribes and pharisees, look at this crucified nation and laugh scornfully: 'Russia is finished. She's lost!' Because reason believes only in what it sees and cannot discern the invisible forces of the martyrdom. But as Christ said, the seed of wheat, in order to become new grain, must first descend into the earth and die. Russia is like the seed, like a great Idea.

"And until there comes—and it surely will come—the Word that will solidify the cry of Russia, the cry will work as an indestructible force on the generations of man, and in the completion of time, it will be incarnated. Let us look at Russia, comrade, with patience and trust."

My comrade again gave me an ironic look. He had become irritated; his voice hissed: "And what shall we call this heretical way in which you see communism?"

"Call it what you like. You still have a need for labels? This is what my heart senses and my mind attempts to clarify. And I would like my actions to follow the road that my heart and mind point to. But in order for your order-seeking Western mind to be satisfied, let it give a name to this heretical faith of mine. Let it be called 'post-communism.'"

■ THE NEW POMPEII

■ SOME YEARS AGO on a spring day, I felt an unexpected, inhuman joy while strolling through the ruins of Pompeii. The sky was lightly clouded; the spring vegetation had covered the thresholds and courtyards; the streets and roads were the way I liked them—deserted. Open houses without doors, without locks, without inhabitants. I was happy going in and out of them. Taverns, temples, theaters, bathhouses, marketplaces—all were deserted. Not just deserted; for there was something that gave me an even greater joy—they were devastated. On the walls of the rich houses, you could still see the washed-out paintings of idiotic, plump, amorous children and of cocks, dogs, and gods in shameless animal mountings.

A voice suddenly rose inside me. It was not my own voice. The voice of someone more worthy and more barbaric than myself had shouted, "May my God one day grant me to be in Berlin, in Paris, in London, speaking Russian with the comrades!" I shivered as I heard this wild cry. Truly it was not I who shouted but some terrible descendant, entrenched in my entrails.

The cellars of Pompeii were full—newly-bathed women, impudent and sterile; rapacious men, satiated, slothful and exhausted from merriment. All sorts of gods—Greek, African, Asian—were thrown together in a mass of egalitarian wretchedness. They were a degenerate and cowardly group, who apportioned the offerings and souls of mortals among themselves with cunning smiles. The entire decadent city stretched out at the feet of Vesuvius in carefree abandon.

To me, the whole earth today appears like Pompeii a little

252

before the eruption. What is the use, I thought, of such an earth with depraved women, with faithless men, with its factories and stock exchanges, with its diseases? Why should all these clever merchants and shopkeepers be alive? Why should children be raised to sit at their fathers' benches in the taverns, courtrooms and whorehouses? All this materialism blocks the way of the spirit. Whatever strength the spirit once possessed was spent in the creation of a great civilization—ideas, religions, paintings, music, song, action. Now it is tired out. Let us open a new channel for the spirit!

Within my chest I felt a savage bird of prey, famished and without love for humans. And I saw with a clear, piercing eye—like the eye of the vulture—the point to which human history has brought mankind; that I happened to be born in a crucial age, when one world staggers toward collapse while another, full of anger and unspent strength, rises.

Such moments are the most fecund in human history, and I am tasting this one slowly and gluttonously. The chimera illumines those who charge out for the new creation. The others, sluggish and drugged from good living, hear the clamor and turn their heads. At first they laugh, then turn pale; they bend anxiously and see their slaves, workers, cooks, rising up. A sacred moment! The greatest feats of thought and action take place during such moments of impetuous ascension.

Whenever I struggle to embrace, as completely as I can, the cycles of human destiny and to divine the wind that propels upward and downward all these waves of humanity, I am seized by a holy terror. And then I struggle to see better, and to focus my glance on the small, difficult to make out arc of the immense circle, the epoch in which I live, and I try to perceive clearly the contemporary duty of man. It is only in this way that a human being will be able, in the ephemeral moment of his life, to accomplish something significant, working in accordance with the great rhythm.

For years now an indomitable faith strengthens and illumines my inner being: A Combatant ascends from inor-
ganic matter to plants, from plants to animals, from animals
to humans, struggling for freedom. In every crucial historical epoch this Combatant assumes a new profile; his face
today: leader of the global proletariat.

A new faith, which has no relation to recognized religions, sweeps the earth today. Slowly, imperceptibly,
human relations change. Morality, education, love, the relationship between the worker and work, the individual and
society, are gropingly striving to take a new shape.

The moment we are going through is a crucial and painful one. Man has grasped the wheels of the machine and
cannot let go. He has unleashed the demonic energies of
matter and can no longer bring them under the mystical
essence of his soul. The Spirit that conquered matter is itself
becoming matter; it becomes an accessory of the machine
and follows its course.

Many visionaries propose: "Our only salvation is to return to the simplicity of former times, to diminish our
needs, to abolish the complexities of contemporary life that
do not allow us to be free for a moment. Only in this way
can each piece of matter that we work on be filled with soul
again. How did they work in the Middle Ages? Stone, wood
and metal became lighter, alive; became spirit under the
patient loving breath of the craftsman. Let us follow the
same road ourselves; let us go back!"

Romantic superficialities. To simplify our lives, to turn
back to the Middle Ages, to the love of the early Christians,
or even further back to the primitive tribal communities—
all these are dreams of impotent men. Life does not turn
backward; it advances, smashing all those who cannot follow its lead. Let us go with it. And more: Let us thrust our
strength behind it so that it can go further. Only in this way

can we help contemporary life pass through this period of mechanization and liberate itself. The solution is always ahead, never behind.

Today's worker cannot love his work as one did in the Middle Ages. In that time, he worked his materials with love and patience. His reward was not just his wages, but more importantly, the recognition of the men and the society that commissioned his work. And he felt the even greater joy that came from creating a beautiful and useful product.

Today the worker feels no personal rapport with his work. How could this be otherwise? For years he works from morning to evening, going through the same motions. He mechanically executes a small detail without concerning himself with the whole or the detail itself, or with the beauty or usefulness of his task. Why should he care? He works, and his personal contribution has no fundamental worth as far as the quality of the product is concerned. And furthermore, he hates the work that he does because he senses that it reduces him to a machine that kills his body and his soul. He also hates it because he knows that all of his efforts fatten and enrich his inhuman capitalist bosses. He, his wife, his children, his grandchildren, will continue to deteriorate as human beings. Consequently, his only care is to shorten his work hours as much as possible and to increase his wages as much as he can.

Do not say to the worker in order to console him that he works for the good of the community and of the state. He detests a society that unjustly distributes the benefits of his labor and that institutionalizes injustice, cruelty, the exploitation of man and the degradation of woman. He dislikes a state that supports a class structure that exploits the sweat and hunger of its people to enrich itself.

What must be done? As the life rhythm accelerates, it becomes necessary for numerous people to work in factories, in mines, at sea. It is not possible for the worker to return to the simplicity and love of the Middle Ages. And yet he cannot accept today's injustices and horrible working conditions. No promises or reward in a future life can lure him. Nothing can any longer give him patience and perseverance. Hell is on this earth; paradise is here as well. This is the place for recompense and punishment.

In the dark, tortured bodies of the workers, new dreams are thriving amid the misery and hunger. Old virtues are displaced, new ones are born and old hopes grow pale and vanish; the homeland takes on a new face. Slowly, in these bodies that are weary of toil, a new decalogue begins to emerge. Traditional marriage loses its prestige and grace; there is no time for the married couple to be together without concerns—economic worries, hard work, ignorance, drink, children, constantly harass them. How can a man and a woman look at each other in serene abandon for endless hours as they did in the stories of times past?

Children go to work at a young age; their tender bodies become deformed; their souls lose their innocence. Women leave their homes at daybreak, work with other women, other men, and return home exhausted. The ancestral fireplace, ancient center of the family, is extinguished. Woman loses her mystique and her true tangible essence.

The homeland is no longer the most beloved corner of the earth. The worker, tied to the factory and the machine, relocates from place to place, feeling that what the bourgeois called homeland is for him the fields, the apartment buildings and factories that are owned by those he hates. And so he becomes "liberated" from traditional notions of homeland and family. And it is not only the workers who are the instruments of today's machines. Little by little other classes of the poor are swept by the same whirlwind of change. People depend on themselves alone, no longer on God, homeland or family. They know that if they do not have the strength to work they will starve to death; the only thing that can save them is the skill of their hands. God and homeland are accomplices of their oppressors.

Is there anything else that can save them? Little by little they are beginning to understand that one person alone has no power but if he joins others like himself, if they become many and organized, then the others—the rich, the exploiters, the enemies—will fear them and respect their rights. And so organizing begins; the weak, the oppressed and the hungry join forces in a fated army that grows and becomes ferocious.

Beyond national borders, they meet in secret cells, new catacombs where workers of different nations and tongues commune with the "body and blood" of the new society, the working class. Just as the early Christians did not ask if one was a Jew, a Greek, a free person or a slave but simply divided humanity into believers and nonbelievers, so too the new faithful have formed a new brotherhood: the comrades. Common hopes and hatreds join them together. They train themselves like all believers; individuality is subsumed to the whole. They are disciplined because they know that they are an army preparing for assault.

And yet there are still many peasants willing to risk their lives for the homeland because their fields are in it. There are also level-headed homeowners and affluent landowners, who are well organized and sit around conference tables. When the great moment arrives, they will oppose change with as much struggle and blood as is necessary to preserve their privileges. But the momentum of the times moves against them. They have eaten, drunk, created their world, and now they have weakened again. The last phase of their duty is to disappear. Seeing the collective reality in a historical perspective, we sense what our duty is today: war against the class that has completed its task and is now an obstacle to the advance of the spirit; collaboration with the proletarians without any reservations. They are hungry, they want to improve their lot, and they are right; they hate, they want to kill, and they are right. And with time, this heavy mass will lighten up; it will become spirit and create a new civilization.

In the midst of the savage groans of the masses, learn to distinguish clearly the cry of the Combatant who is rising. If you lived in earlier times, you would recognize this cry among the masses of the landlords, the small industrialists, the merchants who were moving upward, and you would have allied yourself with them. An eternal surge greater than man drives mankind and transforms it as much as it can—as much as humans can—and then they are spent, it discards them and attaches itself to new unworked material. This force propels everything that can rise and bear fruit and crushes all that is useless.

In different epochs and in a myriad of forms, this is the eternal thrust that stirs and moves life forward. And we have the duty to collaborate with it, to help it along. In our time this energy has merged with those who toil and are hungry. Today the masses are the raw material of this historic force.

This relentless endeavor cannot be understood by the masses themselves. They live it, however, by giving it different names that make it intelligible to their still unenlightened minds and suit it to their desperate needs. They call it happiness, justice, equality, brotherhood, peace . . . But the invisible Combatant does not get trapped in the nets spread out by the masses. Harsh and uncompromising, it struggles to overcome this flesh and matter that beckon it, and from all these contemporary cries of slavery, it creates a Word of freedom.

■ GENERAL OVERVIEW

■ THIS IS SOVIET RUSSIA TODAY. Without prejudice, with all the emotion and clarity of mind that I could muster, I tried to see her and to live her present ferment. I often imposed discipline on my heart in order to let my mind see and speak freely. Often I did not see what I wanted to see and I said so. Often I saw what I expected and I said so. I did not consent to hide either the good or the bad. I endeavored to follow the most difficult of all roads, that is, the most honest.

Now at the end of the journey, after reviewing the whole experience, after putting details aside and concentrating all my attention on the nucleus that is still forming, I have arrived at the following conclusions:

The historical moment that we are going through is exceptionally crucial for mankind; one world is crumbling, another world is rising. Over a large sector of the globe the proletarian class, its vanguard, has already taken power.

Naturally this change has not taken place without violence; this is always the case in history; the history of man drips with blood; the way in which mankind moves forward on the earth may be in accord with our idiosyncrasies or it may offend our morality. But there is no other way.

On the 7th of November it was not one revolution that broke out but two essentially different ones: the revolution of the peasants against feudal lords, a revolt clearly of the petite bourgeoisie; and the revolution of the workers against the bourgeoisie, a revolt clearly socialist.

At the time of the common danger, the two revolutionary currents fought together. When the common enemy disappeared, however, the two allies—peasants and workers—

separated, and a savage undeclared war broke out between them. And Soviet Russia came to the brink of the precipice.

At this crucial moment one man, Lenin, saved the Soviet Idea. He understood—a simple truth which other leaders at crucial moments usually do not understand—that there was only one way for the Idea to survive: Compromise; adapt the still-fluid, contradictory, disordered reality. Many solutions proved to be only temporary. Various persistent bloody measures for the solution of the problems lasted for years. New difficulties raised their heads like Hydras, but the main road had already opened. The Idea was victorious, a gigantic, epic undertaking, which history will someday characterize as the "Russian miracle."

The Idea was victorious—socially, economically, politically, militarily. Today it stands at the summit of responsibility. The Soviet Idea, as ideology and not as a state manifestation, needs to spread and grow like every new organism. It cannot remain within one country, within one society. It will suffocate. It needs to shatter frontiers, to take hold of the entire earth. For this reason—this is the nature of every great new idea—the Soviet Idea disturbs and worries the rest of the world; nothing can happen anywhere in the world anymore which is not related to the new Idea, whether as action or reaction. The destruction of the Greco-Roman world was a provincial event compared to today's violent stirrings of the communist tempest across the five continents. Today, because of the new technology, man has armed himself with ships, railroads, airplanes, telephones, telegraph, radio. The world has become one. Distance has been abolished, time has been vanquished and an idea, a message, can be transmitted with lightning speed from one end of the earth to another.

The consequences of this unified global ferment are incalculable. How can there be peaceful coexistence with this flaming center in Russia that awakens and enlightens the masses of the entire earth? A confrontation between capitalist actuality and communist ideology is inevitable. The more slowly this confrontation occurs the better for communism; time is its best ally. The capitalist countries know this well, but they do not dare declare war against Russia because they themselves are divided into conflicting camps. There does not exist among them any ideological or economic unity. And sooner or later—and sooner is more likely, for such is the contemporary rhythm of the globe—terrible wars will break out.

We are entering a long period of adventurous wars; if communism is indeed a great Idea, capable of inflaming and renewing the world, then we have already entered the first zone of fire in our succeeding history. We live in it and consequently do not see our epoch clearly; but centuries later our time will surely not be called a Renaissance but a Middle Ages; that is, an interregnum, a period in which a civilization is collapsing while another is being born. The former will be in the throes of death for generations; the other in labor pains for generations. Between them, long wars will rage. From the Russian Revolution onward we are going to live through the bloody turmoil of the birth of a new civilization.

In every country, the responsibility of every thinking and acting person is immense. If this world is to be saved, we know that sooner or later, through peace or war, the new Idea will become dominant. We must therefore directly face the nature of the historical moment in which we live without fear and with responsibility. Any other attitude would be blindness or cowardice and subterfuge.

And when we look our fate straight in the eye, what will be our duty? To become conscious collaborators with history. By "conscious" I mean: to comprehend with as much freedom in ourselves as is humanly possible the future that is approaching and to prepare our people to receive it. To strive from now, by scrutinizing the psychological, economic and spiritual condition of our nation, that we might be ready, when the moment comes, to accept the Idea, not in a passive but in a dynamic fashion, making it, in spite of its international nature, as Greek as possible. Only in this way will the arrival of the Idea not be dangerous. Its adaptation will be quicker and more fertile, and the face of Greece will not be distorted.

Great and crucial is the moment we are going through. If you are a true human being, my reader, if you feel compassion for mankind and understand the fiery storm that envelops us, then you have a duty to think with care and make, if you can, a decision.

■ AFTERWORD

■ NIKOS KAZANTZAKIS wrestled with communism for a little over a decade, from 1922 to the mid-thirties. He embraced it after he had been convinced by the First World War and the disastrous defeat of Greece by Turkey in Asia Minor in 1922 that bourgeois capitalist civilization in Europe was in decline, whereas the "barbarous" peoples of the East—including the Russians—were the carriers of a future Renaissance.

By 1929, however, following a prolonged sojourn in the Soviet Union, he had revised his estimate of the Russians, seeing them no longer as heralding something new but rather as carrying to an extreme something old—the materialism of the West. Thus in Kazantzakis we have one of the earliest and most interesting examples of disenchantment. What annoyed him was not Bolshevism's *threat* to the West but rather its *imitation* of the West. His disenchantment is all the more interesting because, after his eyes had been opened by Russian reality, he did not renounce communism in order to defend the bourgeois status quo; nor did he retreat to universal embitterment, like Alexander Solzhenitsyn, proclaiming West and East equally abhorrent. Instead, Kazantzakis in his disenchantment remained a "post-communist," a believer in the maturation of youthful communism into something supramaterialistic who was, at the same time, aware of the role the great personality played in human history. He embraced a position that may be called "homeopathic," proclaiming that since Soviet communism is a disease extending the West's worst characteristics, let us have more of that disease rather than less, so that the patient may come to a crisis and be cured—or die.

Kazantzakis' reactions to his involvement with Soviet communism are recorded most extensively in a political novel called *Toda Raba,* written in 1929, in which the hero cries out: "Yes, Yes, let us be communists! Let us go on intensifying this cult of the machine and of matter. . . . Let us drive the world to an exaggerated Americanism! There is no other way to liberate ourselves from the machine." But the same reactions are also summarized in the following encyclical letter to Michael Anastasiou, which is printed by kind permission of Mrs. Helen Kazantzakis, using the text preserved in Pandelis Prevelákis' *Tetrakósia Grámmata tu Kazantzáki ston Preveláki (Four Hundred Letters of Kazantzakis to Prevelákis).* Characteristically combining lucidity with fervor, Kazantzakis formulates here, for himself and others, the residue remaining after one of the most tempestuous decades in his extraordinarily engaged life.

—Peter Bien

Peter Bien, Professor of English at Dartmouth College, is a leading specialist on Kazantzakis. He has translated *Report to Greco, The Last Temptation of Christ* and the forthcoming *Selected Letters of Nikos Kazantzakis.*

August 28, 1929

Dear Michael,

After my long journey to Russia, where I saw and experienced many people, events and places, and after my solitude here in the calm of this deserted mountain, and on the eve for me of the important moment when I again begin my work on the *Odyssey*, I truly sense that I have a duty to speak with you and to clarify for you the stage—a very intricate and vibrant one—that I have reached as I struggle to confront the contemporary world problem.

I am beginning to understand the Russian reality—to comprehend, that is, all of the complexity, obscurity, contradictions and, above all, the necessity that it unwillingly serves. For this reason, it is now exceedingly difficult for me to speak about Russia. Earlier, when I knew her incompletely, I could talk for hours and with certainty, filling in with my own desires and ideas what I did not know, seeing straight geometrical lines where I now discover curves, angles, backward turns and inconsistencies resulting from a multitude of opposing ideologies and practical necessities.

I will only try, very imperfectly, to help you perceive the general outline that my mind follows when it wishes to think about this problem. Many things in my sketch fill in or bring to consciousness several earlier pathways that my mind has taken; and it is precisely for this reason that you should confront my conclusions with caution and skepticism because it may be that I have channeled all the events and the ideas that I experienced during those years into my own predetermined intellectual and psychological needs. Perhaps it is impossible for a person to escape from this kind of setback. Only he who does not have a strong drive within him—that is, the lifeless person—can confront these ideas and the world with an impeccable impartiality. But his view consequently has no value whatsoever.

For this reason, I do not address myself primarily to your reason but to the impetus within your own being that wishes to mobilize others in harmony with its own rhythm. But since I am in fact obliged to formulate my own drive in words—that is, to transform it into something inert—it is first necessary to keep this in mind: Confront the words I use as "matter"—as if each one were a very hard, dormant seed, which nevertheless holds explosive forces within it. In order to find out what I wish to say, you must let each word explode within you and in this way free the spirit that it imprisons. Perhaps you know the wonderful anecdote of the great Rabbi Nahman: Whenever he went to the synagogue to pray, he made out his will and said a tearful good-bye to his wife and children, because he did not know if he would emerge alive from his worship since, as he used to say, "when I use a word—for example, 'Lord'—I am possessed by fear. I start to collapse, not knowing if I can make the leap to the next words: 'have mercy.'" Oh, if only one could recite a poem or speak to his wife or read a letter from a friend in such a way!

Now that I have given you these instructions, I can begin without being afraid of using a logical outline:

1. After my firsthand experience of Russia—that is, of a dream that became reality—I have reached the following conclusion: Attainment is inferior to the struggle. It is a dangerous and painful conclusion that can never be used as a practical basis for human action. The sublime moment of intoxication cannot last; inspiration out of necessity constricts and degrades itself when it seeks durability in words—all this we know. But the pain is great when you see this awesome law of human impotence in contemporary Russia's consolidation of its own vast inspiration. The realization of the ideal has reduced the spirit of those struggling for it; having reached a balance they find convenient, they do not wish to go any further. The revolutionaries have

become comfortable; the comfortable quickly degenerate into conservatives, and little by little, the conservatives develop into reactionaries.

I do not wish to make a judgment about this curve, a necessary and, in some cases, useful thing for the waves of human progress. It is natural that souls cannot long endure continuous exaltation; they want to rest, to live without anxieties like forgetful plant life. The soul is not that much different from matter. It easily settles, becomes inert, turns into material. However, in Russia specifically, we have the following dual problem:

a. The natural evolution of the soul into matter is occurring very quickly.

b. The Russian proletariat is profoundly linked with its worldwide counterparts. A premature decline such as this is extremely dangerous and demoralizing for those comrades who still find themselves in the preceding and onrushing stage of the assault.

If we were together here, we would not stop talking about this. But it is a very real and bitter fact that we must confront without any faintheartedness. Summarizing then, I repeat my first conclusion: The valuable and productive stage of human motion is not the attainment of the ideal but the struggle.

2. In order for the masses—and not just the masses but the elite—to be drawn into an assault that contains so many dangers, there is a need for the appropriate slogan, one that has certain elements:

a. It answers the needs of the age.

b. It does not simply answer but exaggerates and distends, giving them a tragic quality that surpasses reality.

c. It states its purpose simply.

Every era that created a civilization had a slogan, which often took the form of a religion. For our age, the slogan without doubt is the communist one. It has all the elements, it responds and exaggerates—and this is proper; otherwise it would not have become the slogan of contemporary reality. Actually, classes as clearly distinct as proletariat and bourgeoisie do not exist; they are not two battalions with separate boundaries and a deep trench between them. But Marx, formulating the two classes with a sudden logical clarity, helped them to separate abruptly and achieve a class consciousness that they had not previously possessed; they now began to place themselves in camps that Marx with his logic had outlined for them in advance. For once a riverbed had opened up in reality, countless phenomena that had been wavering and unclear, that had cascaded to the left or to the right, began to align themselves and to follow the channel laid out for them—some in a conscious way, others because of laziness, and still others by imitation.

The lawgiver of our age is Marx, whose name today means "Leader" for our time. Defining the fluctuating reality around him with a logical and inexorable consistency—and therefore with considerable arbitrariness, since life never flows in such a fashion—he forced it to enter forms that it loosely set for itself and that he carved out for it with a very strict and logical precision.

And at this point we would really have to talk, if we were together, about the role a great man plays in his age—that is, until what point his intervention is still a creative one. The outstanding individual is only he who expresses the needs of his time; however, if he mirrored simply those needs or those of this own age, he would be average; he must always add the totally new tint of his individuality, a reflection of his own epoch of course, but also a pioneering one, a bridge between his age and the one to come. In him, this appears for the first time with such intensity that it is almost entirely new.

But the question—until what stage is the great man a slave, and from where does his free creative intervention begin—would take us far from the issue.

For our age, Marx found the appropriate slogan, one that consolidated the masses, gave them an illusion, presented it to them as a realizable goal (in fact as historically determined) and assured them that, after the triumph of the proletariat, the class struggle would end, so would war, and justice would arrive. In other words, he gave them a faith.

What are the major characteristics of this faith? Two: materialism, and worship of the machine. The ideal for the Soviet Union is America. This is a very natural want. Communism is not something entirely new, a change in the battlefield of the human struggle; it is simply the most extreme and logical consequence of bourgeois civilization, which, with its development of the mind's critical faculty, tore down every religion and created what we call science; that is, the laws by which we can recognize and subjugate natural forces. Communism deifies these fruits of bourgeois efforts and only attempts to achieve—and does so—a more equitable distribution of material wealth. These two chief elements that characterize the contemporary slogan bring us to the third rather frightening conclusion:

3. The mission of communism is not the creation of a new civilization but the decomposition of bourgeois society. Communism is the end, not the beginning. It has all the symptoms of finality: unadulterated materialism, excessive logic, deadly analysis of every faith that transcends the senses, deification of practical goals.

4. What then is our duty? This is the age in which we have been born, and if we want our actions to have worth and help mankind, we have an obligation to be communists. But aware communists—that is, enlightened, implacable, fully knowledgeable, without any superficial, limitless hope. We cannot be naive communists who believe that prosperity and justice will follow the triumph of communism. We must feel distaste for such a simpleminded and superficial

optimism, and fulfillment in our passion and strength by this severe, sober conception of communism.

Just as a driver who has entered a burning forest must, instead of turning back, move ahead as quickly as possible at double speed to escape the conflagration, so we who have entered this awesome age must intensify, as much as we can, all the tendencies of communism to the utmost so that the hour for salvation will come more quickly. What will be our deliverance? The destruction of this world and the beginning of the creation of another on different foundations in which the worship of the machine, of logic and of practical goals will appear as unworthy satisfactions. A new slogan.

If, on the other hand, we are not men of action, we have the right, if we are capable, to desire this post-communist slogan right now, to live it and to divine its meaning. Communism is the end, but naturally, as in every end, there are many elements of the new beginning. What are they? From all the desires, needs and premonitions that encircle us, which will survive and be of value in the coming civilization? From all that are transient, which of them have the likelihood of relative permanence?

This is the awesome anxiety and the great duty for those among us today who are creative in the realm of theory.

This is my very general outline. In every word that I have written to you, I feel as Rabbi Nahman did. For this reason, rather than writing words, I wish we could have talked together. I personally found myself at one moment in Russia in the midst of a terrible dilemma that would have given a sudden turn to my life. Before making a decision, I concentrated all my strength and focused my own possibilities, because I know that today the person who dedicates himself to action also leads an integral life, uprooting unnecessary aesthetic and metaphysical hair-splitting and contradictions and willingly narrowing his thought so that his action will be more fruitful.

But I saw what a responsibility it is for each person to follow his nature to the utmost, to the very extreme, with such unyielding obstinacy that he gradually ceases to be a human being and becomes a monster.

After my long trip to Russia, I feel as if I have entered the second period of my life. For me Russia is now a violent drive that has already begun to place itself, not in my immediate activity or in my thinking, but in my memory. I experienced this country, I saw her, I enjoyed her, and words cannot express the emotional riches I received from her people, rivers, oceans, mosques, churches, peasants, deserts, ideas and aspirations. But now she has shifted away from the immediate circle of my anxiety and desire; she has placed herself with somewhat reduced energy, a glowing treasure, in memory.

For the next two or three years, I will assign one purpose to my life: to create in the *Odyssey*—with images, flesh, perfect verse and an impetuous love for all the elements of earth, water and air—the cry of future man.

That is the duty I give to my life. Everything else—the salvation of the proletariat, the cultivation of the mind, the curiosity of the eye to see and the ear to hear, the heart's desire to love—can only be for me the painful march toward this cry.

I am pleased that I have spoken with you, my dear Michael. I have again felt sadness that it has been years since I have seen you and that I no longer know when we will meet again. But you know the marvelous line from our own Cretan ballad: "Freedom washes and combs its hair in the dark and glows."

Love too is like that.

—Nikos

Translated by Michael Antonakes and Peter Bien.